IMAGES
of America

INDIANA'S OHIO RIVER SCENIC BYWAY

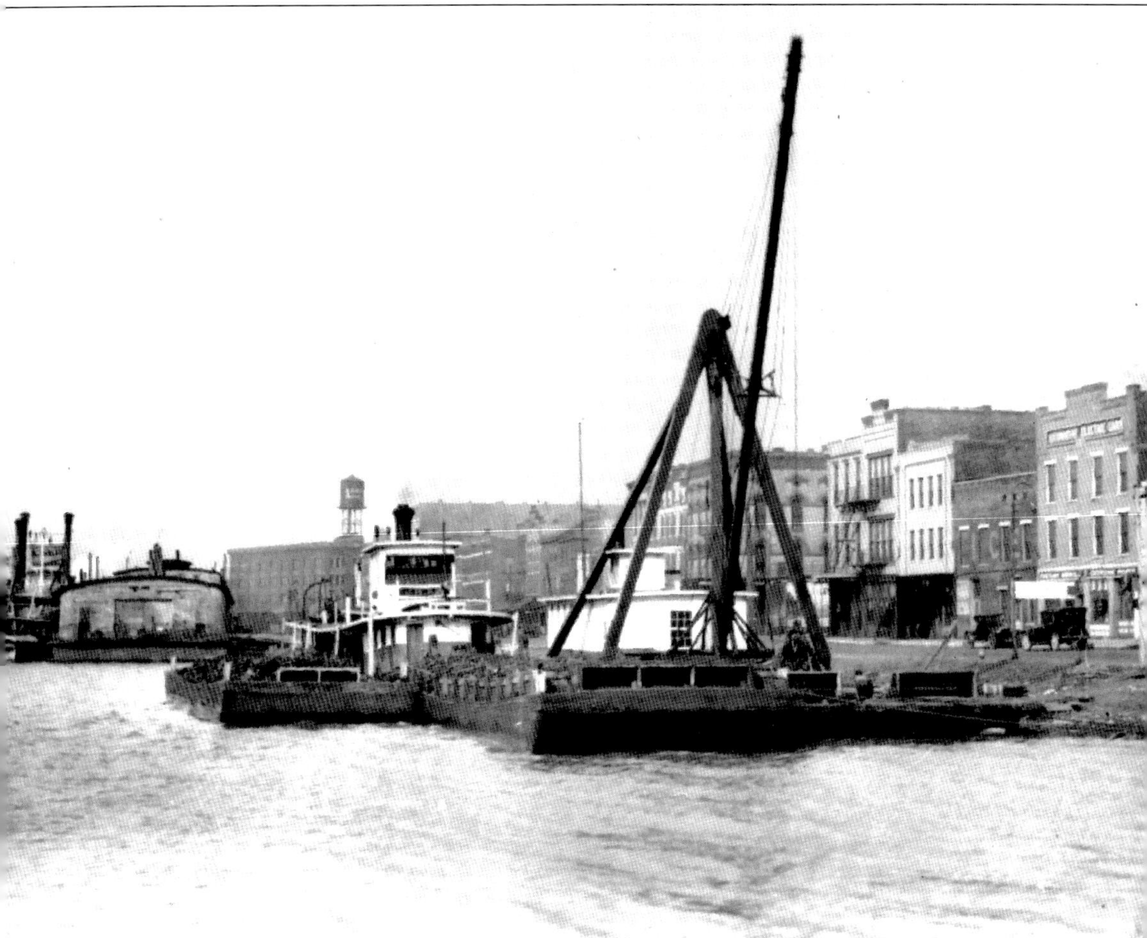

This portion of Evansville's riverfront has changed considerably since this photograph was taken. In 1936 Dress Plaza, a major riverfront improvement project which provided a buffer from the river to the downtown, was completed. The river contributed to the local economy as is evident by the barges and riverboats docked at the wharf. This scenic view is indicative of many cities and towns along the Ohio River.

On the cover: A group of people boards the boat the *Wanderer* at the Evansville Boat Club and prepare for a day on the Ohio River. This photograph was taken in Evansville in 1915. (Courtesy of Willard Library.)

IMAGES
of America

INDIANA'S OHIO RIVER SCENIC BYWAY

Leslie Townsend

ARCADIA
PUBLISHING

ISBN 978-0-7385-4085-6

Published by Arcadia Publishing
Charleston, South Carolina

Printed in the United States of America

Library of Congress Catalog Card Number: 2006924921

For all general information contact Arcadia Publishing at:
Telephone 843-853-2070
Fax 843-853-0044
E-mail sales@arcadiapublishing.com
For customer service and orders:
Toll-Free 1-888-313-2665

Visit us on the Internet at www.arcadiapublishing.com

To Jon, without whose help and support this would not be possible. And to the other men in my life—my boys, Ethan and Christian, and my dad, Ray.

Contents

Acknowledgments 6

Introduction 7

1. Historic: Major Events and Everyday Life 9
2. Natural: Geological Features and Forces of Nature 59
3. Recreational: Fun and Play Along the Byway 83
4. Scenic: Vistas and River Valleys 111

ACKNOWLEDGMENTS

Since the Ohio River Scenic Byway formed in the early 1990s, it has been guided by a group of dedicated people who want to see wonderful things happen along the byway. I want to thank everyone on the board that offered assistance when needed.

This book posed some challenges in traveling the length of the 302-mile byway to select photographs from each of the counties. I spent a lot of time driving the back roads and enjoying the beautiful southern Indiana countryside. I would like to thank the Dearborn County Historical Society; the Ohio County Historical Society; the Switzerland County Historical Society and Museum; the Jefferson County Historical Society; the Jeffersonville Township Public Library; the New Albany-Floyd County Public Library; the Harrison County Public Library; Willard Library; the Evansville Museum of Art, History, and Science (EMAHS); the University of Southern Indiana (USI) Special Collections; and Ben Hubbard with the Indiana Department of Natural Resource's Division of Forestry. I would also like to acknowledge Darrel Bigham, my boss, who inspired me to write this book and provided much support. Historic Southern Indiana provides administrative support for the Ohio River Scenic Byway and has made this book possible.

Lastly, I want to thank my editor, Anna Wilson, for being so patient. I had several unavoidable delays, and she was very understanding.

Introduction

The Indiana Ohio River Scenic Byway was designated a national scenic byway in 1996. The byway travels through 13 counties on its 302-mile journey. Traversing the lush hills and farmland of southern Indiana and paralleling the mighty Ohio River, the Ohio River Scenic Byway marks a timeworn and history-rich corridor that has profoundly influenced the people and communities through which it passes. As in all areas, fortunes have been won or lost, and communities have seen good times and bad. What has remained constant is the Ohio River and the beautiful landscape it has sculpted over the centuries. Whether clinging to the shores of the river or traveling inland as it links together farms and historic river communities, the Ohio River Scenic Byway is the common thread, joining a geographically broad and culturally diverse region together.

Much of Indiana's early settlement happened along the Ohio River, and the communities along the byway have rich and wonderful stories to tell. The river has been a blessing, encouraging economic development in many communities. It is also a force of nature to be reckoned with, as some of the devastating floods have shown.

National scenic byway designation depends on possessing at least one intrinsic quality: historic, natural, recreational, scenic, cultural, and archaeological. These are the qualities that make a place what it is—the places, views, and activities that, when viewed as a whole, make each byway special. While the Ohio River Scenic Byway possesses all six, it mainly focuses on four: historic, natural, recreational, and scenic. This book will explore all of these qualities as they relate to life in the communities along the byway.

While there are many common characteristics and themes, each community is distinctive. In fact, each could have a book on its own. Starting upriver by Cincinnati and traveling west to the Illinois border, the Ohio River Scenic Byway includes Lawrenceburg, Aurora, Rising Sun, Vevay, Madison, Charlestown, Jeffersonville, Clarksville, New Albany, Corydon, Leavenworth, Cannelton, Tell City, Troy, Grandview, Rockport, Newburgh, Evansville, and Mount Vernon. This book will weave together some common threads and unique stories from communities all along the byway.

The Ohio River Scenic Byway was one of the first byways in the country to receive designation. The effort began in the early 1990s and was led by Historic Southern Indiana, a regional outreach program of the University of Southern Indiana, whose mission is to promote, enhance, and preserve the heritage of southern Indiana. Historic Southern Indiana gathered interested individuals from each of the 13 counties. Today the byway board and advisory committee is comprised of people from convention and visitors bureaus, economic development agencies, parks and recreation departments, and small businesses. It also includes staff from state agencies such as the Office of Tourism, the Indiana Department of Transportation, and the Indiana Department of Natural Resources, as well as federal agencies like the Hoosier National Forest and the Federal Highway Administration. Historic Landmarks Foundation of Indiana, a historic preservation organization, also is heavily involved. Historic Southern Indiana provides administrative assistance to the Ohio River Scenic Byway, which is mainly a volunteer organization.

The Ohio River Scenic Byway is developing interpretive panels that will be placed along the byway and will further tell the stories of the communities. The byway also is working to develop an artisan trail, called By Hoosier Hands, in which the Ohio River Scenic Byway will serve as the backbone. The trail will feature artisans producing their crafts in a traditional manner. It will include such things as wood crafts and furniture, pottery, paintings, textiles, candles, musical instruments, and much more. It will also include agricultural products such as locally made wine, cheese, and jams and jellies. The artisan trail will add another layer to the story of the byway.

The communities and countryside along the Ohio River Scenic Byway are rich in history and beauty. This is their story.

One

Historic
Major Events and Everyday Life

Historic can encompass many things. Along the Ohio River Scenic Byway, it includes the development of communities. How did a place come to be where it is, and what has happened to it over the years? Has it seen its fortunes rise or fall or both? How has it changed over the years?

Transportation plays a major role in the history of communities. Riverboats and trains brought people and goods and contributed to a town's success. Bridges opened up new possibilities and ended isolation.

Historic includes the events that impact lives. World War II touched almost everyone in some way, whether a family member served in the armed forces, or worked on the home front. Historic includes famous people and places. The boyhood home of Abraham Lincoln and the first state capital in Corydon are pieces of Indiana history.

It can also deal with the stuff of everyday life. How did people make a living? While industry is important, agriculture is also an integral part of life in southern Indiana. Religious affiliation and customs also are part of the fabric of life.

Today historic qualities are an important part of the Ohio River Scenic Byway. Visitors travel to see historic sites and places. Aurora, Madison, Jeffersonville, New Albany, and Evansville all have historic house museums that depict life in the 19th century. The Falls of the Ohio State Park in Jeffersonville is a 400 million year old Devonian fossil bed. It is also the spot where Meriwether Lewis met up with William Clark to begin their exploration of the country in 1803. In addition to being the site of the first state capital, Corydon also holds the distinction as the site of the only Civil War battle fought in Indiana.

The Ohio River Scenic Byway possesses a wealth of historic qualities. They affect every community along the byway.

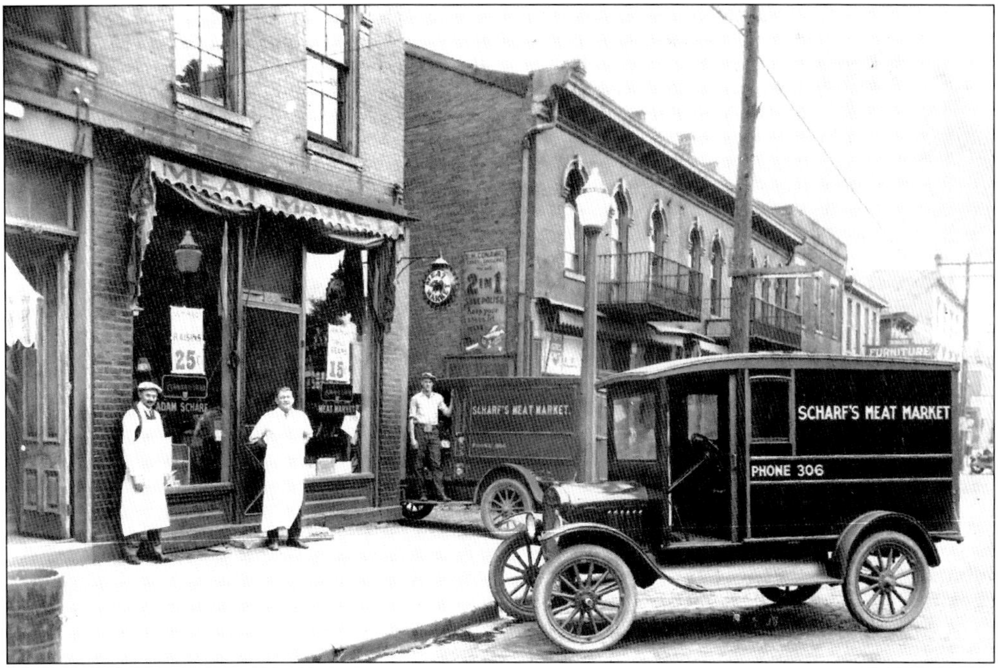

Lawrenceburg is on the far eastern end of the Ohio River Scenic Byway near Cincinnati. It is Indiana's fourth oldest city and the county seat of Dearborn County. This photograph from the early 20th century shows Scharf's Meat Market in the downtown business district. (Courtesy of the Dearborn County Historical Society.)

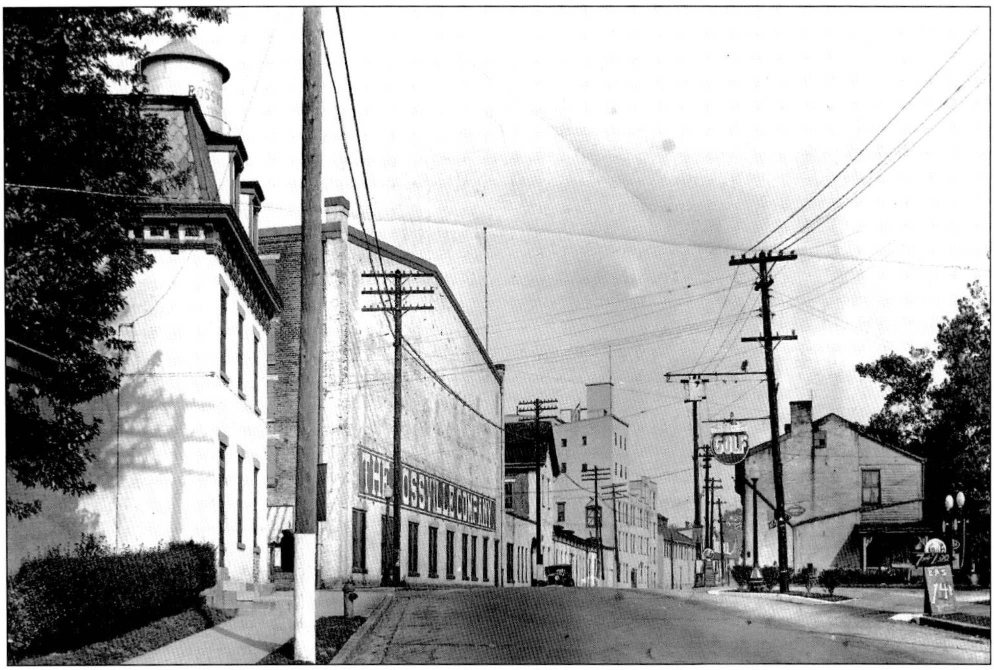

Warehouses and other industrial buildings are visible in this street scene from Lawrenceburg. Today Argossy Casino, a floating riverboat casino, is located near this area. (Courtesy of the Dearborn County Historical Society.)

Firemen stand outside Lawrenceburg's Fire House No. 2. For some inexplicable reason, the entrance is blocked by piles of wood. (Courtesy of the Dearborn County Historical Society.)

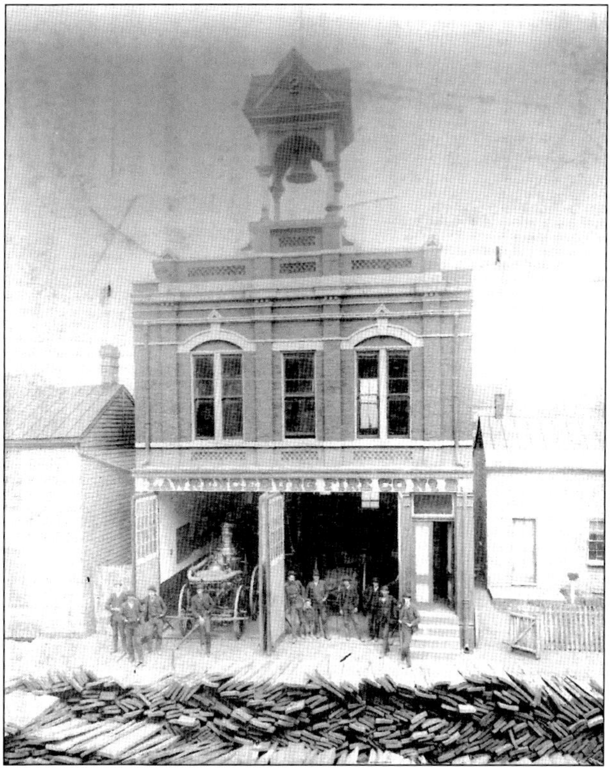

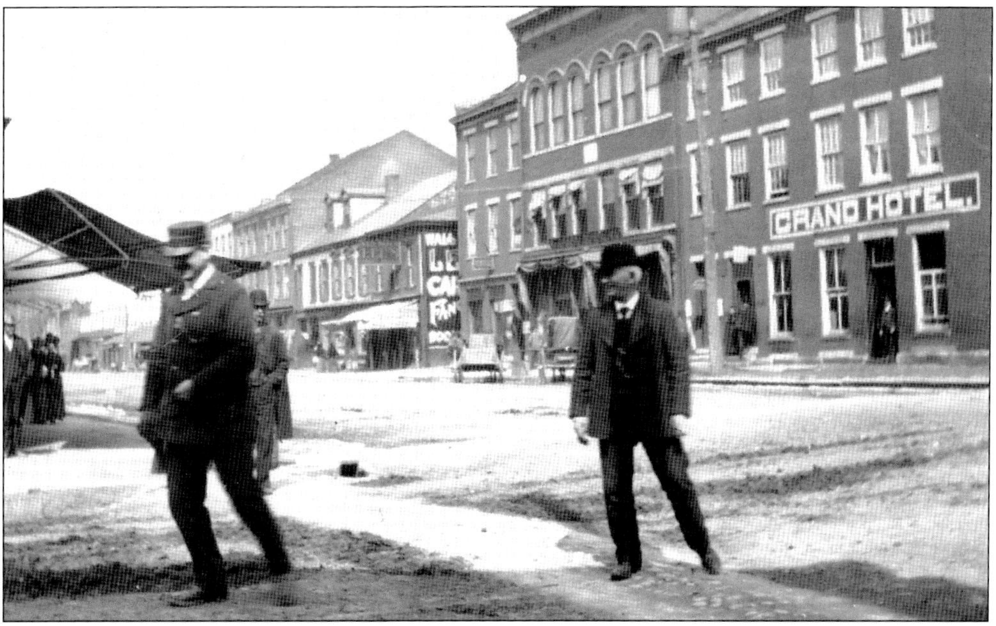

This is another view of Lawrenceburg's downtown. In 2003, Historic Landmarks Foundation of Indiana, a historic preservation organization, and the City of Lawrenceburg received grants to help preserve High Street, one of the main thoroughfares in downtown Lawrenceburg. The street features many old businesses and row houses. (Courtesy of the Dearborn County Historical Society.)

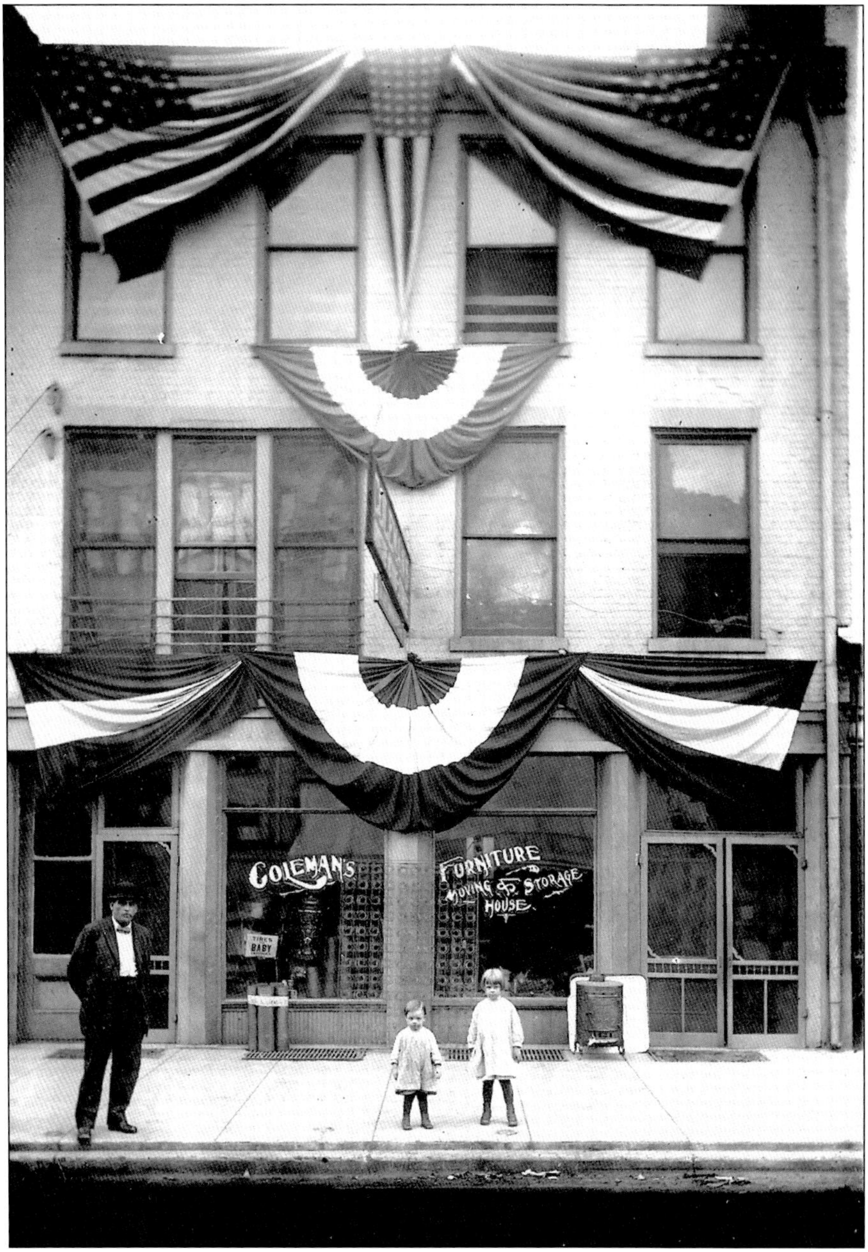

Coleman's Furniture, Moving, and Storage House is decorated in American flags and red, white, and blue bunting to celebrate New Albany's centennial in 1913. Indiana became a state in 1816, and many cities and towns experienced centennial anniversaries of their settlement in the early 20th century. New Albany was settled in 1813 by brothers Joel, Abner, and Nathaniel Scribner who came to the area from New York City. Named for the capital city of the founders' home state, New Albany became the seat of government for Floyd County, which recently had been formed from portions of Clark and Harrison counties in 1819. Located on the Ohio River, just downstream from Louisville and the Falls of the Ohio, the only natural obstruction in the Ohio River, New Albany experienced growth and economic success from the steamboat industry and was the largest city in Indiana by 1850. (Courtesy of the New Albany-Floyd County Library.)

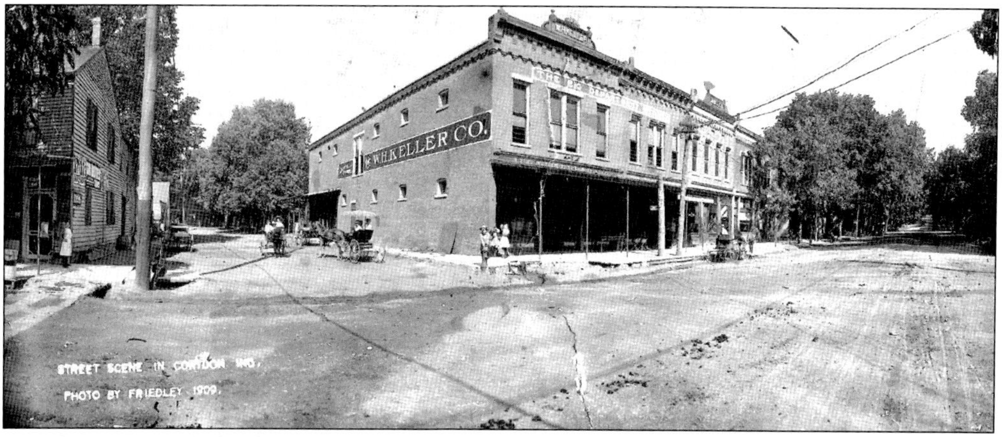

Corydon is one of the few communities along the Ohio River Scenic Byway, located inland from the Ohio River. It served as Indiana's first state capital from 1816 until it was moved to Indianapolis in 1825. Prior to that it served as the second Indiana territorial capital, which was moved from Vincennes in 1813. This photograph shows downtown Corydon in 1909. (Courtesy of the Harrison County Public Library.)

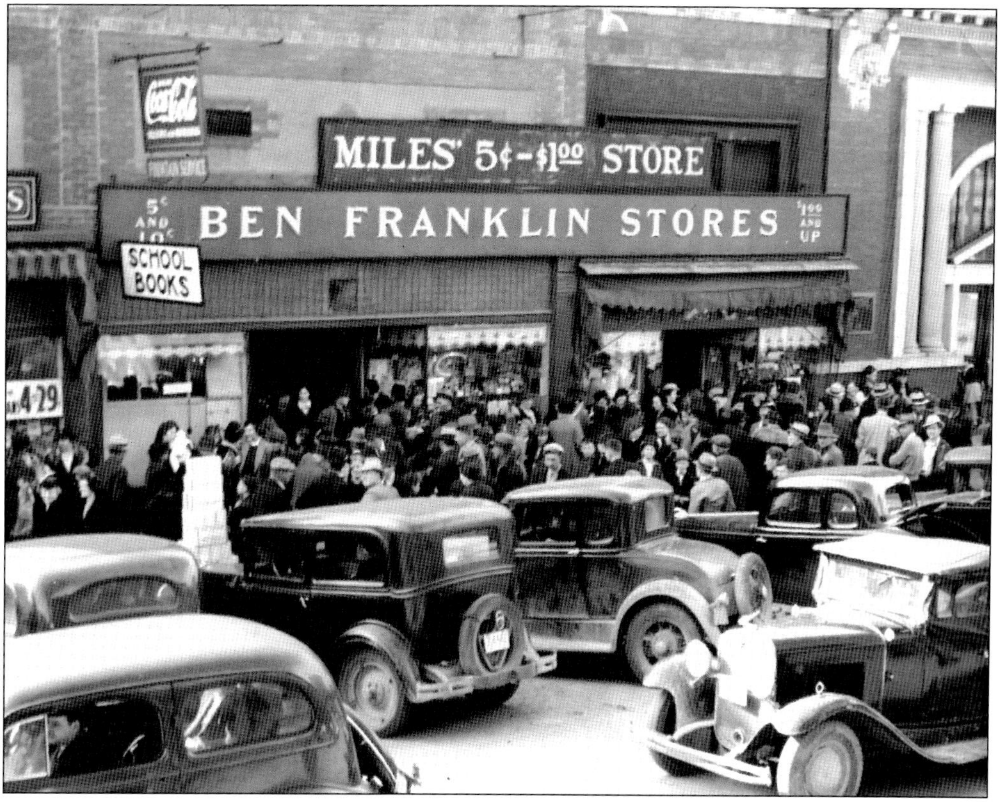

Cars and pedestrians pack the front of Corydon's Ben Franklin Store, a five and dime discount store popular in small towns across the United States. Ben Franklin Stores began in 1927 and were perhaps the first retail franchises in which individual stores were owned by independent operators. (Courtesy of the Harrison County Public Library.)

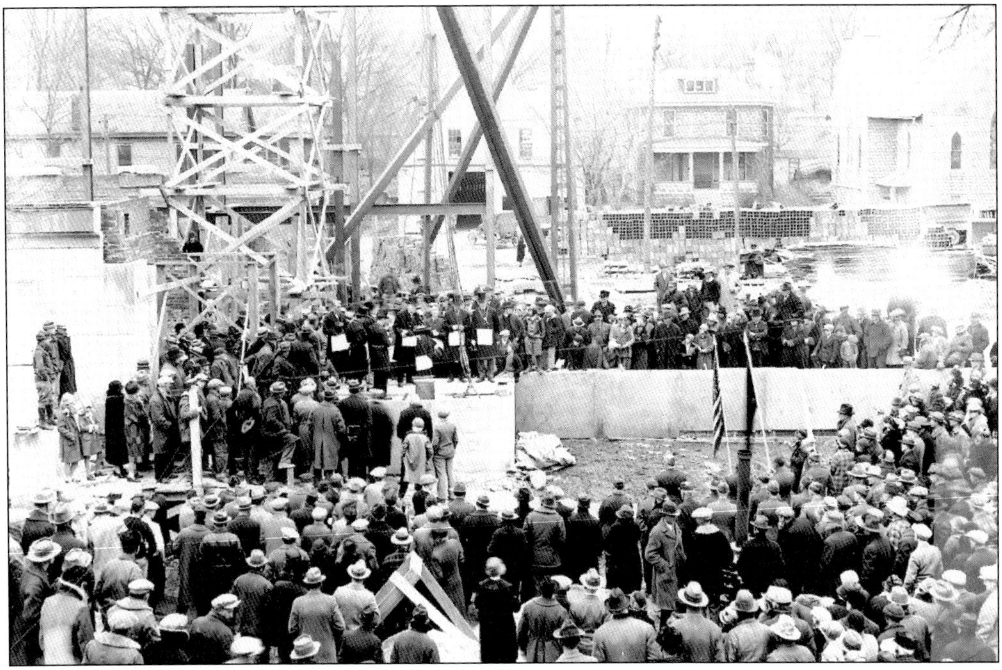

The old state capitol in Corydon served as the Harrison County Courthouse for over a century. A large crowd gathers as the cornerstone is laid during construction of the new Harrison County Courthouse in 1928. The building is next to the old capitol and is still in use today. (Courtesy of the Harrison County Public Library.)

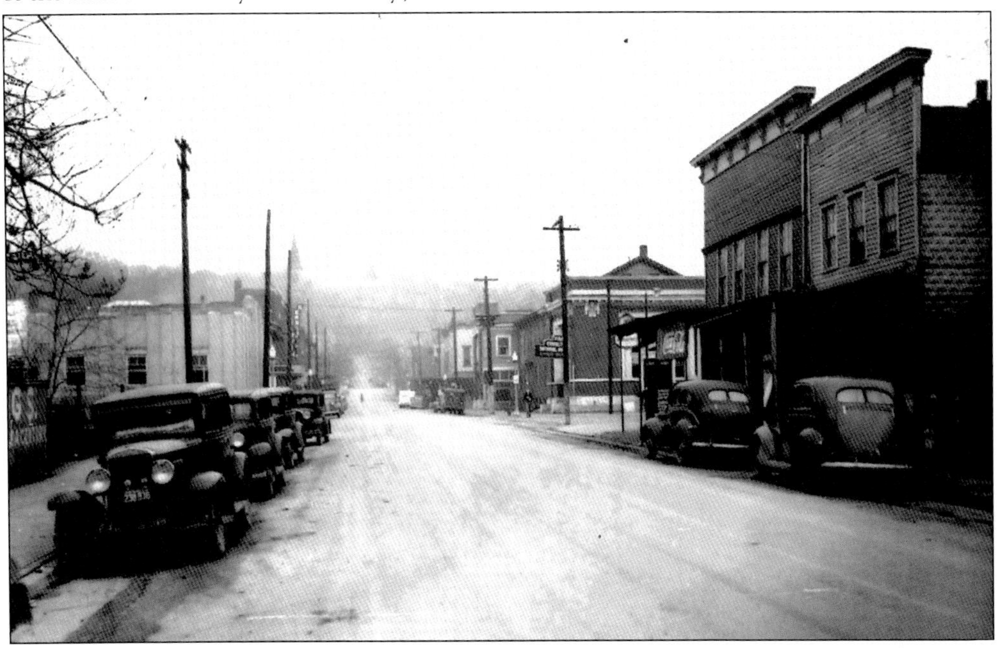

Cannelton is located on the Ohio River in Perry County. It served as the county seat after it was moved from Rome in 1859. The county seat eventually moved to the neighboring community of Tell City. Cannelton got its name from the high grade of semicannel coal found in the hills overlooking the Ohio River. (Courtesy of USI Special Collections.)

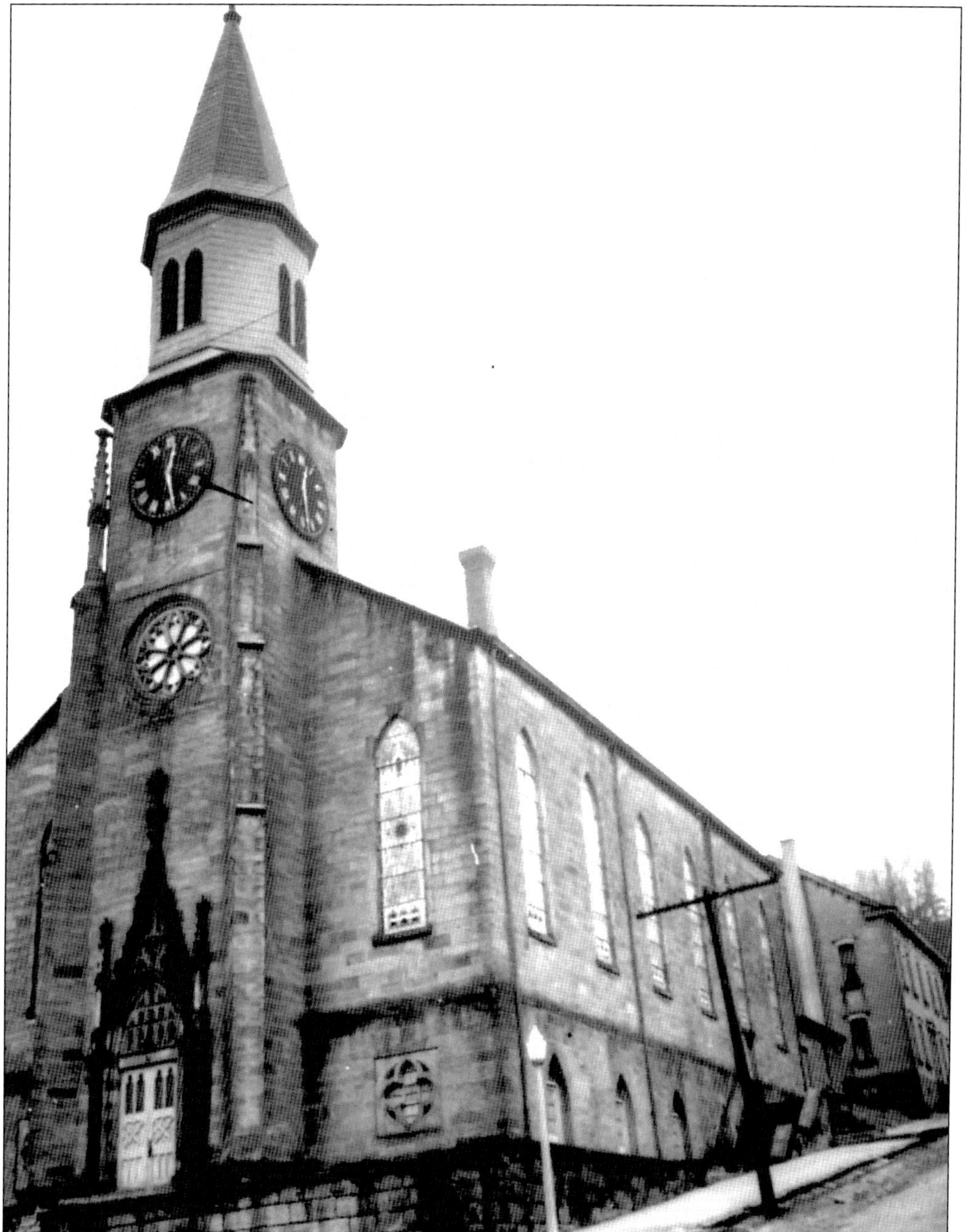

St. Michael's Catholic Church in Cannelton sits at the bottom of a large hill that overlooks the town. It is one of the few remaining structures in Cannelton built with sandstone quarried from the nearby hills. The church is constructed with finished sandstone blocks on the exterior and interior walls, and loose rock chips and mortar on the inside with walls 38–41 inches thick. The spire was added in 1860 and rises 156 feet and contains four bells. One weighs 1,060 pounds, and the other three weigh 623, 336, and 119 pounds. (Courtesy of USI Special Collections.)

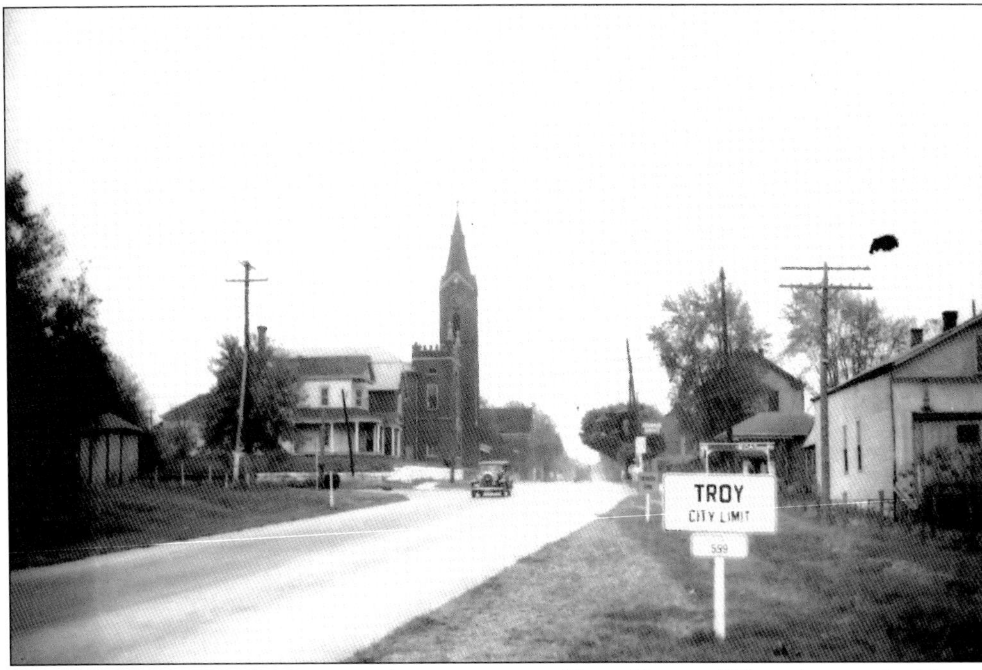

Like Cannelton, Troy also was once the county seat of Perry County. When the state legislature formed Spencer County in 1818, Perry County's boundary shifted eastward, and Troy was no longer centrally located. St. Pius V Catholic Church, with its imposing 142-foot high steeple, is visible in this photograph. (Courtesy of USI Special Collections.)

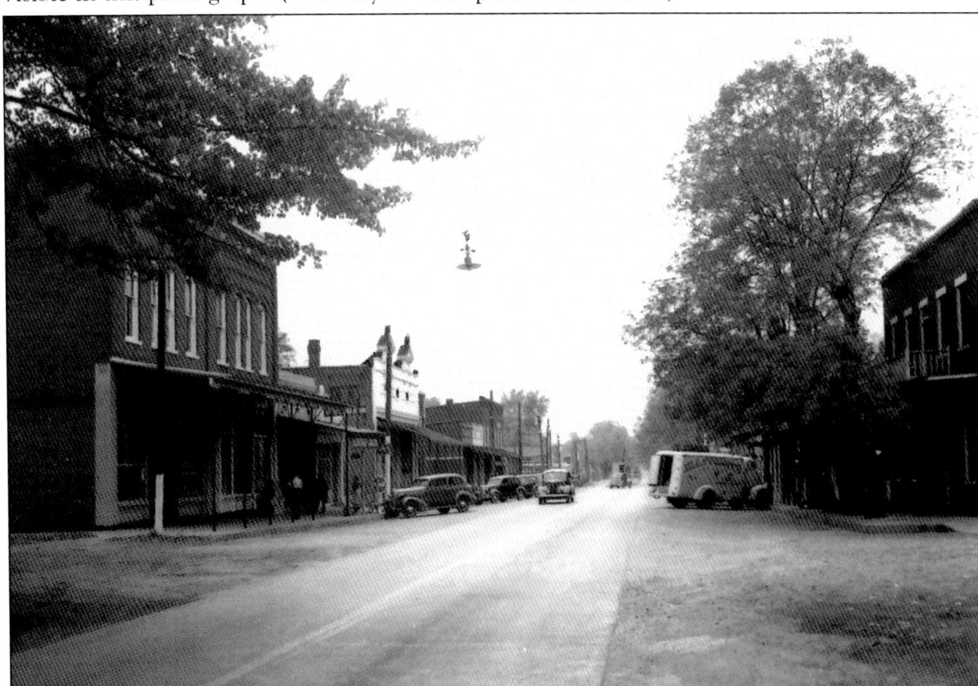
Troy's downtown has changed considerably since this photograph was taken. Few of these buildings remain. (Courtesy of USI Special Collections.)

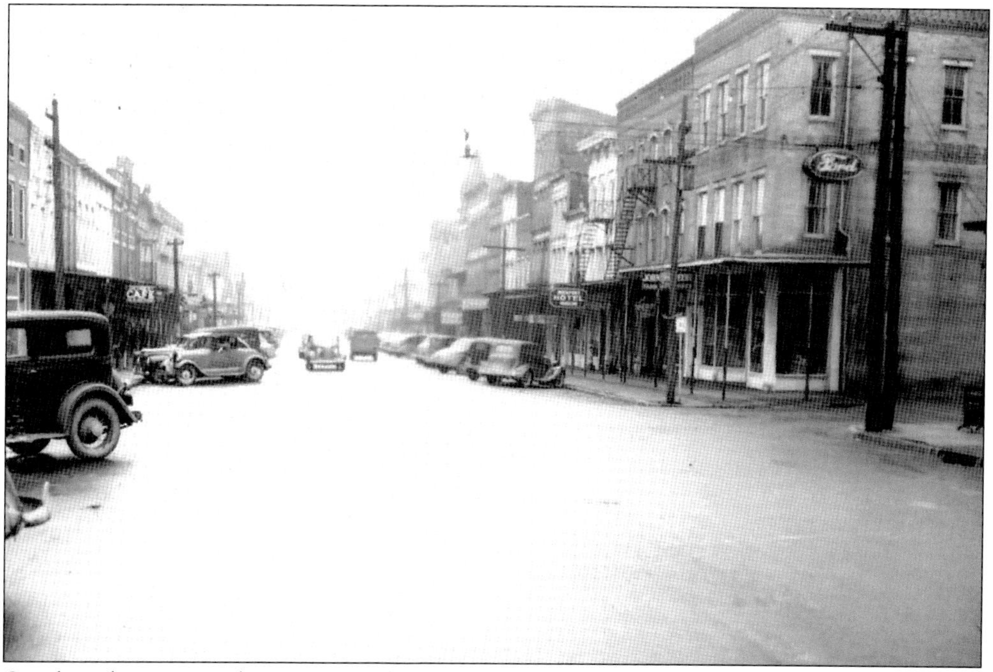

Cars line the street in downtown Rockport. Rockport is the county seat and the largest town in Spencer County. (Courtesy of USI Special Collections.)

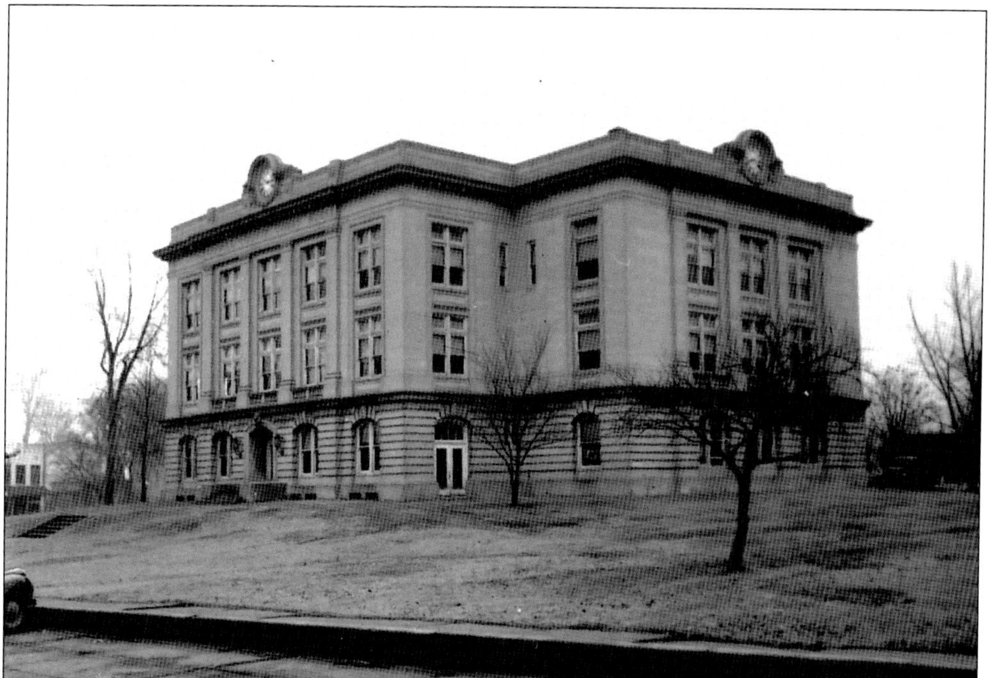

The Spencer County courthouse was completed in 1921. It is the fifth courthouse in Spencer County since it was established in 1818. In October 1844, Abraham Lincoln delivered a speech in the county's third courthouse on behalf of Henry Clay, the Whig presidential candidate. (Courtesy of USI Special Collections.)

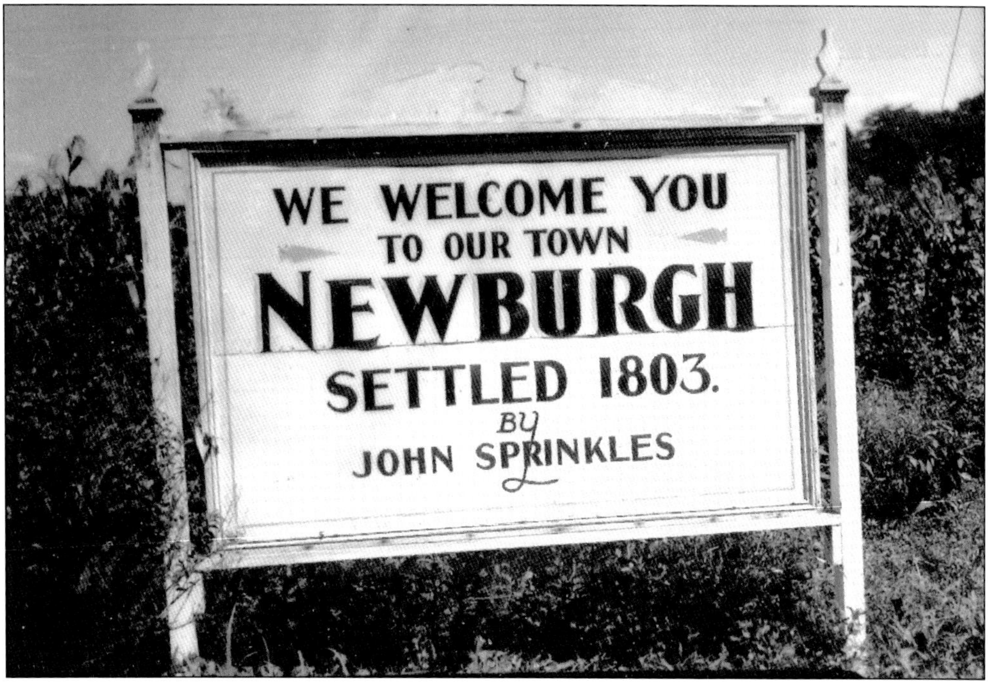

The town of Newburgh sits on the Ohio River in Warrick County. It dates from 1803 when the Sprinkle family from Henderson, Kentucky, settled on the town's present site. It was known as Sprinklesburg or Mount Pleasant. In 1829, Newburgh was platted and bordered Sprinklesburg. The state legislature merged the two towns in 1837 under the name Newburgh. (Courtesy of USI Special Collections.)

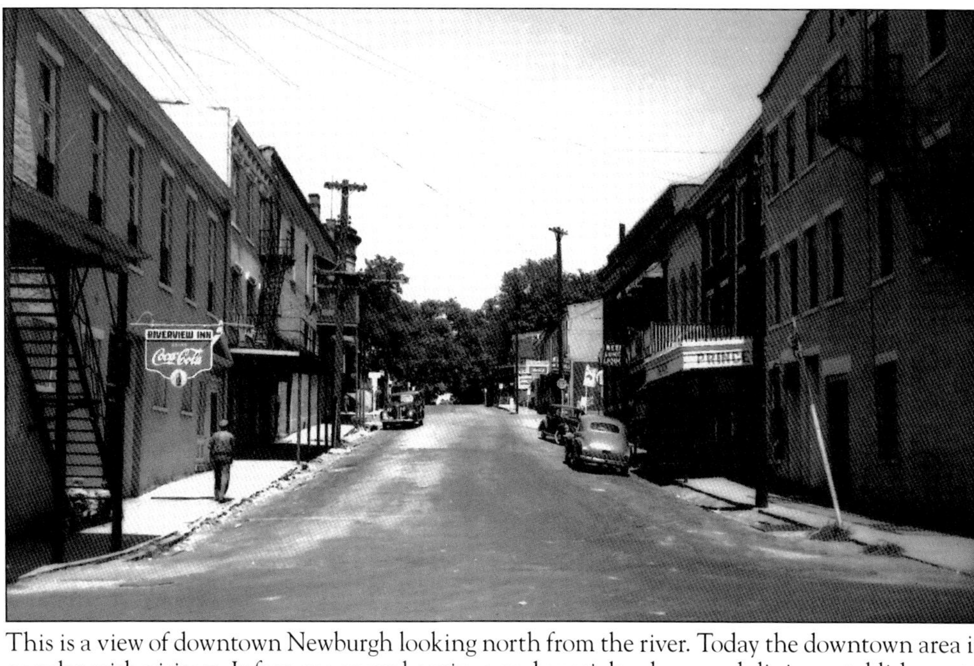

This is a view of downtown Newburgh looking north from the river. Today the downtown area is popular with visitors. It features several antique and specialty shops and dining establishments. (Courtesy of USI Special Collections.)

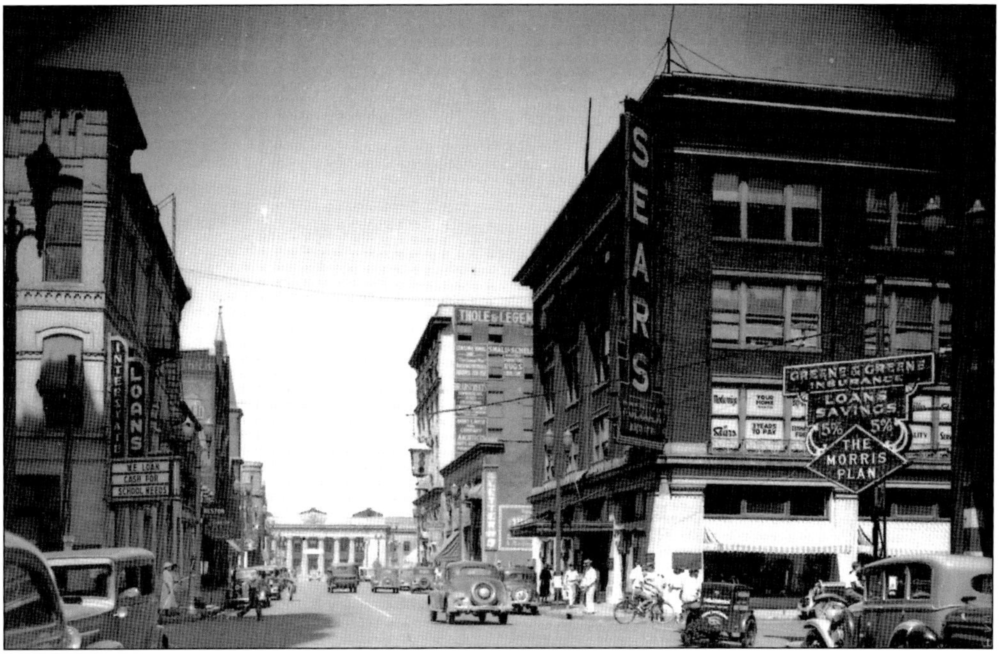

Evansville is the largest city in Indiana along the Ohio River. This photograph of the downtown shows the Soldiers and Sailors Memorial Coliseum at the far end of the street. The Sears Department on the right opened in 1925 and was the first retail store that Sears opened outside of its catalog business. (Courtesy of USI Special Collections.)

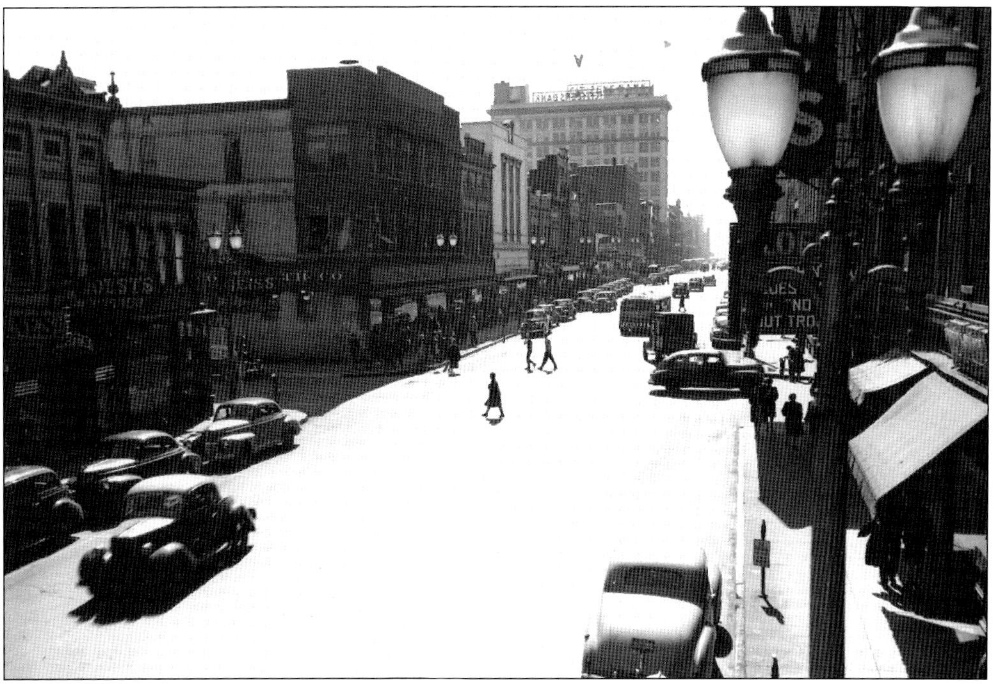

This is a photograph of Main Street in Evansville. As part of the push for urban renewal in the late 1960s and early 1970s, Main Street was blocked to traffic and became an open air walkway. It has once again opened to vehicular traffic. (Courtesy of EMAHS.)

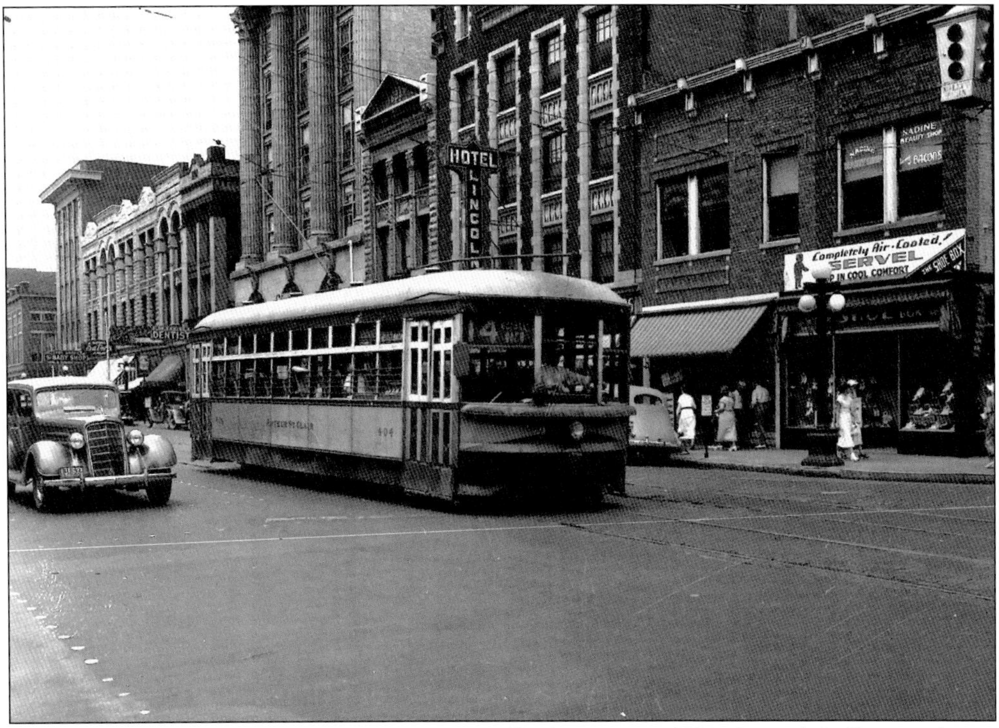

A streetcar travels down Main Street in Evansville. (Courtesy of USI Special Collections.)

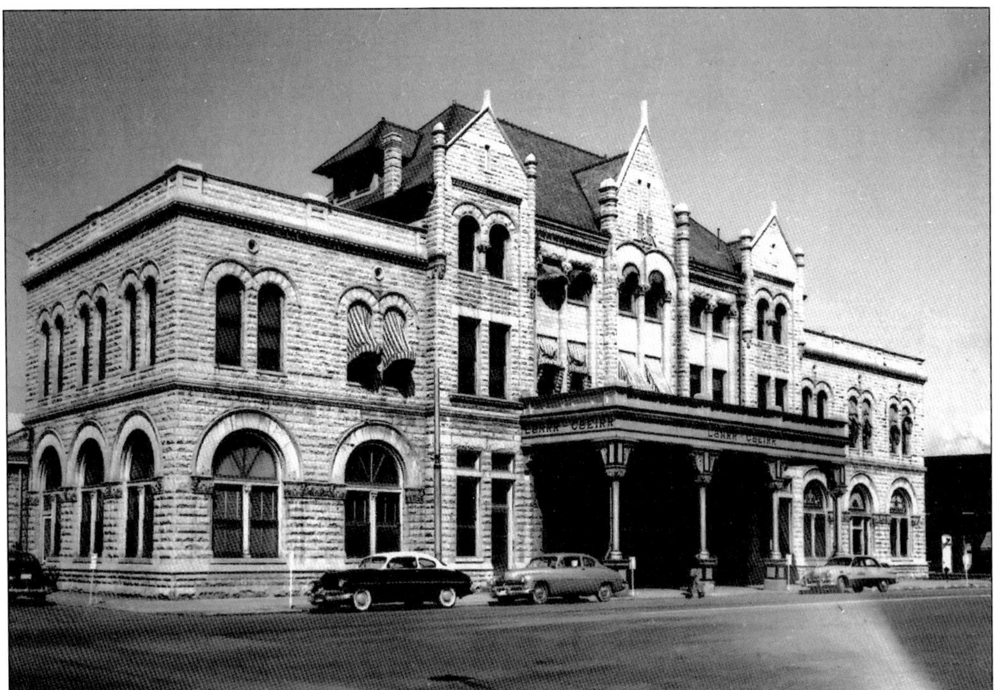
The Louisville and Nashville Railroad station in Evansville is pictured here. It fell on hard times after World War II and was eventually razed in the 1980s. (Courtesy of USI Special Collections.)

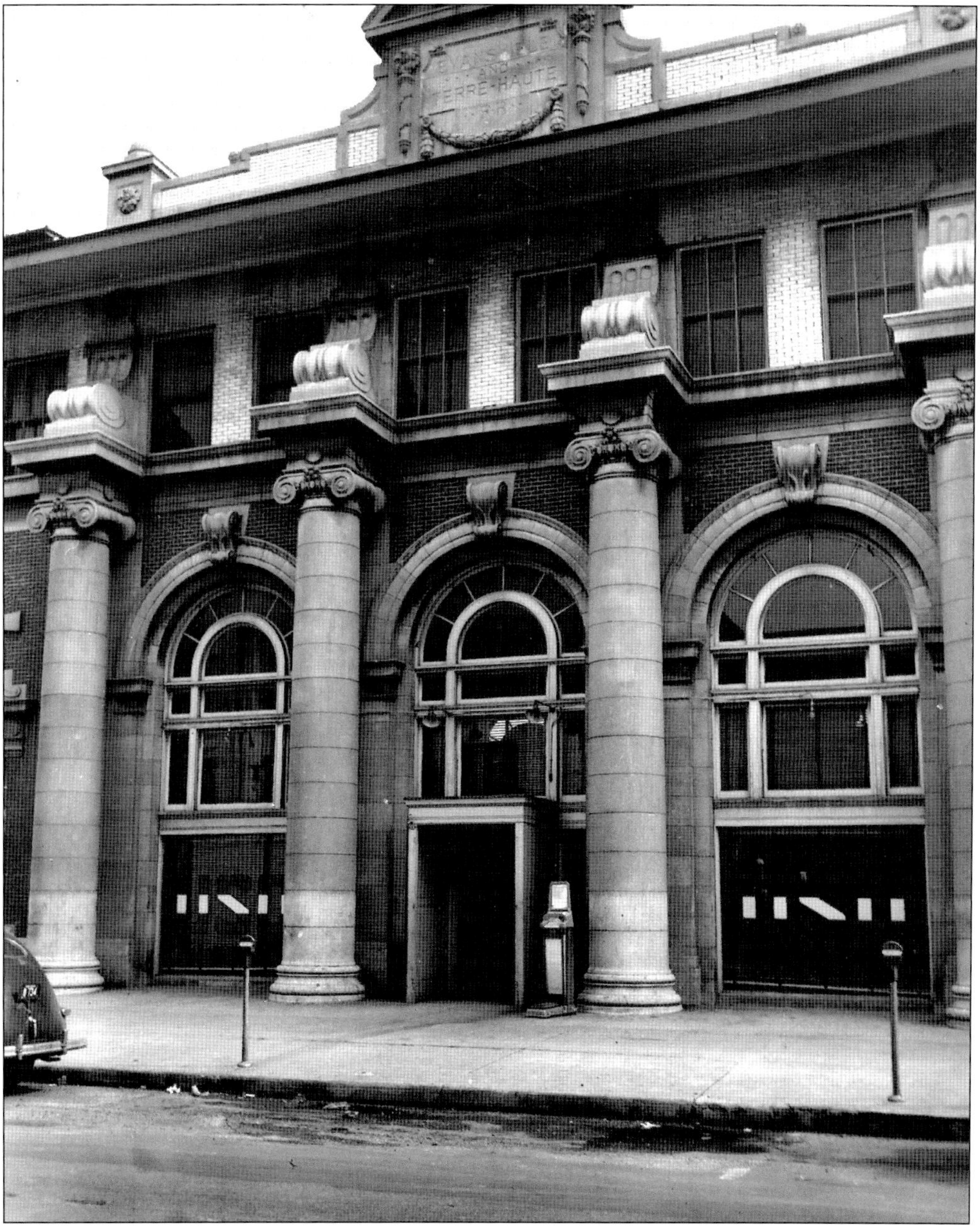

The passenger terminal of the Chicago and Eastern Illinois Railroad was built in 1882 and stood at Eighth and Main Streets in Evansville. It was abandoned in 1942 after the line was purchased by the Louisville and Nashville Railroad. During World War II, it became Evansville's USO, and after the war, it was a community center. Its columns are now a riverfront monument, titled the Four Freedoms. They represent the freedom of speech, freedom of religion, freedom from fear, and freedom from oppression. The circular base is believed by some to symbolize a circle of unity, as well as a fifth freedom, the right to peacefully assemble. (Courtesy of EMAHS.)

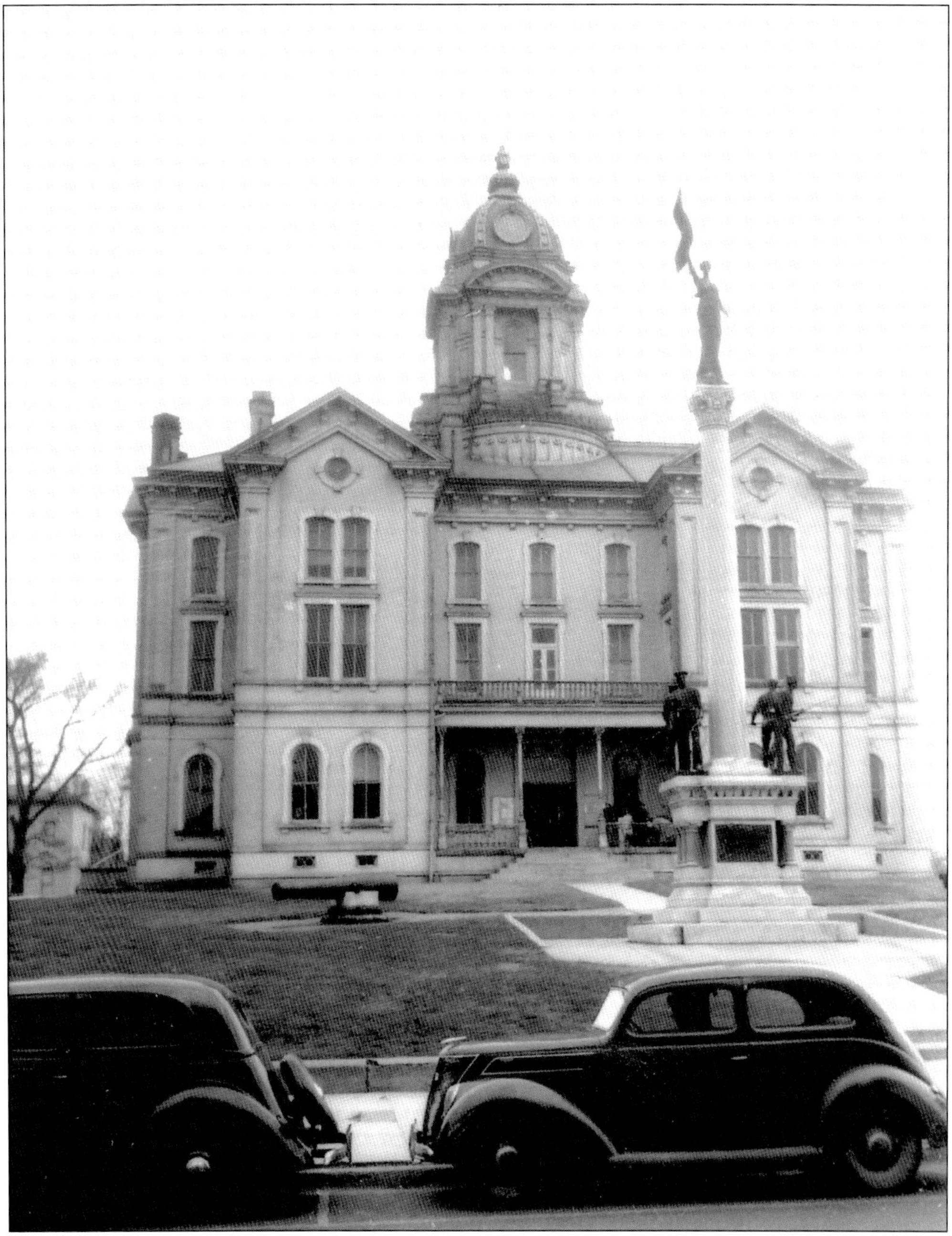

The Posey County Courthouse in Mount Vernon was built in 1876. Rudolph Schwartz, sculptor of the 284-foot high Soldiers and Sailors Monument in Indianapolis, designed the Soldiers and Sailors Monument that is seen here on the town square, where it was erected in 1908. (Courtesy of USI Special Collections.)

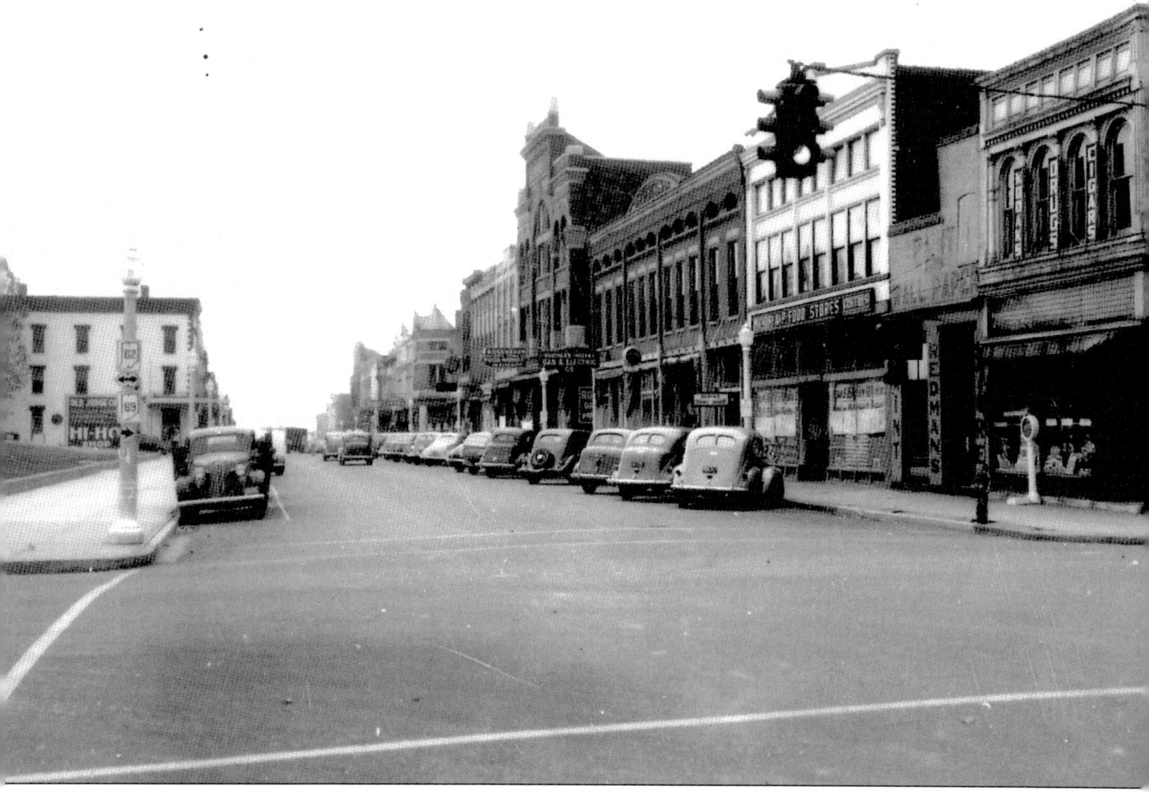

Mount Vernon is the westernmost town along the Ohio River Scenic Byway in Indiana. It became the county seat in 1825. Alvin P. Hovey, governor from 1889 until his death in 1891, was from Mount Vernon. This is a photograph of the downtown square. (Courtesy of USI Special Collections.)

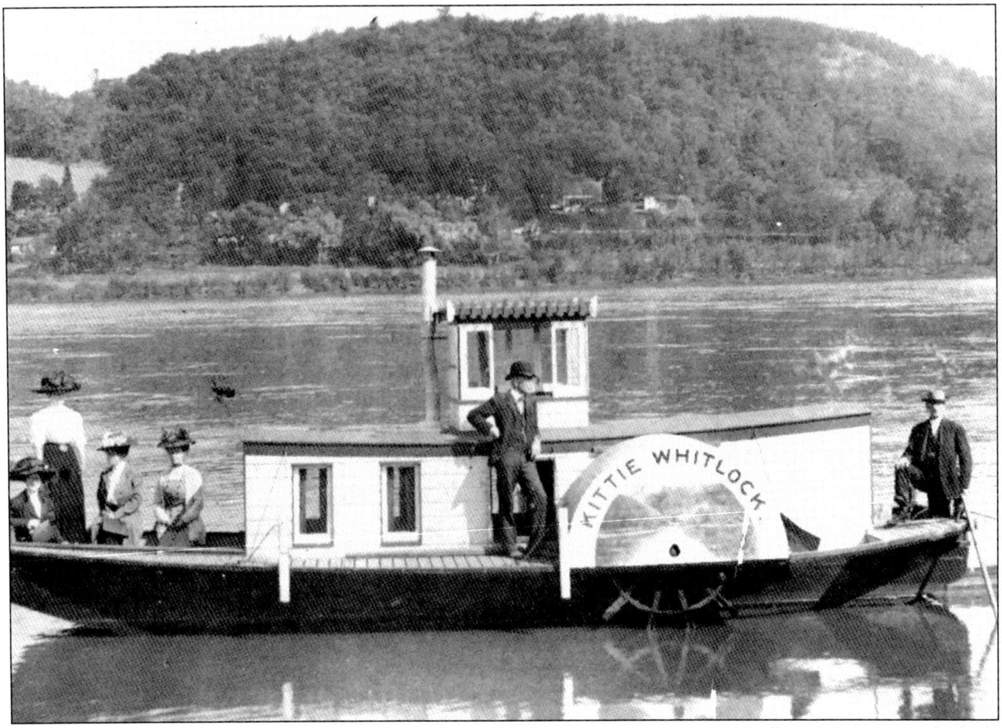

A group of people are photographed enjoying a ride on the *Kittie Whitlock*. The *Kittie Whitlock* was a pleasure boat, but it also served another purpose. William Whitlock and his son J. W., the owner of the famous Hoosier Boy, would travel up and down the Ohio River selling yawls, or small boats. The *Kittie Whitlock* was used to push the small barge to which the yawls were attached. Whitlock named the boat after his daughter Kathleen. (Courtesy of the Ohio County Historical Society.)

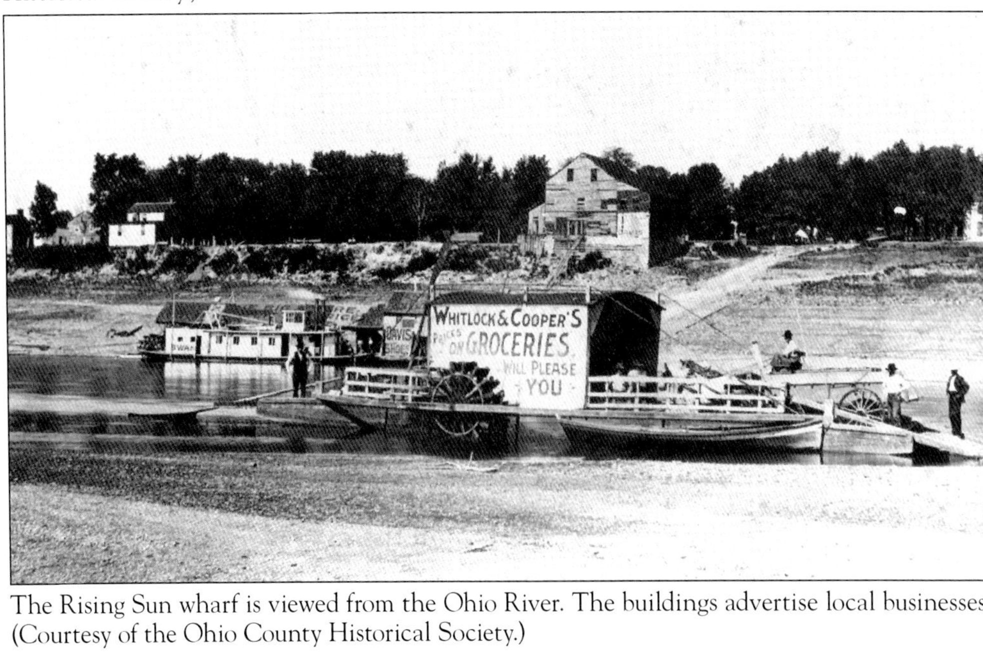

The Rising Sun wharf is viewed from the Ohio River. The buildings advertise local businesses. (Courtesy of the Ohio County Historical Society.)

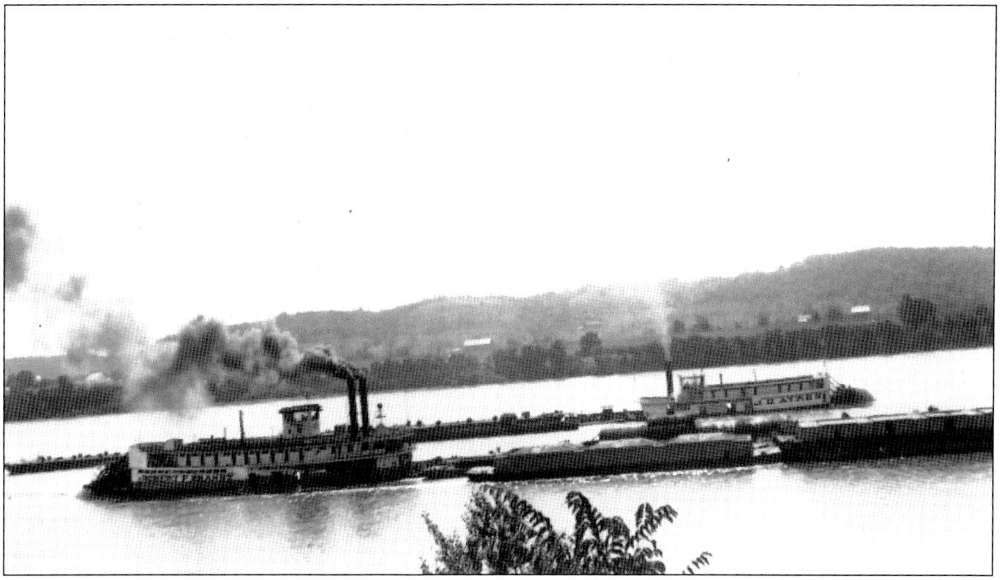

From the time the first settlers arrived in the region, the Ohio River has proved a useful tool for transporting people and goods. Many of the cities and towns that dot the shoreline owe their fortunes to their place on the river. Here barges travel along the river near Vevay. (Courtesy of the Switzerland County Historical Society and Museum.)

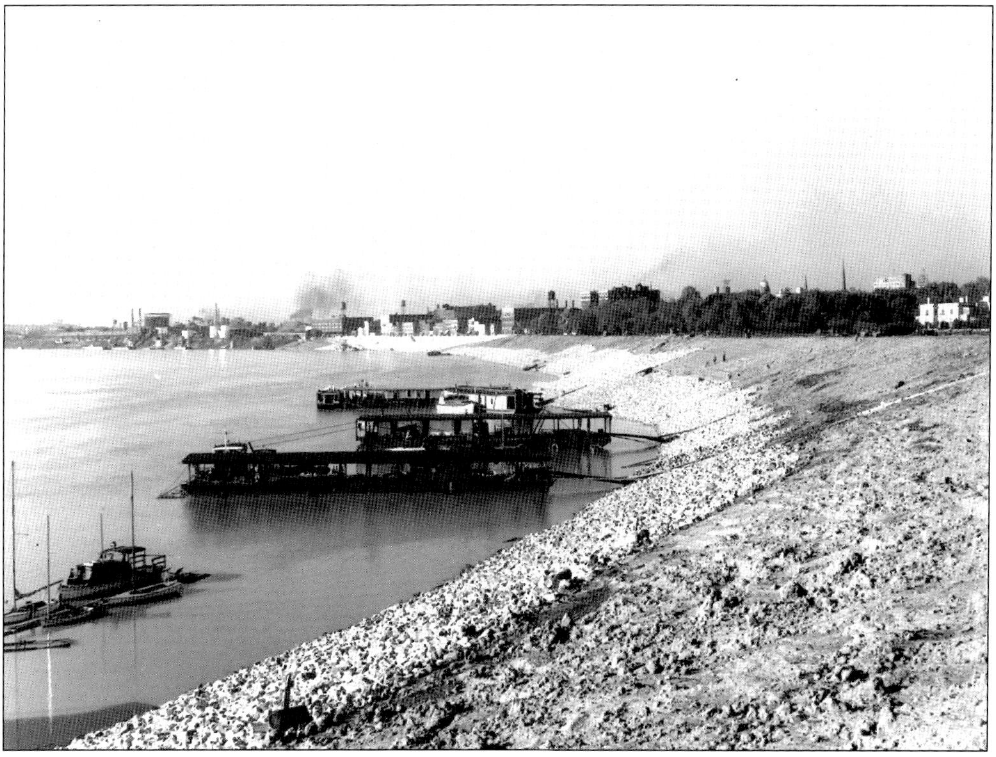

Boats are docked at a marina on Evansville's waterfront along Riverside Drive. This photograph was taken after 1936, because Dress Plaza can be seen in the background. Dress Plaza opened in 1936, just months before the flood of 1927. (Courtesy of Willard Library.)

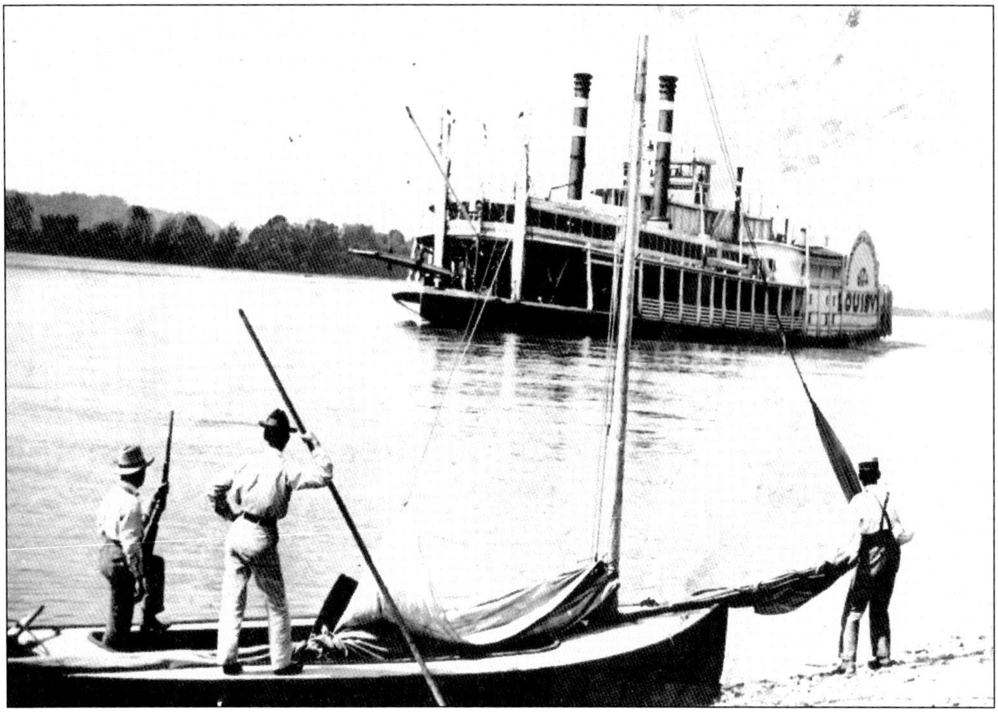

The riverboat *Louisville* gets ready to dock at the landing in Rising Sun. (Courtesy of the Ohio County Indiana Historical Society and Museum.)

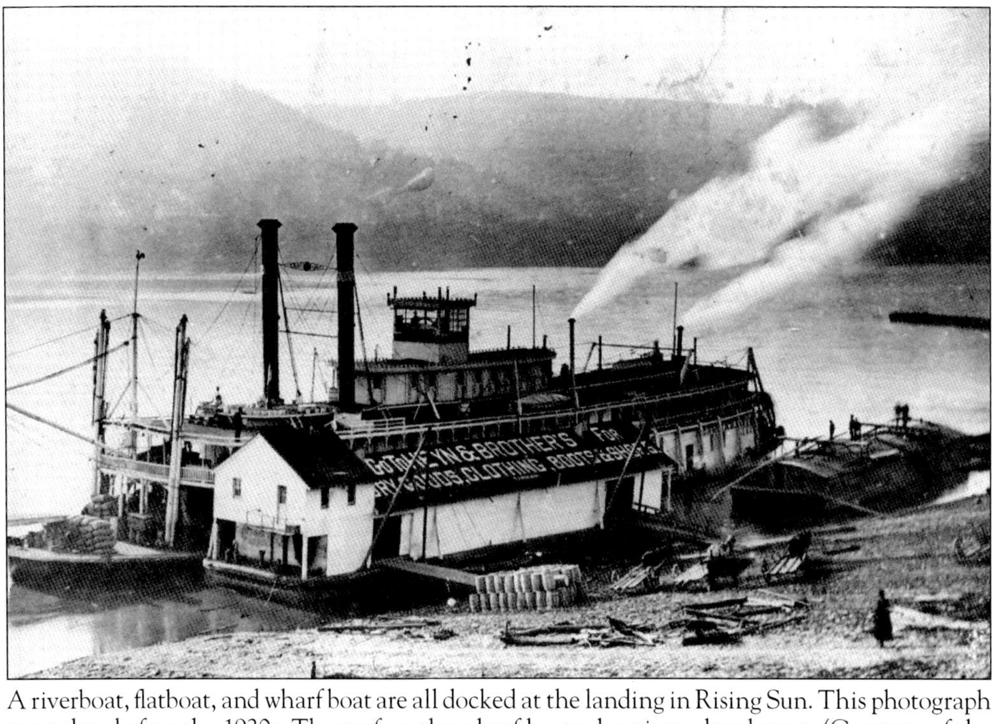

A riverboat, flatboat, and wharf boat are all docked at the landing in Rising Sun. This photograph was taken before the 1920s. The roof on the wharf boat advertises a local store. (Courtesy of the Ohio County Indiana Historical Society and Museum.)

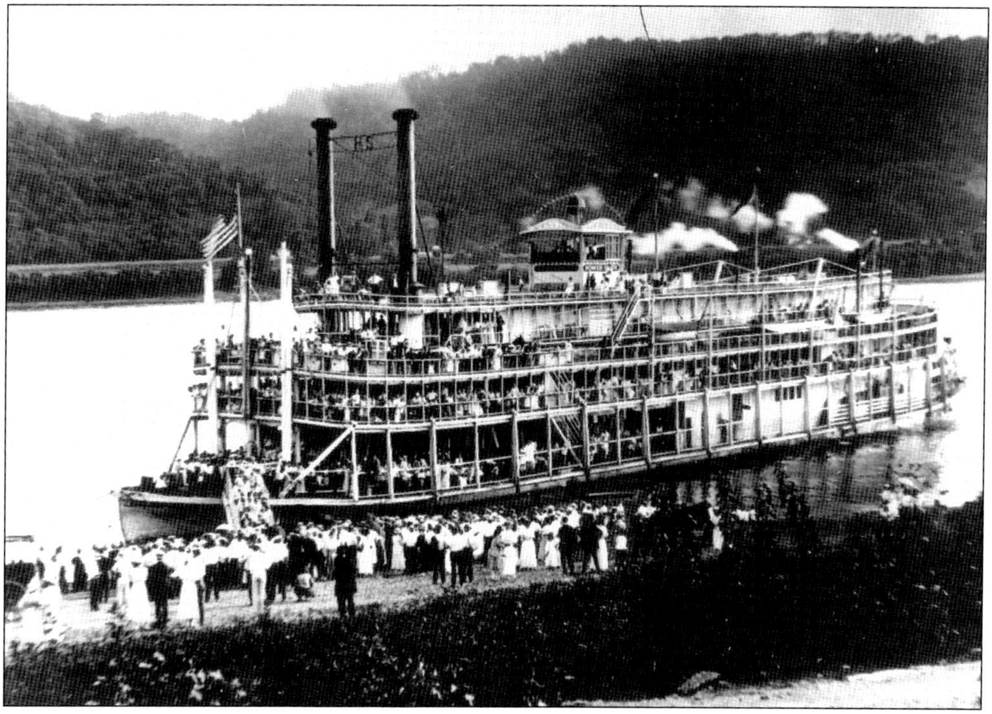

People line the banks to greet a crowded riverboat. (Courtesy of the Switzerland County Historical Society.)

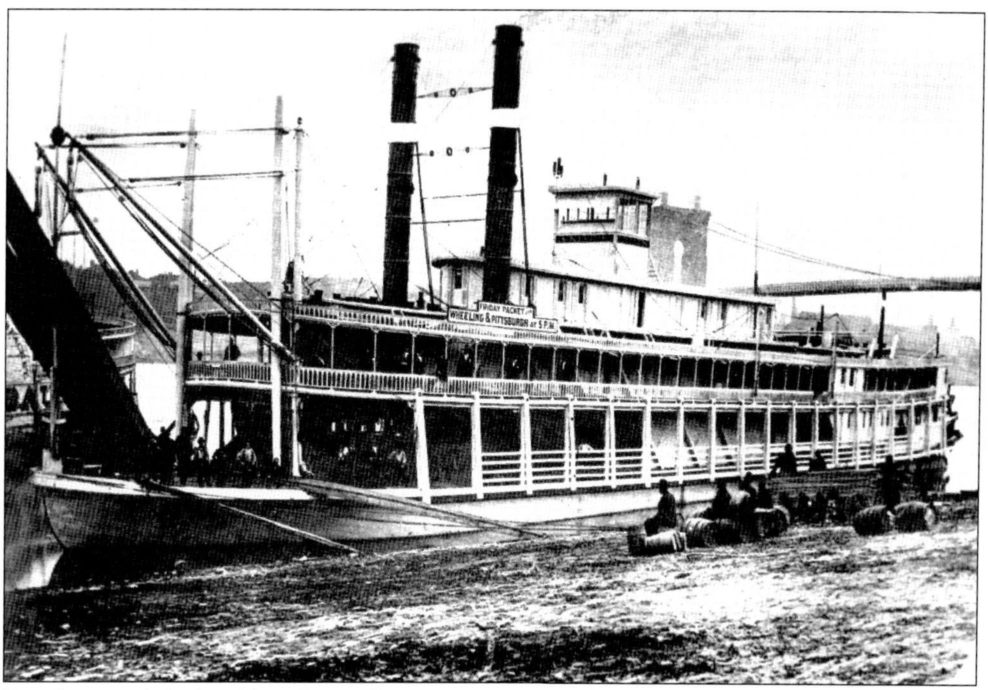

Riverboats ruled the Ohio River for many years, until train travel became more popular. Riverboats transported both people and goods. This riverboat is loading up with barrels as it is docked in Vevay. (Courtesy of the Switzerland County Historical Society and Museum.)

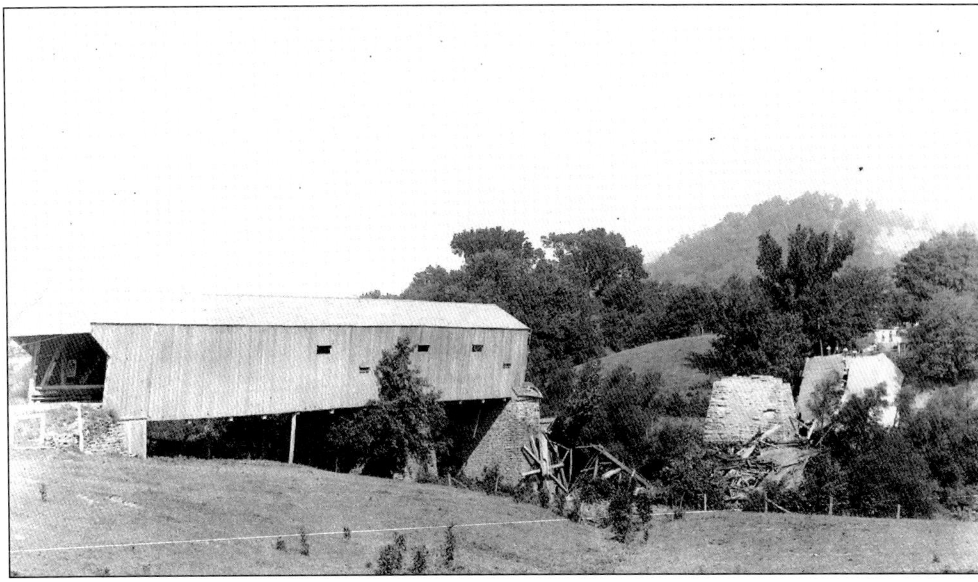

Indiana's covered bridge era began in the early 1830s, and it is estimated that between 400 and 500 covered bridges may have existed in Indiana. The Brooksburg covered bridge, located in Jefferson County near Madison, collapsed in the 1880s. (Courtesy of the Jefferson County Historical Society.)

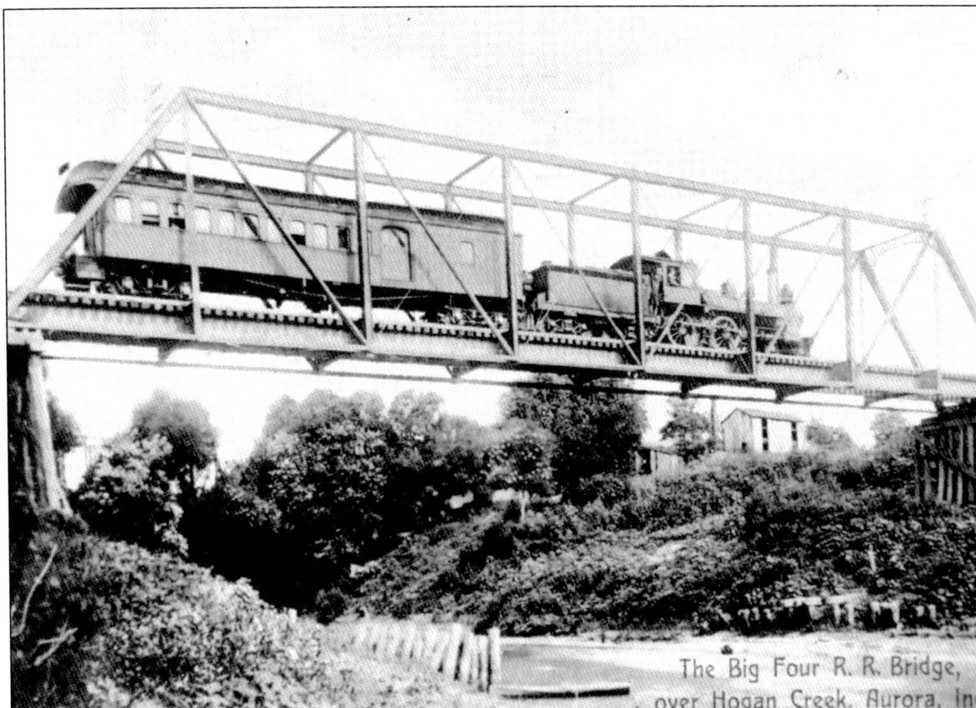

The Big Four Railroad Bridge is pictured at the mouth of Hogan's Creek in Aurora. The railroad car was used for passengers and for transporting freight. Drinking water was available from a container, in which a block of ice was placed each day. A tin cup with a chain was attached. (Courtesy of the Dearborn County Historical Society.)

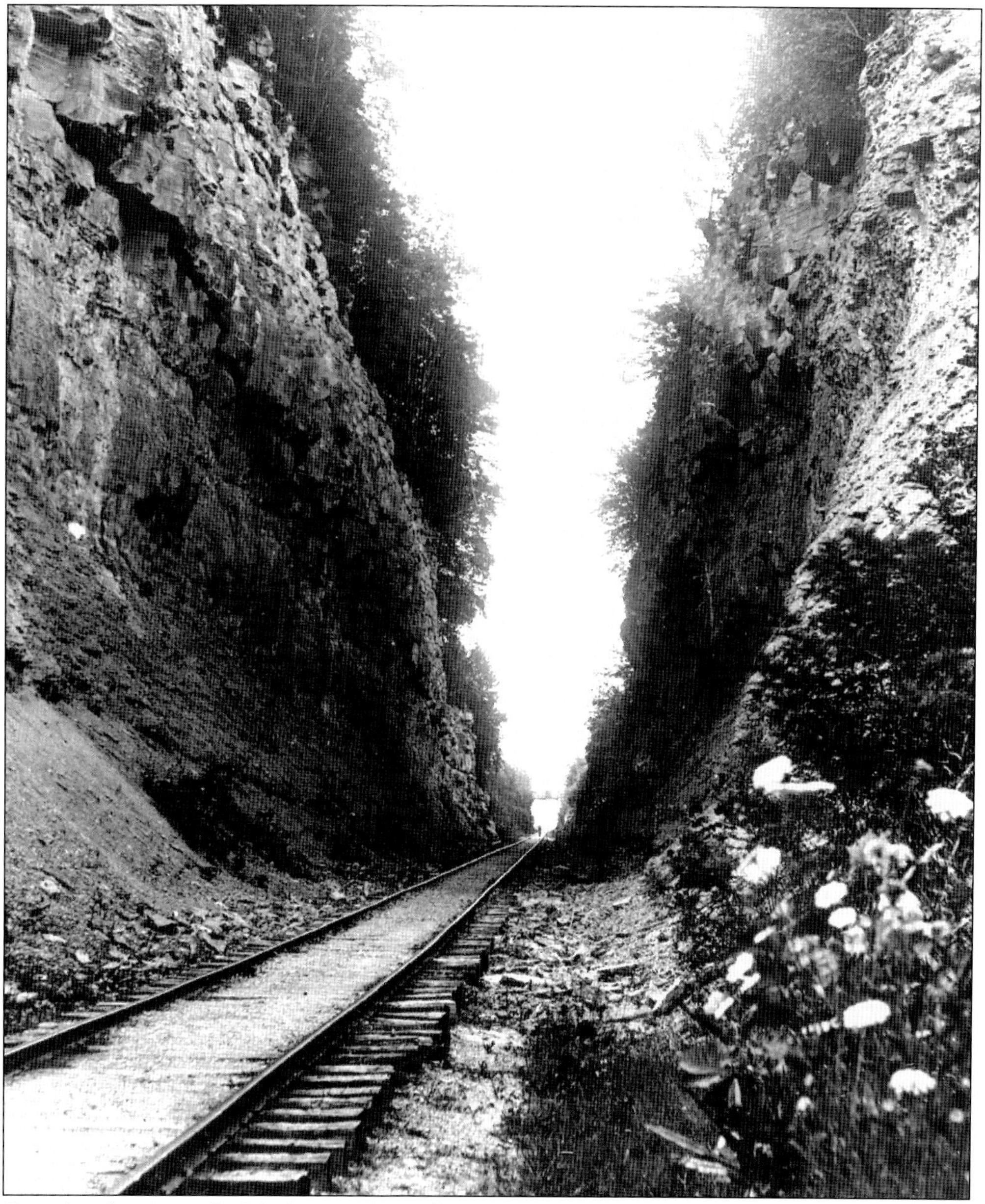

Completed in 1841, the Madison incline of 7,012 feet was, and remains today, the steepest grade of any line-haul railroad in the country. The incline ascends 413 feet, or 311 feet per mile, giving the tracks a 5.89 percent grade. In January 1836, Gen. Noah Noble signed a huge internal improvements bill for Indiana that provided for a Madison-Columbus Indianapolis-Lafayette railroad. At that time, Madison was Indiana's largest city. Construction started September 16, 1836. Hundreds of Irish laborers came to Madison to build the incline. The principal obstacle confronting the workers was the rugged terrain. The largest obstacle by far was making a cut 1,150 feet long, 40 feet wide, and up to 125 feet deep. It has been estimated that this big cut produced no fewer than 175,000 yards of materials, or 250,000 tons of earth and rock. That much excavation might take a month or so today, but back in the 1830s, it took five years of hard, backbreaking labor. (Courtesy of the Jefferson County Historical Society.)

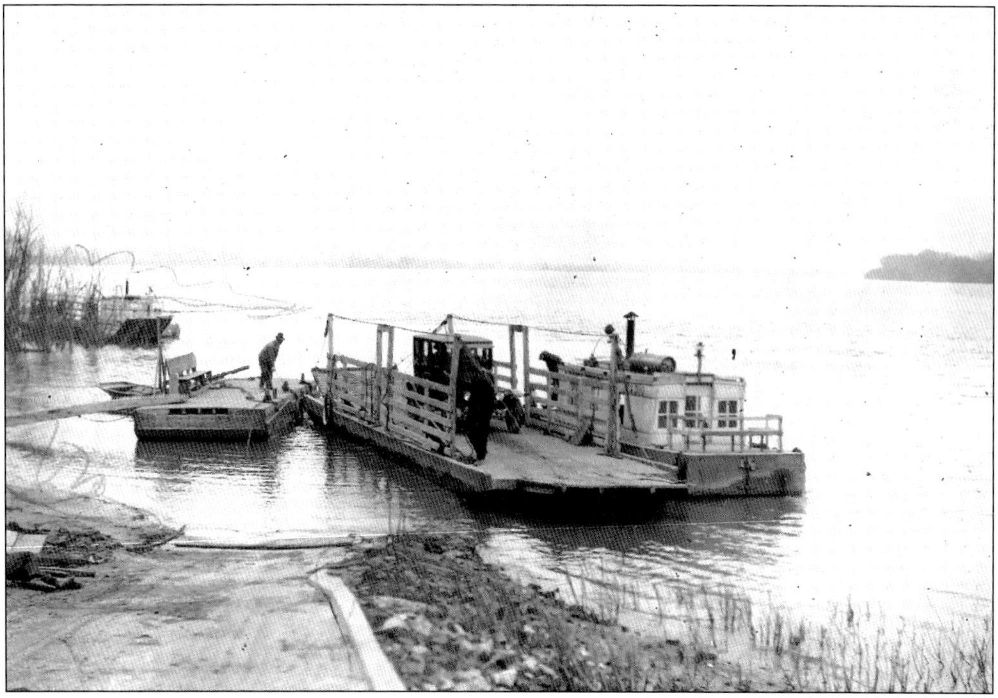

The Rockport Ferry, pictured around 1910, was a vital means of river transit until a bridge was constructed long after World War II. Before the Evansville-Henderson vehicular bridge was completed in 1932, all river crossings between Louisville and Paducah, Kentucky, were provided by ferry. (Courtesy of Willard Library.)

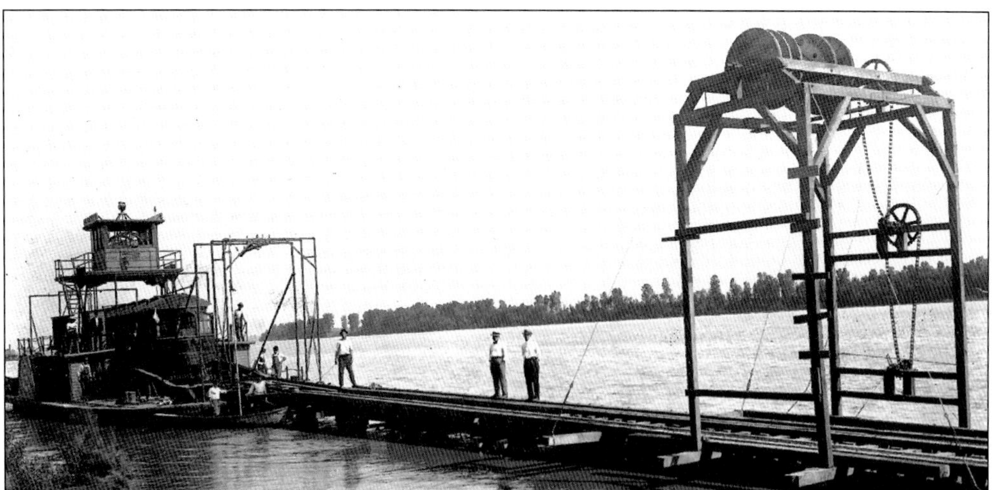

The lack of bridges isolated contact between Indiana and Kentucky. Pictured here is the Evansville-Henderson ferry for the Interurban Railroad. It is located near the present Henderson Bridge and Ellis Park. (Courtesy of Willard Library.)

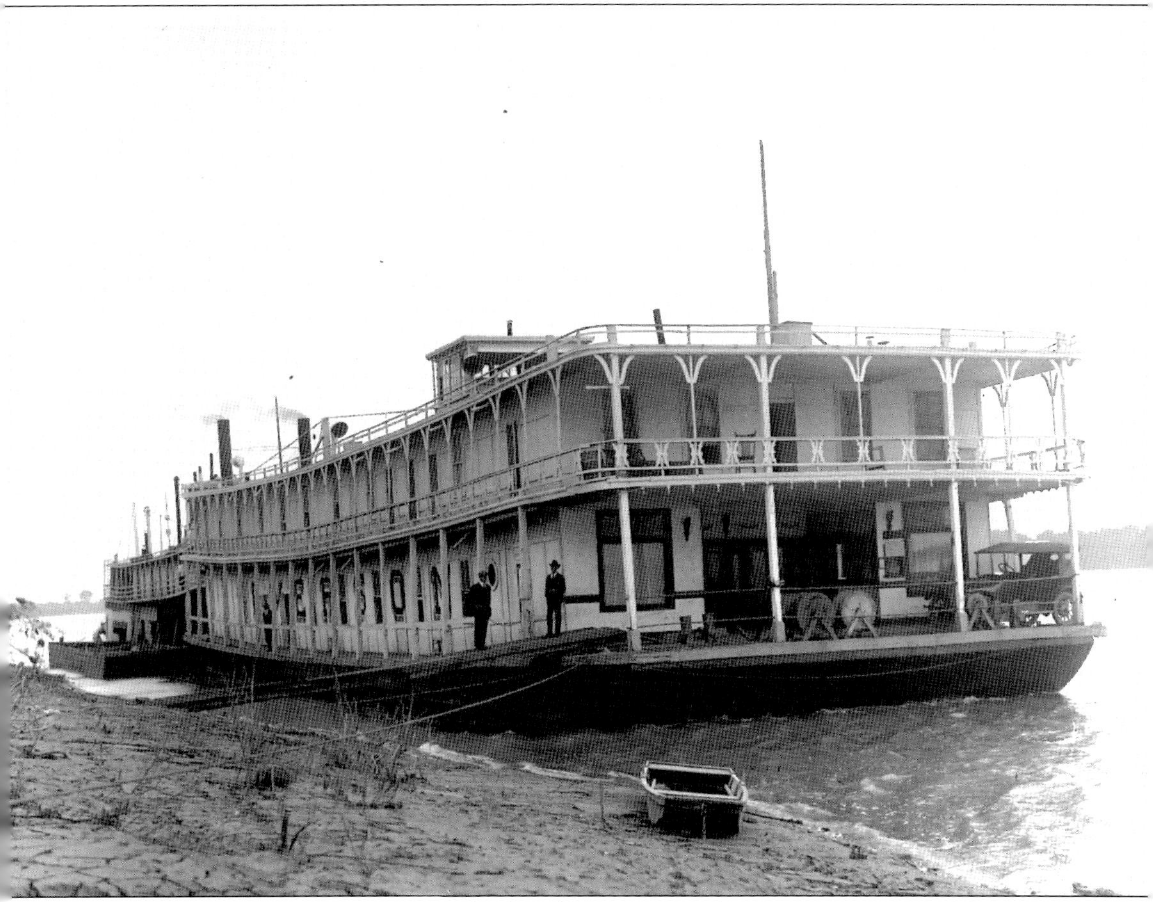

The *Emerson Goldenrod* showboat, and others like it, provided entertainment up and down the river. These flat-bottomed boats depended on the pushing of a steamboat for power. The boat was large enough to accommodate an automobile for transportation on its stern. (Courtesy of USI Special Collections.)

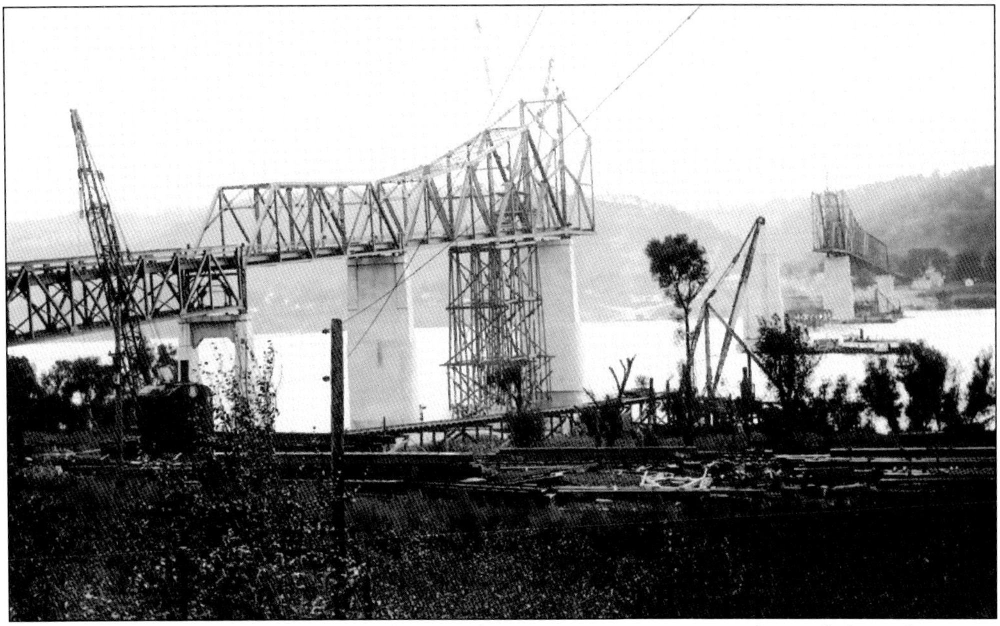

The Madison-Milton Bridge, shown here under construction, is a cantilevered through a truss bridge over Ohio River on U.S. Route 421 between Madison, Indiana, and Milton, Kentucky. It opened in 1929 and is the only vehicular crossing for 40 miles upstream and downstream. (Courtesy of the Jefferson County Historical Society.)

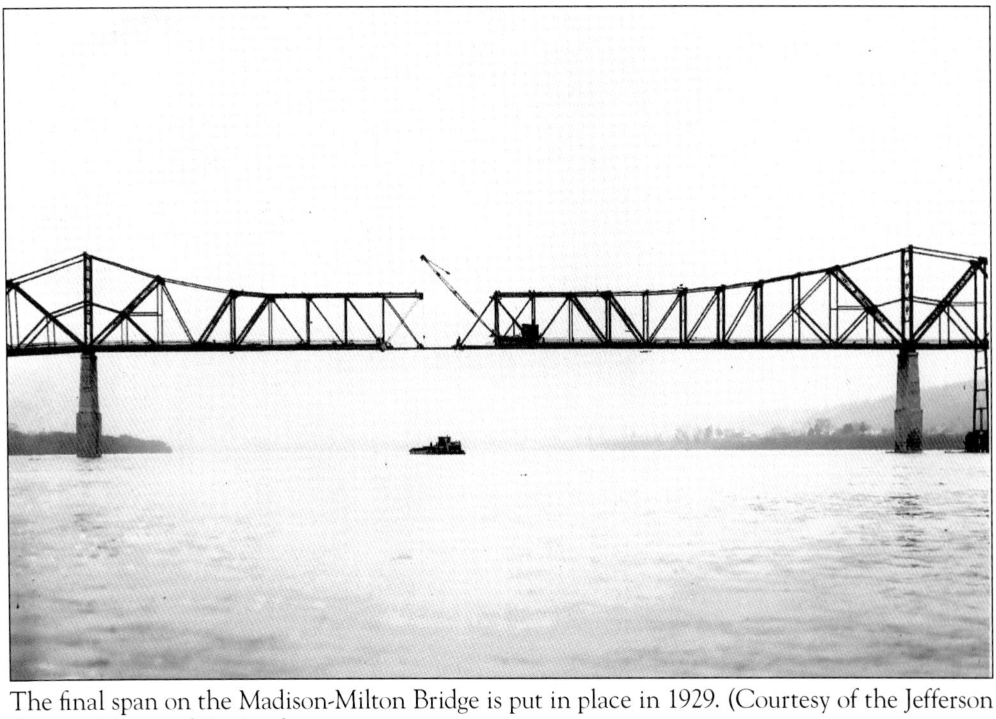

The final span on the Madison-Milton Bridge is put in place in 1929. (Courtesy of the Jefferson County Historical Society.)

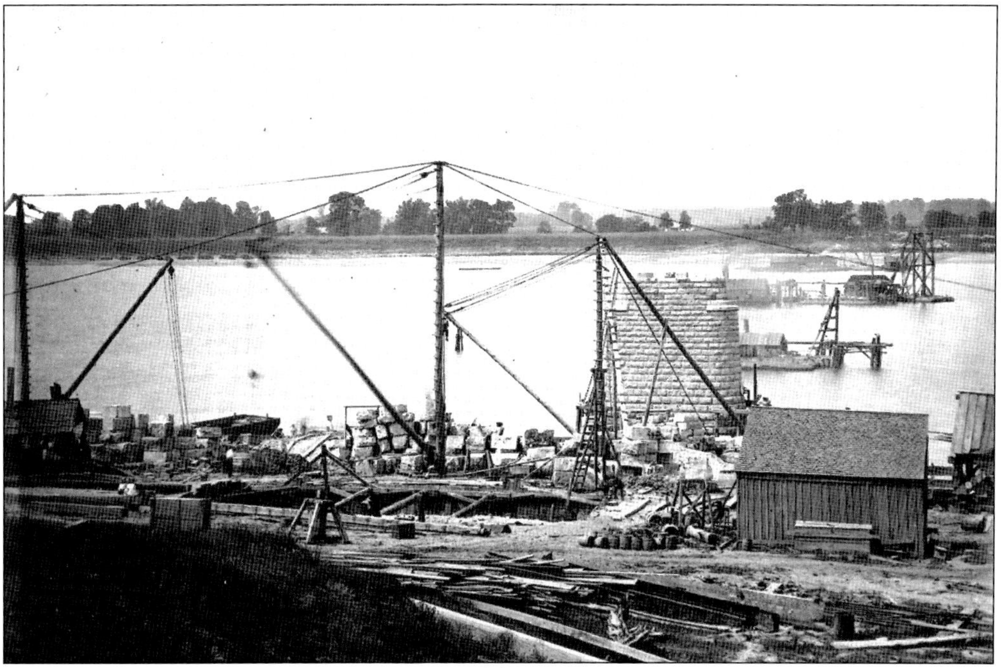

The girders of the original span of the Audubon Memorial Bridge are under construction. (Courtesy of Willard Library.)

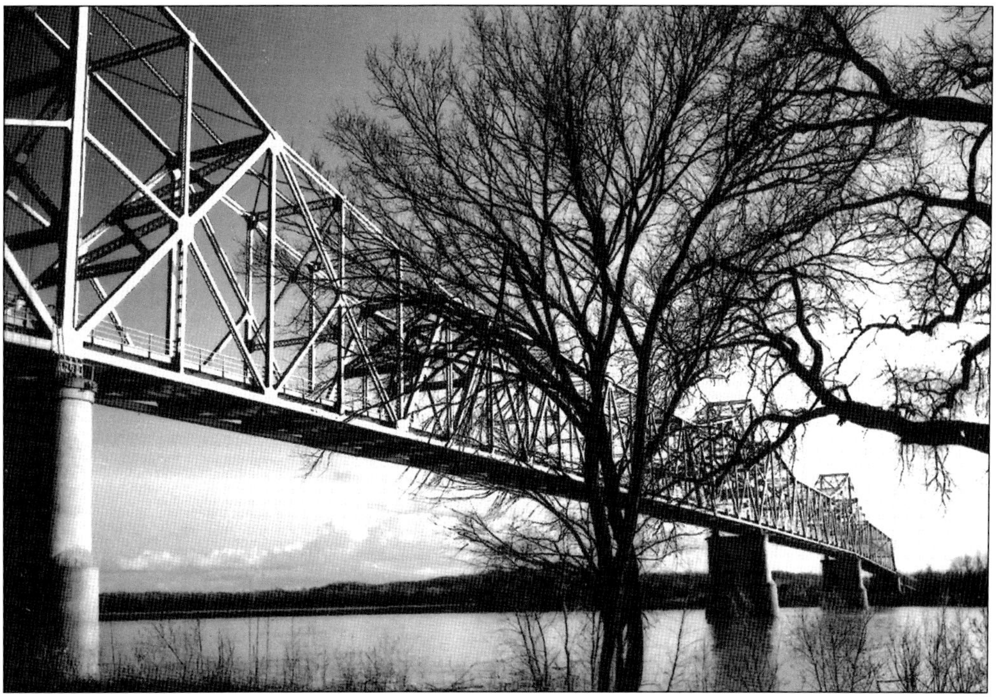

The Audubon Memorial Bridge, which linked Evansville and Henderson, Kentucky, was built in 1932. In 1965, an identical bridge was built next to it, which became the southbound lanes. The original structure handles the northbound traffic. The pair is often referred to as the twin bridges. (Courtesy of USI Special Collections.)

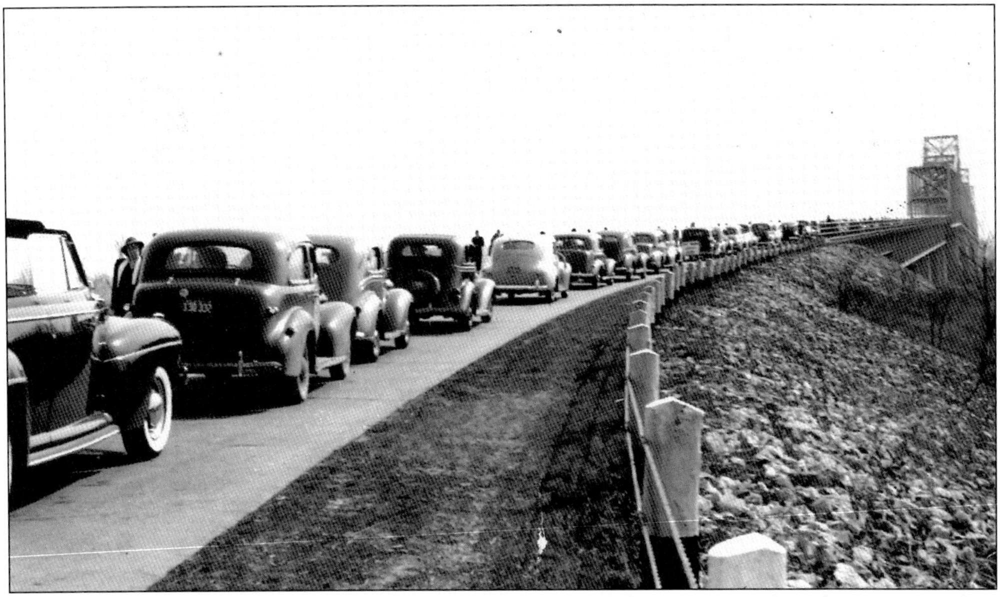

Cars line up for the grand opening dedication of the Audubon Memorial Bridge. Prior to this, crossing the river meant taking the ferry. (Courtesy of Willard Library.)

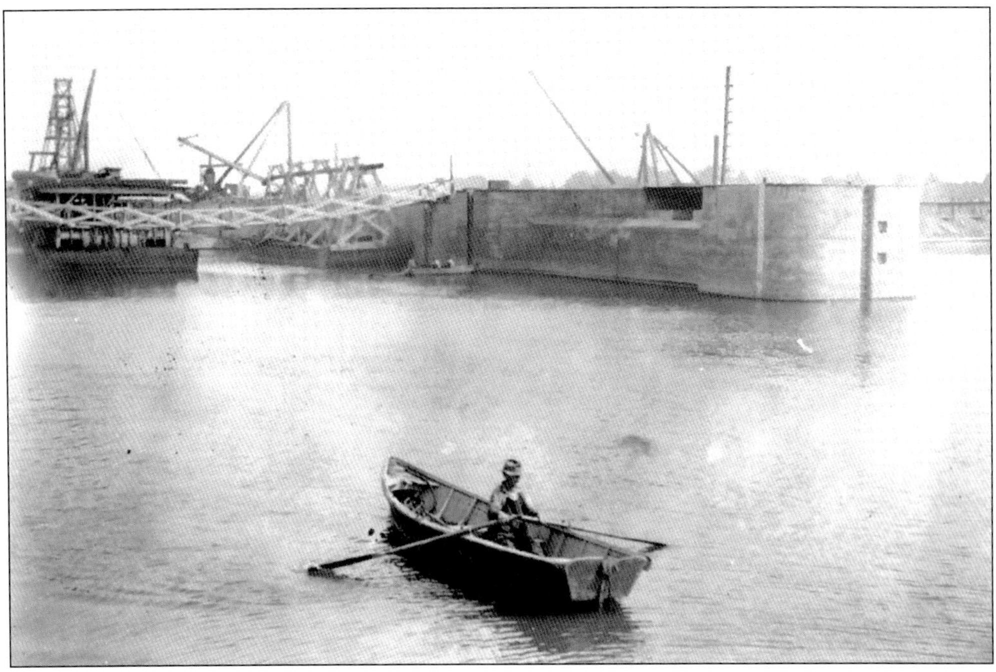

Construction takes place on the original Newburgh Lock and Dam No. 47 in the 1920s. In 1953, a federal program was instituted to modernize the Ohio River's locks and dams erected in the 1920s. The newest dam was completed in 1975. The hand-operated wickets on the old dam gave way to push button controls. Over the last 60 years, the string of dams has raised the water level and created a succession of moving lakes. (Courtesy of Willard Library.)

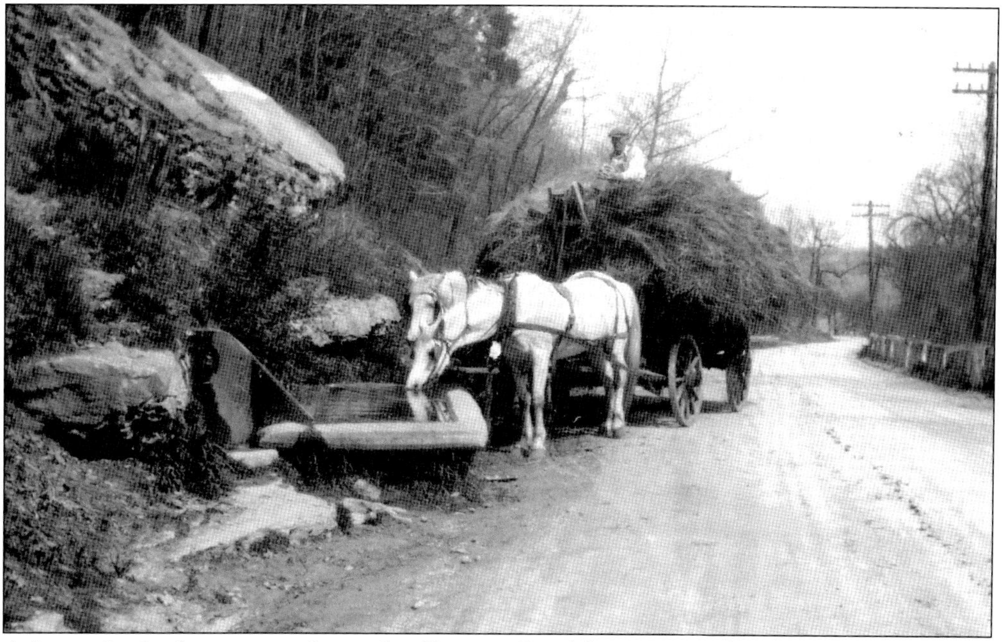

A horse drinks from a trough on the Hanover Road between Madison and Hanover while pulling a hay wagon. The road was very hilly and steep, and the trough accommodated horse traffic. (Courtesy of the Jefferson County Historical Society.)

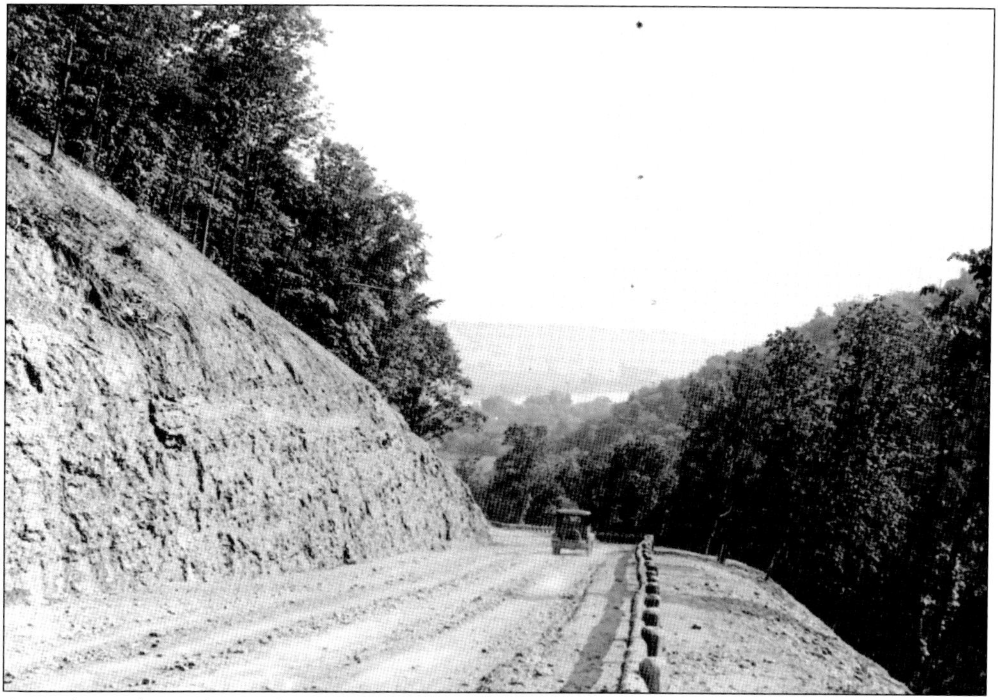

A car drives down the south entrance road to Clifty Falls State Park in 1938. The park is located in Madison, between state roads 56 and 62. The park is known for its deep gorges, waterfalls, and sheetrock walls. This road is indicative of many of the roads around Madison and shows the difficulty of early car travel. (Courtesy of the Jefferson County Historical Society.)

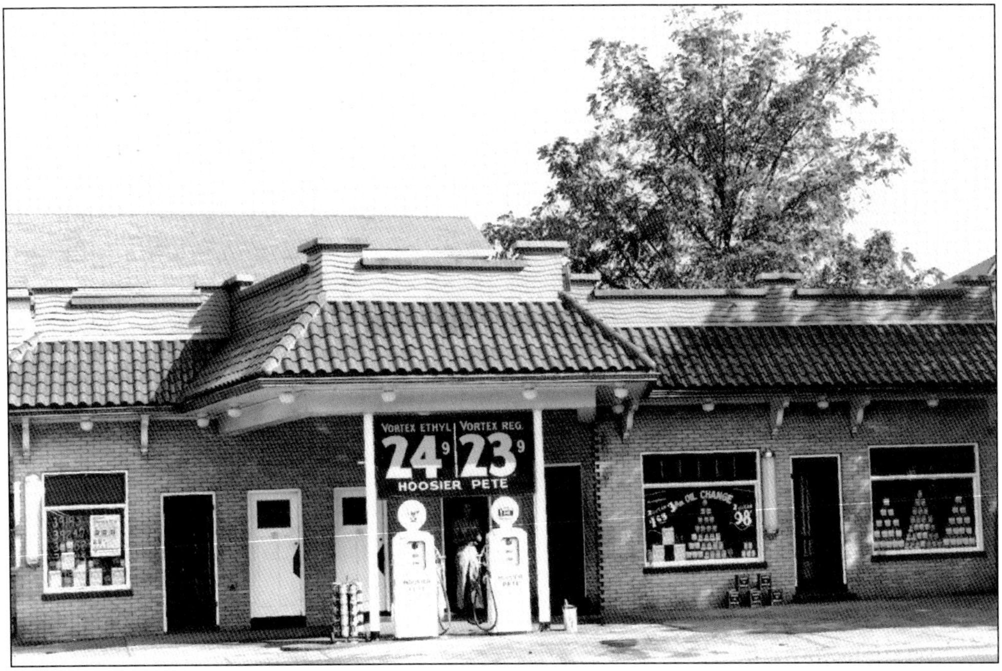

A Hoosier Pete gas station sits along the roadway in Rising Sun. Stations like this sprung up in small towns all across the country to handle the increase of vehicular traffic after the early part of the 20th century. (Courtesy of the Ohio County Indiana Historical Society and Museum.)

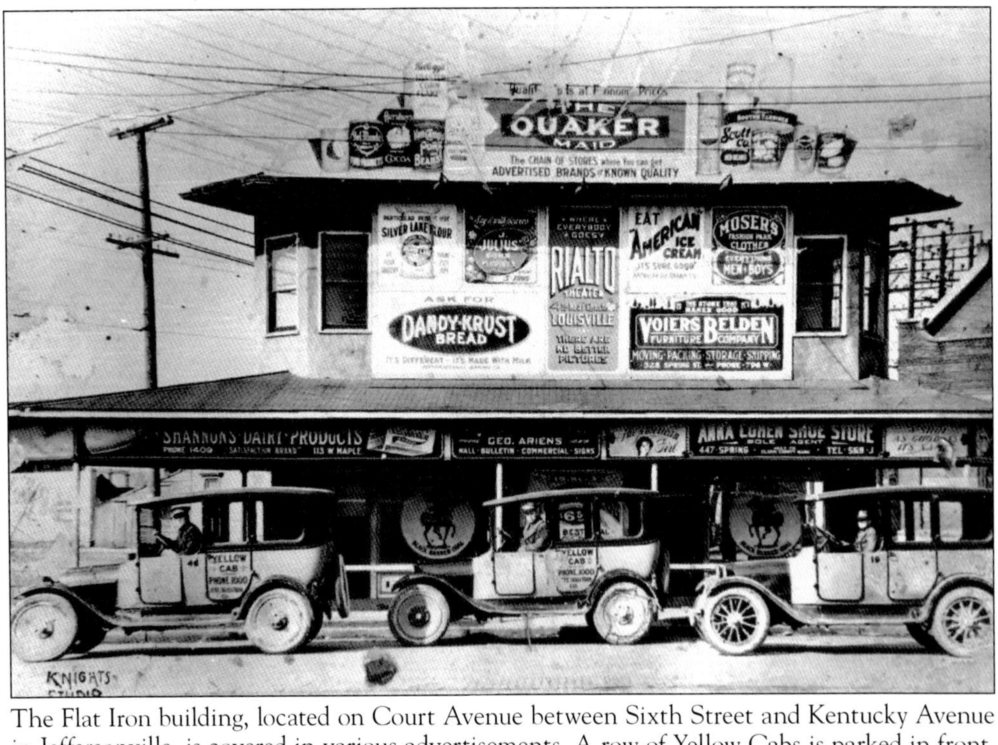

The Flat Iron building, located on Court Avenue between Sixth Street and Kentucky Avenue in Jeffersonville, is covered in various advertisements. A row of Yellow Cabs is parked in front. (Courtesy of the Jeffersonville Township Public Library.)

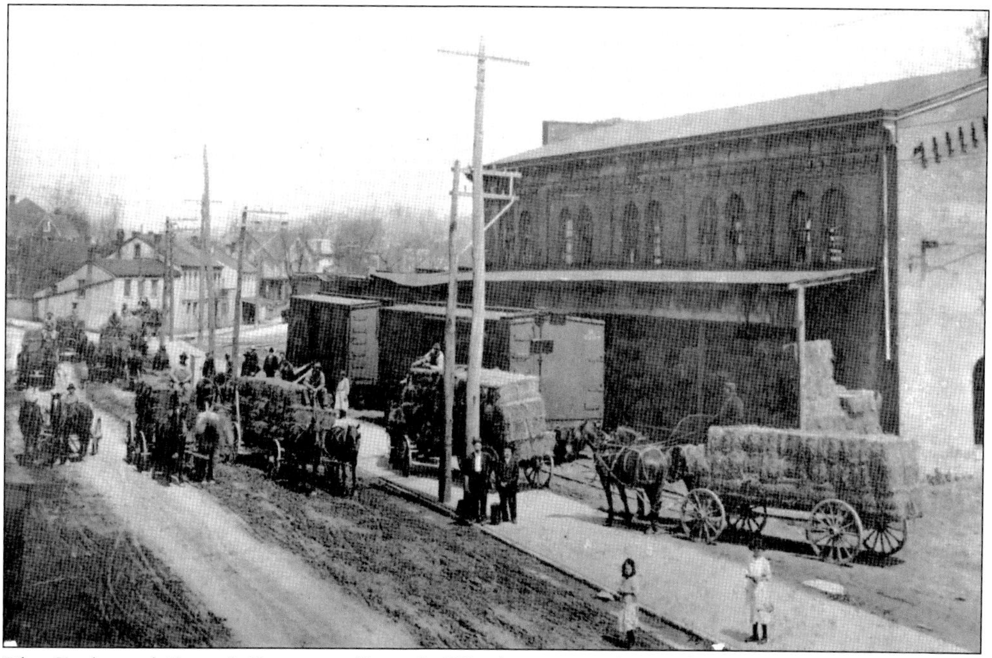

The Early and Daniel Company Branch Warehouse was located in Aurora. Hay and other grains were brought by area farmers to be shipped on rail or by boat. Warehouses like this were common along the Ohio River since it provided an easy way to ship materials. (Courtesy of the Ohio County Indiana Historical Society and Museum.)

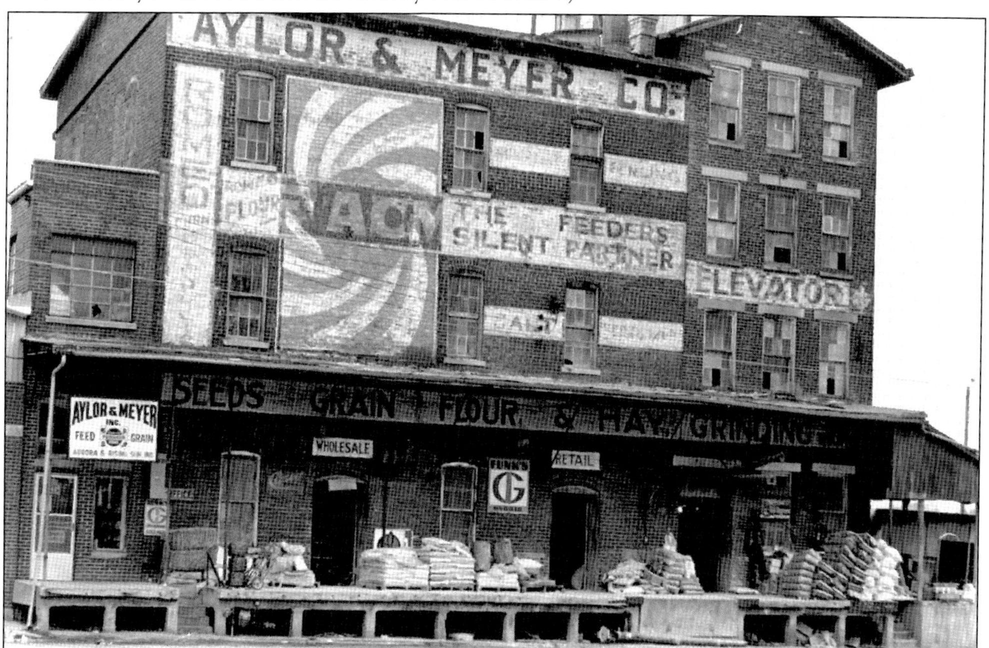

Farming was common in many of the communities and throughout the countryside along what is now the Ohio River Scenic Byway. The river bottoms yielded rich farmland. Feed stores, like the Aylor and Meyer Company in Aurora, were located in most of the small cities and towns along the river. (Courtesy of the Dearborn County Historical Society.)

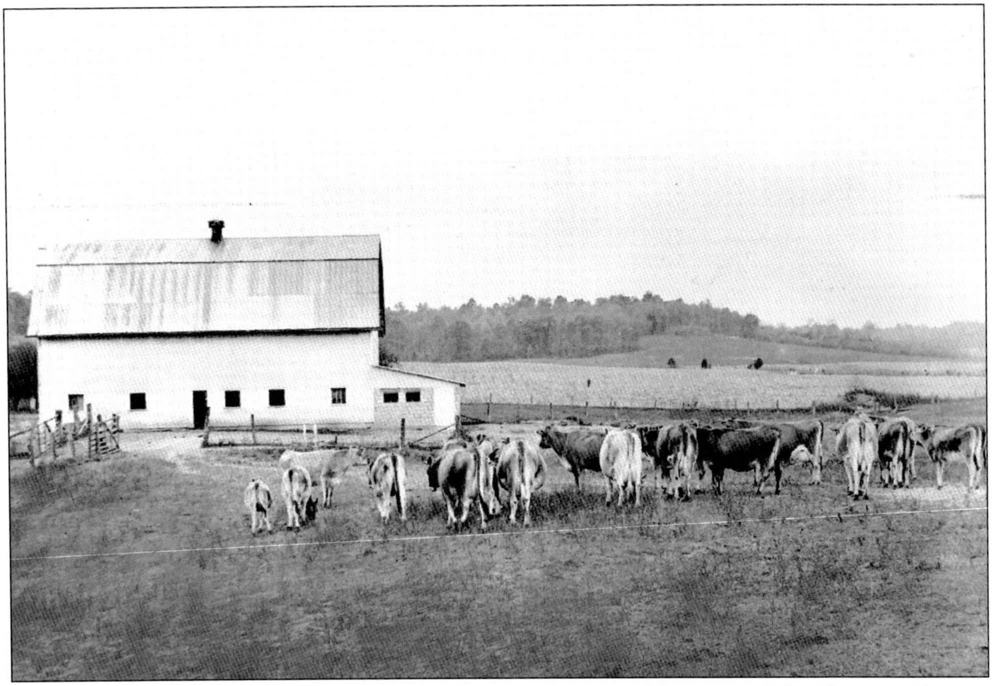

Cattle graze outside a barn near Corydon in Harrison County. (Courtesy of the Harrison County Public Library.)

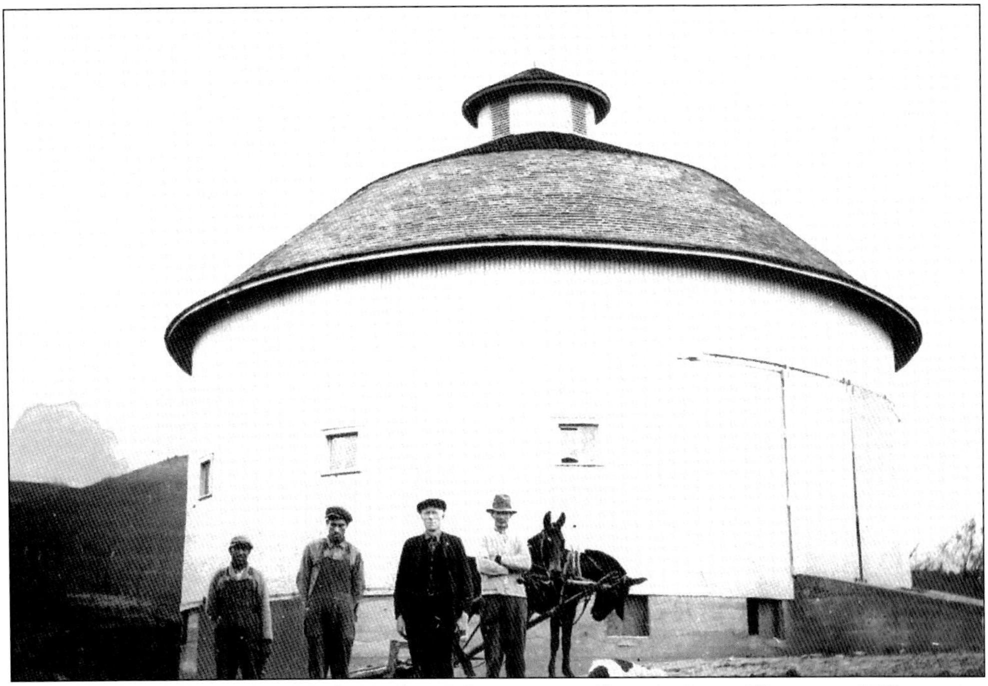

Round barns like this were popular in the Midwest, especially in Indiana, Illinois, and Wisconsin. The barns were typically built with the silo in the center of the barn. Their shape was to make feeding, milking cows, and other work more efficient. This barn was located in Switzerland County. (Courtesy of the Switzerland County Historical Society.)

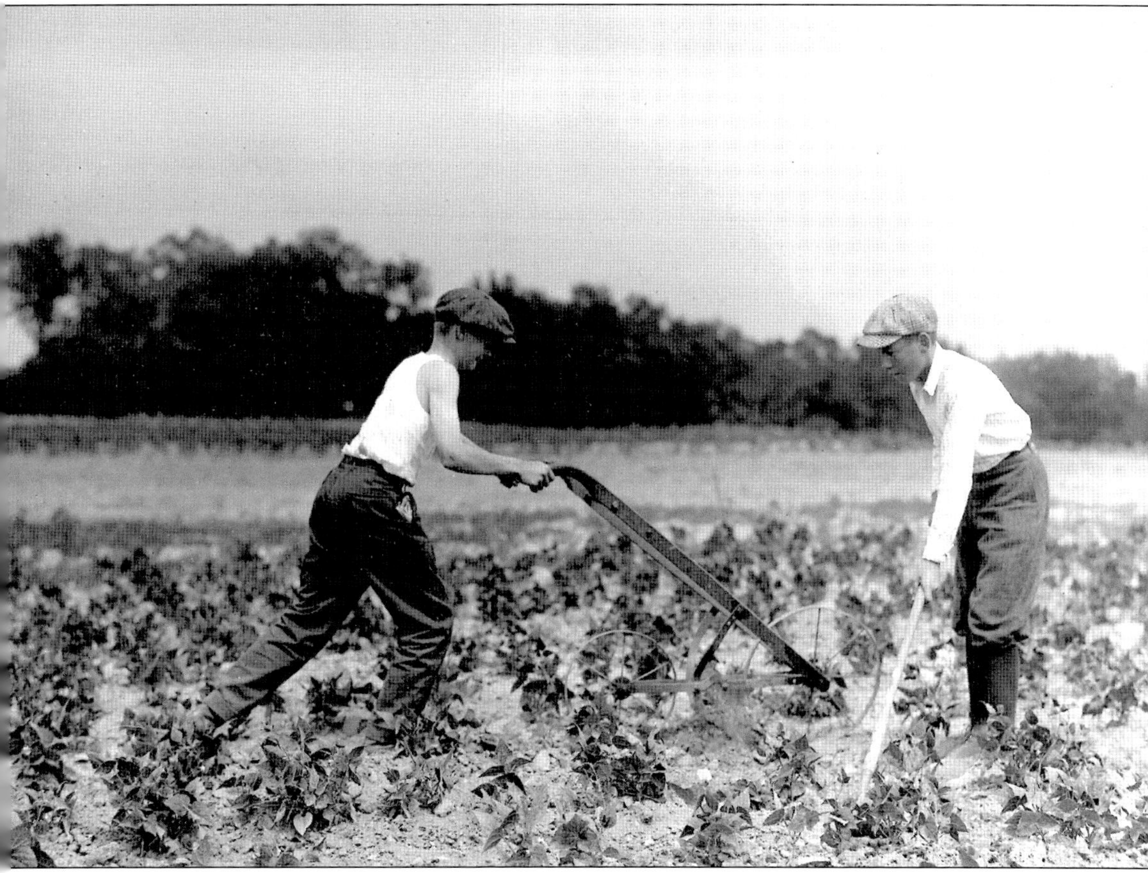

Two young boys work in the fields. Children often helped with the manual labor required in farming. (Courtesy of USI Special Collections.)

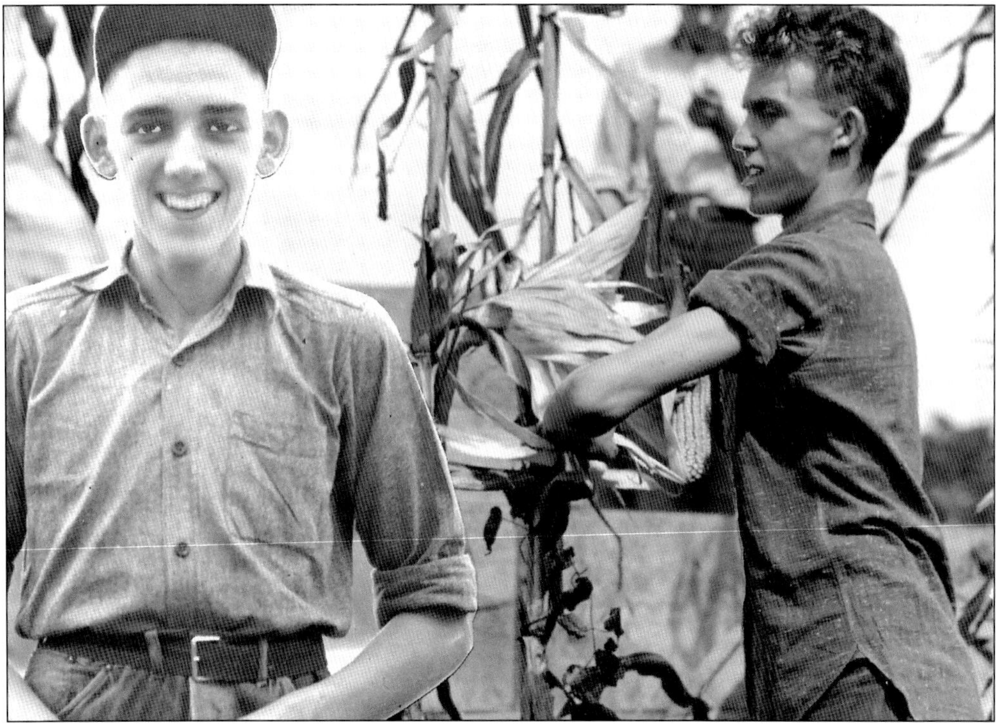

Stanley Miller and Orville Duncan pick corn on a farm in Harrison County near Corydon. As is evident from this photograph, farming was still done much by hand with little assistance from mechanized machinery. (Courtesy of the Harrison County Public Library.)

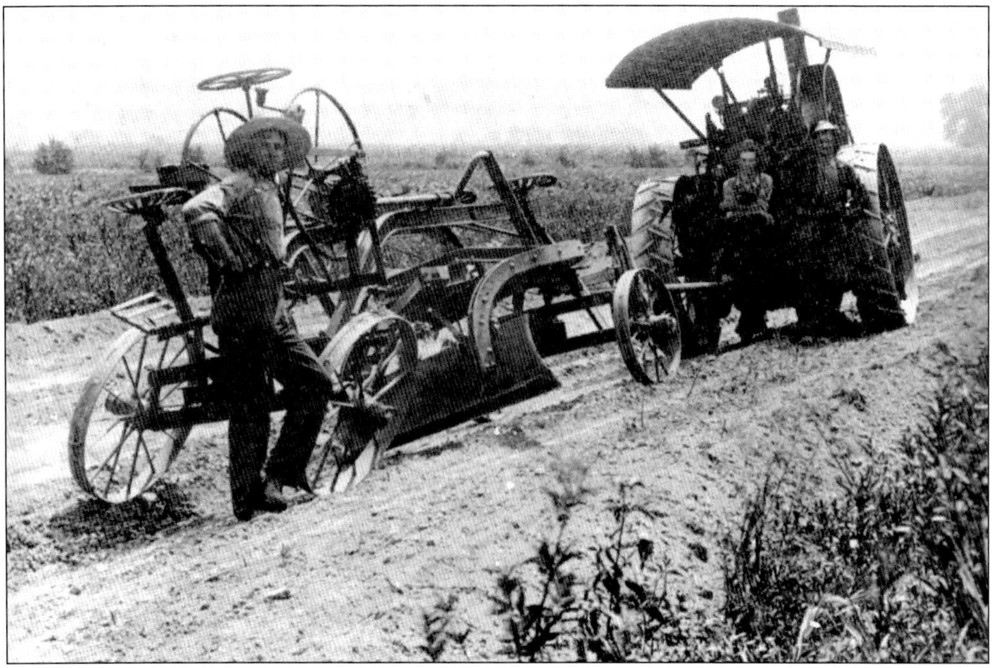

In this photograph, tractors make plowing easier for these farmers in Ohio County near Rising Sun. (Courtesy of the Ohio County Indiana Historical Society and Museum.)

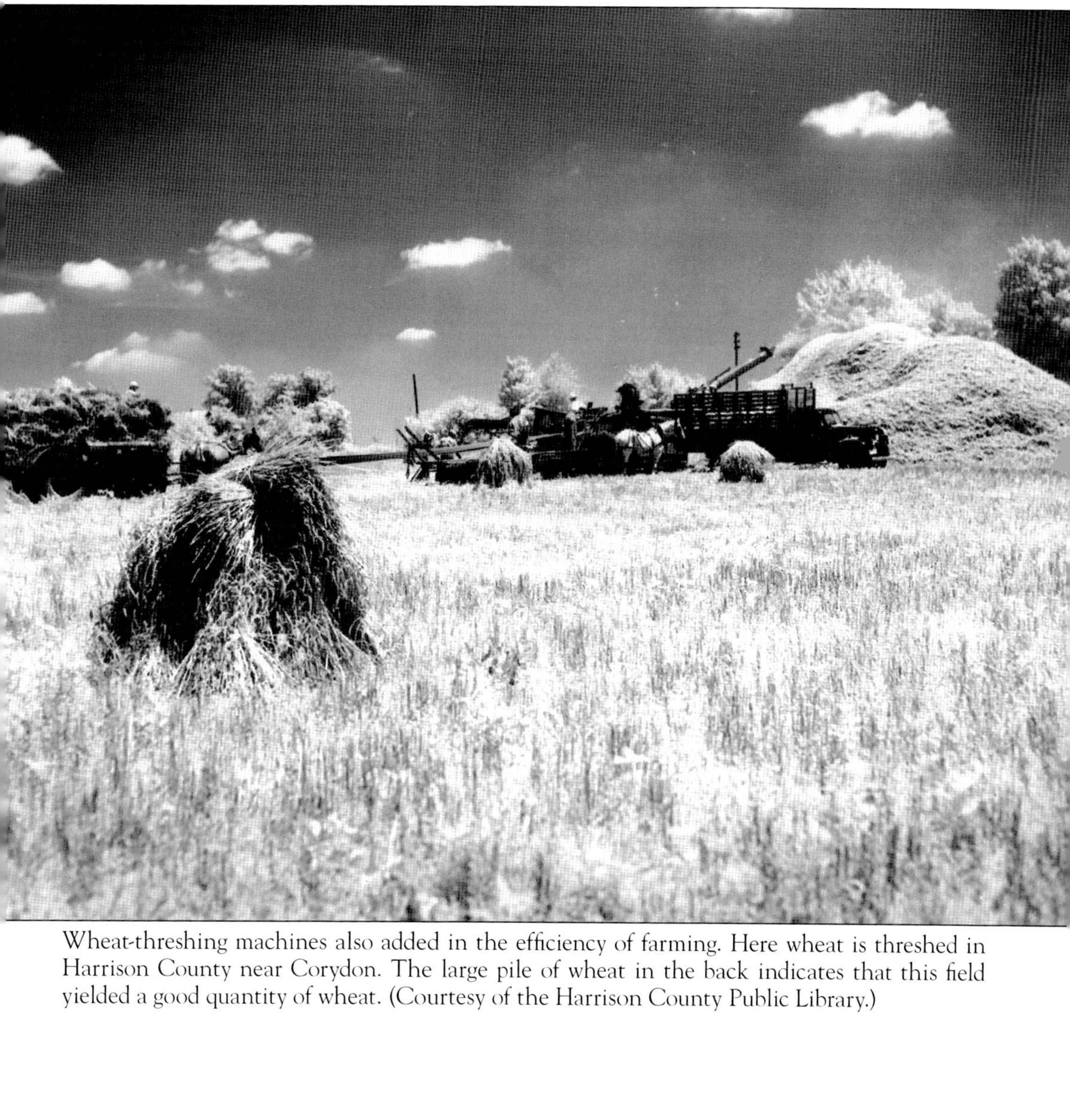

Wheat-threshing machines also added in the efficiency of farming. Here wheat is threshed in Harrison County near Corydon. The large pile of wheat in the back indicates that this field yielded a good quantity of wheat. (Courtesy of the Harrison County Public Library.)

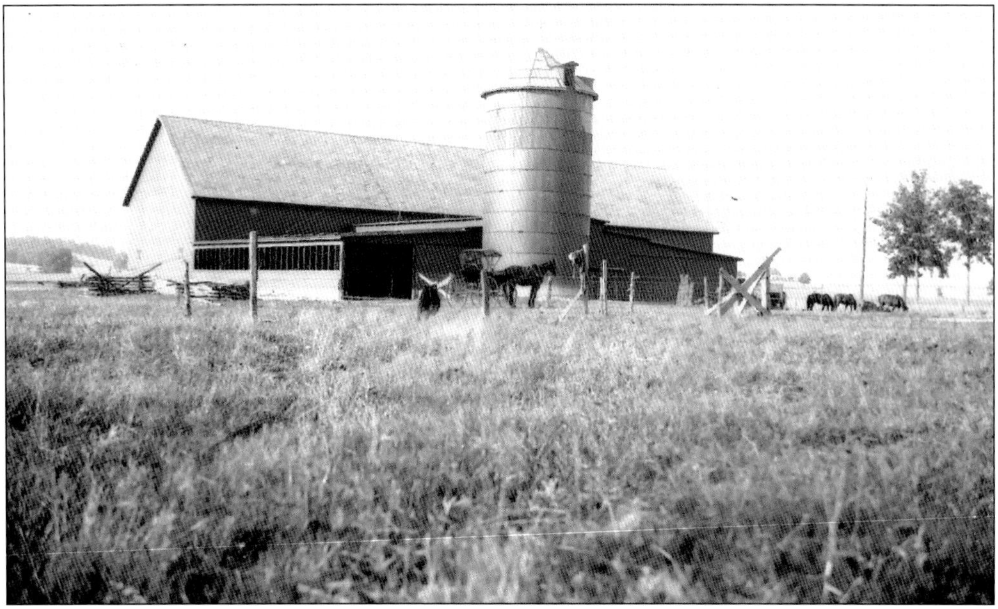

This is a typical farm in southwest Indiana. (Courtesy of USI Special Collections.)

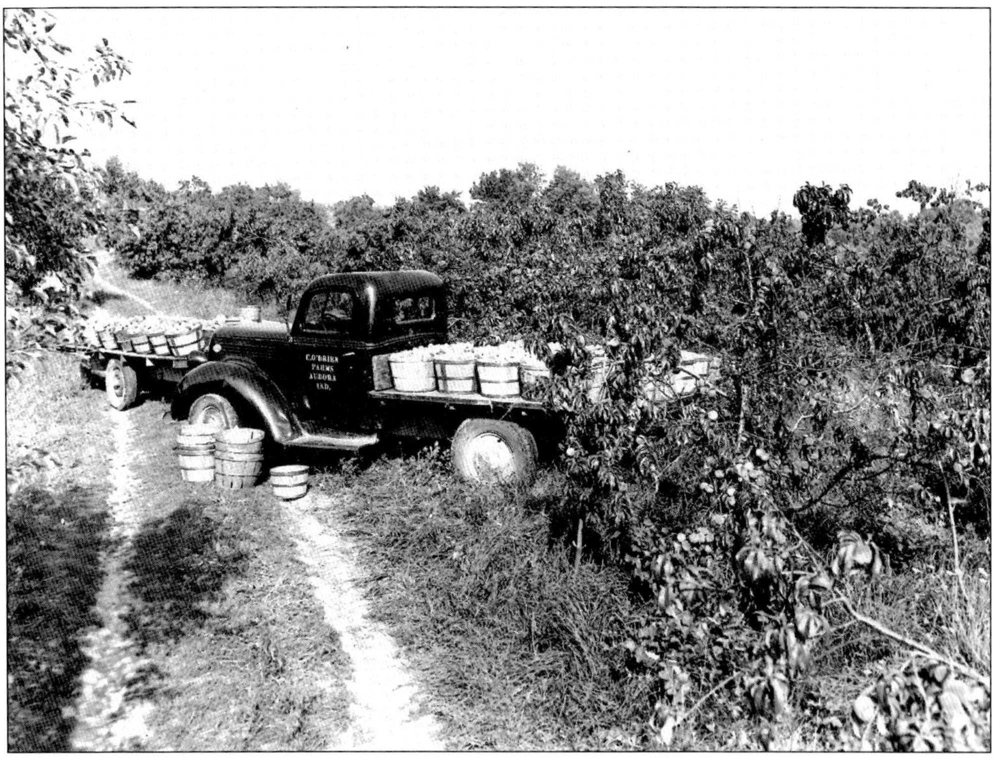

Fruit is harvested at the Cornelius O'Brien farm in Aurora. O'Brien purchased the property, with its house known as Veraestau, in 1935. The name Veraestau is derived from the Latin roots for spring, summer, and fall. Determined to make it a productive farm, O'Brien brought in blooded livestock and cultivated apple and peach trees. (Courtesy of the Dearborn County Historical Society.)

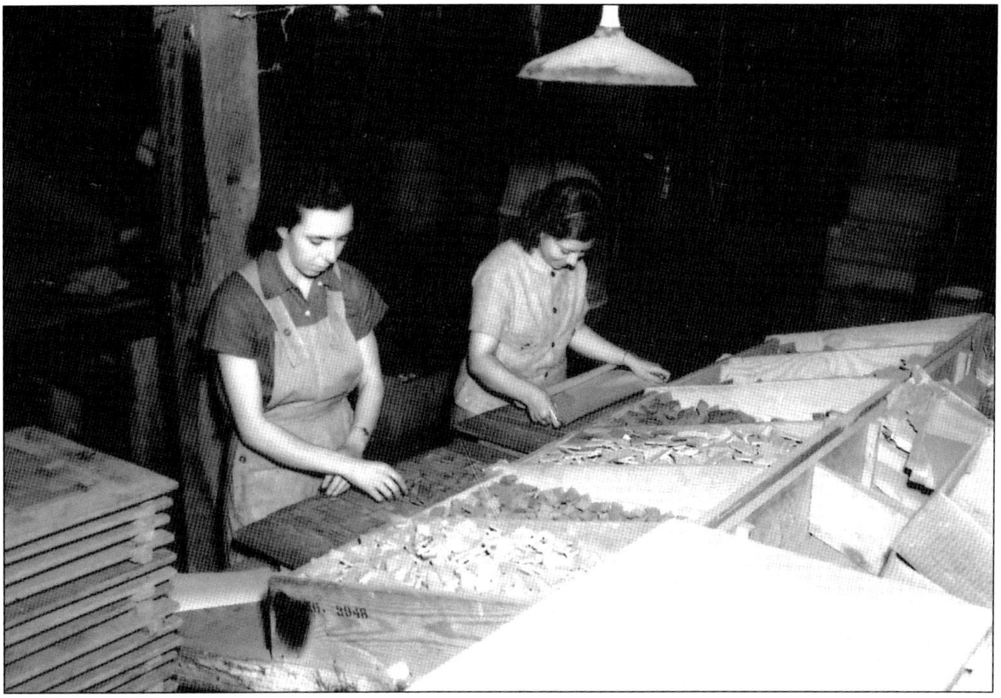

Two women perform industrial work at a Rockport factory. (Courtesy of USI Special Collections.)

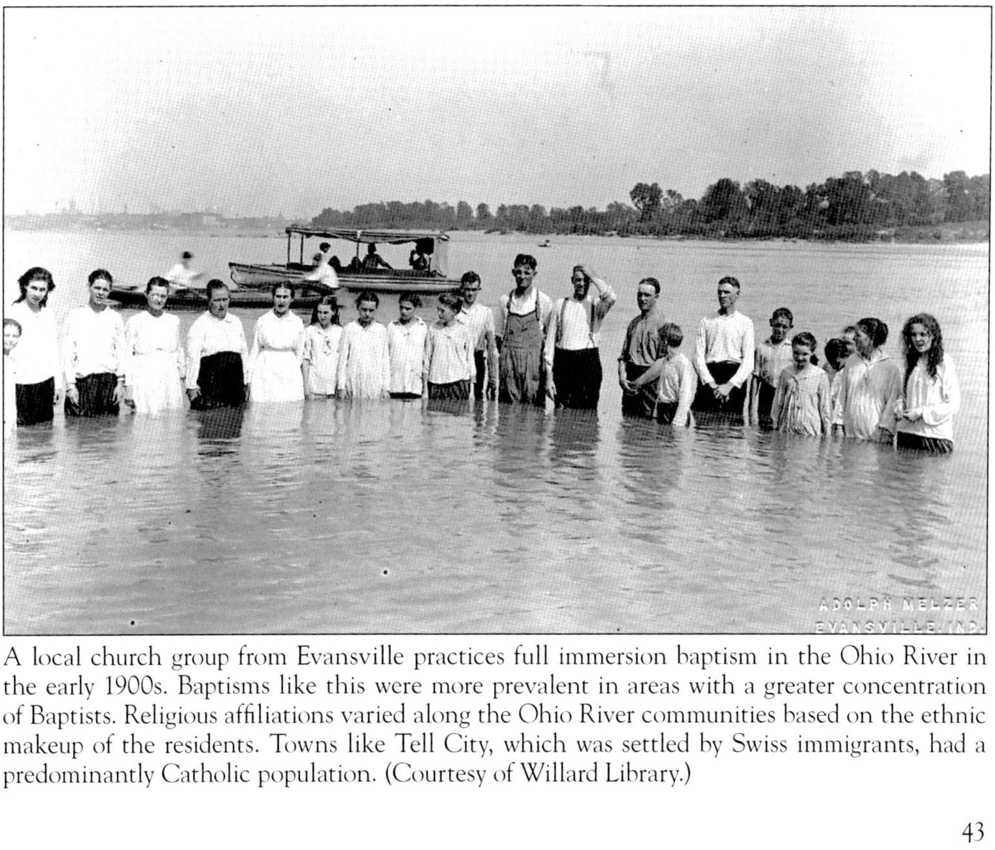

A local church group from Evansville practices full immersion baptism in the Ohio River in the early 1900s. Baptisms like this were more prevalent in areas with a greater concentration of Baptists. Religious affiliations varied along the Ohio River communities based on the ethnic makeup of the residents. Towns like Tell City, which was settled by Swiss immigrants, had a predominantly Catholic population. (Courtesy of Willard Library.)

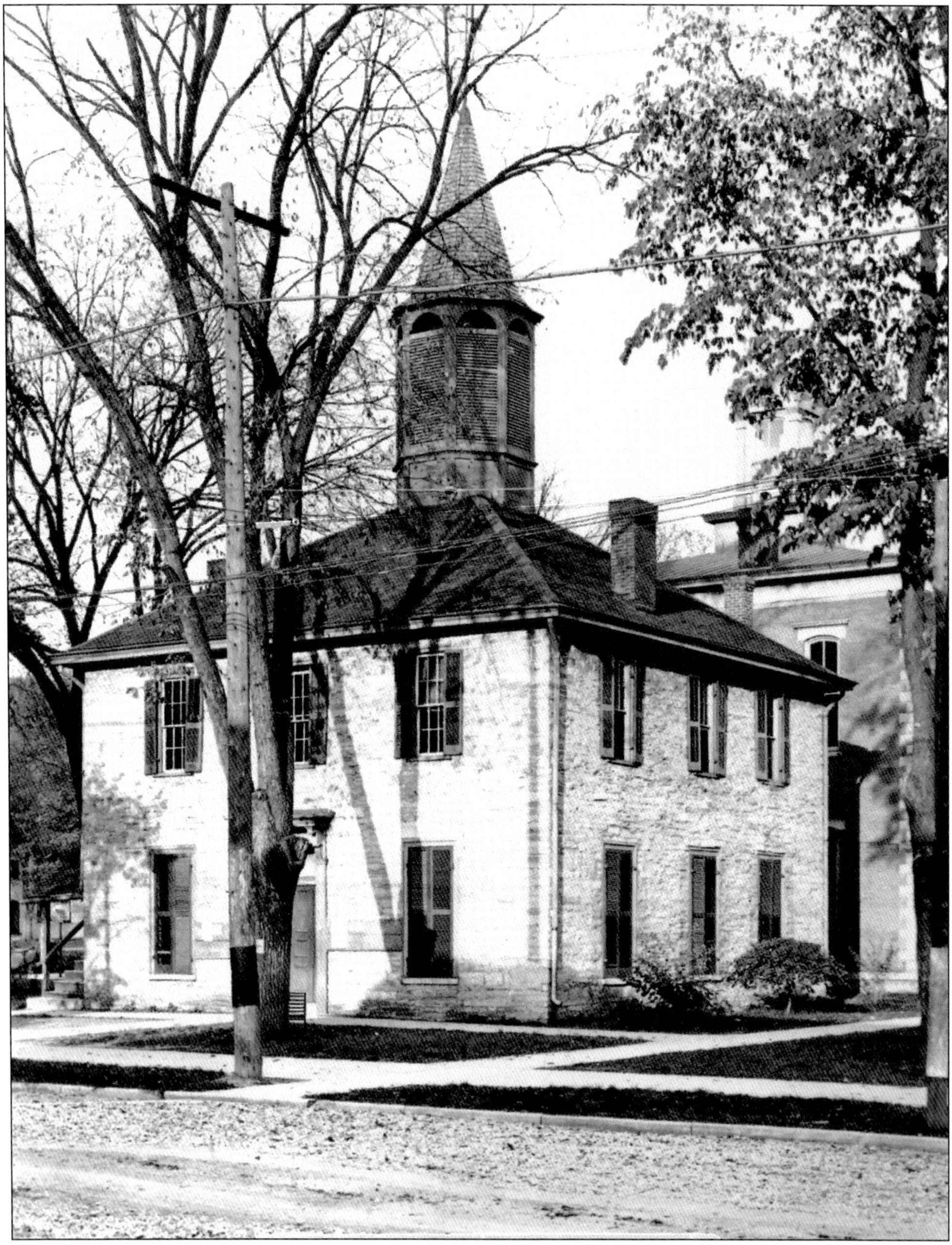

Corydon served as the capital from 1816 (when Indiana achieved statehood) until 1825, when the capital was moved to Indianapolis. The square, Federal-style limestone capitol building, built between 1814 and 1816, was originally intended to serve as the courthouse for Harrison County. Limestone was hauled from nearby quarries to erect the 40-foot square walls, and poplar and walnut logs were cut from virgin forests for the ceiling and roof supports. The building was constructed after the great New Madrid earthquakes of 1811 and 1812, and the building has special rods that were added for support. The House of Representatives met on the first floor, while the second floor housed the Senate and the Supreme Court. This is the way the building looked in 1916 during the state centennial. (Courtesy of the Harrison County Public Library.)

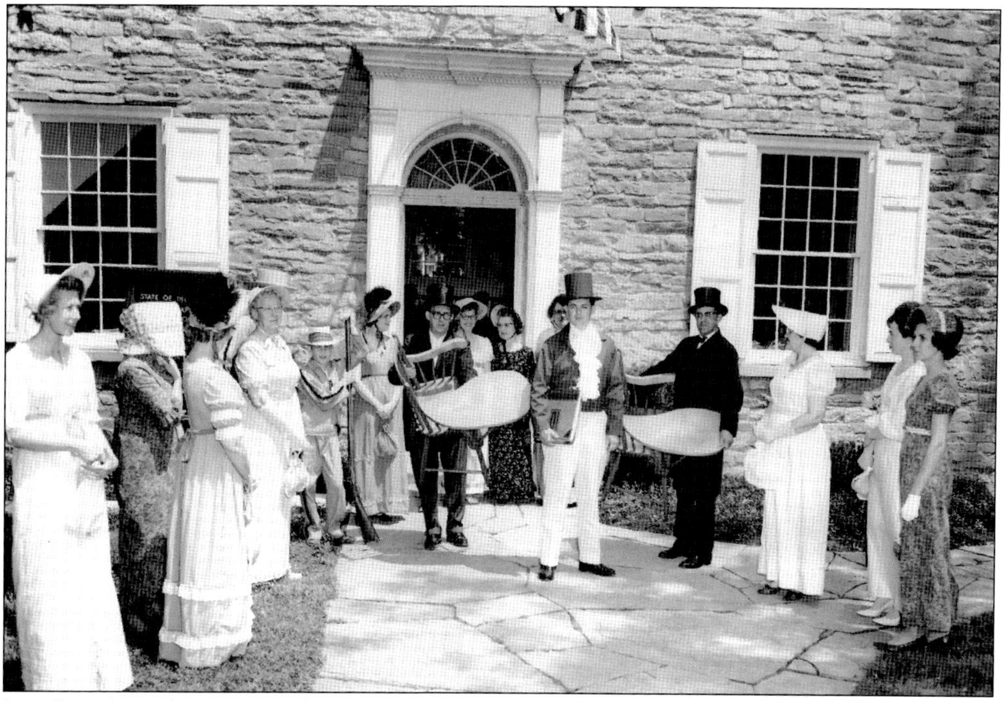

Local residents dress in period costume outside the original state capitol building as they celebrate Indiana's sesquicentennial in 1966. (Courtesy of the Harrison County Public Library.)

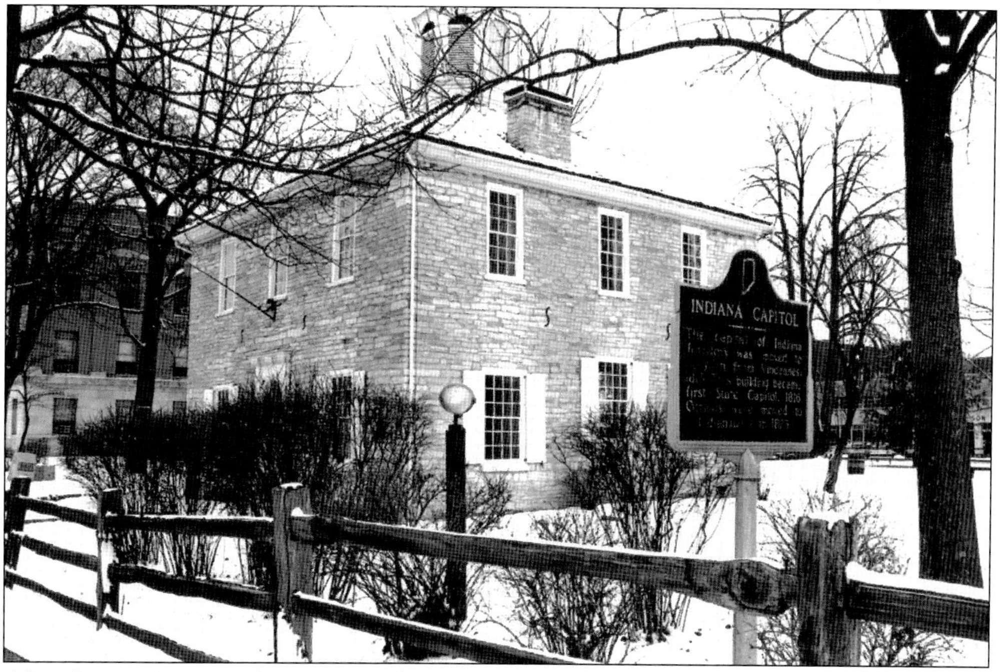

After the new Harrison County Courthouse was completed, the old state capitol building, which had served as the county courthouse, was restored to its original appearance. It is now a state historic site and is operated by the Indiana Department of Natural Resources. A historical marker interprets the history of the state capital. (Courtesy of the Harrison County Public Library.)

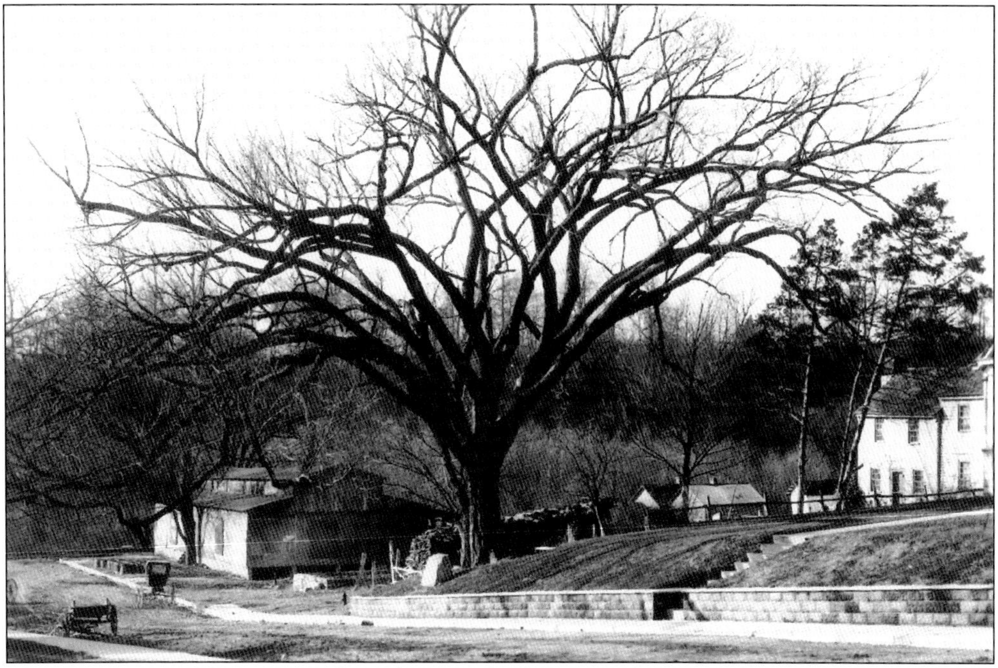

The Constitution Elm in Corydon, photographed in 1913, has special significance in Indiana history. Due to the heat, delegates to the first constitutional convention that began on June 10, 1816, met underneath its shade. The first constitution was completed 19 days later. The tree died of Dutch elm disease in 1925. (Courtesy the Indiana Department of Natural Resources, Division of Forestry Archives.)

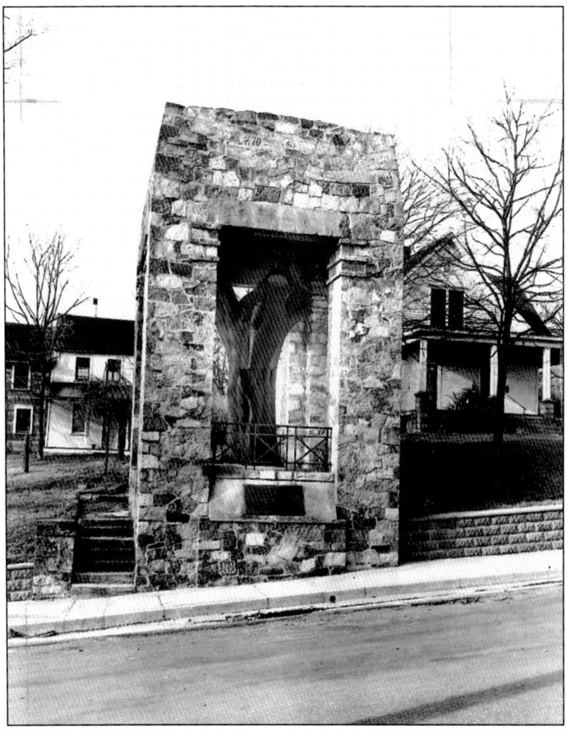

After the Constitution Elm died, the stump was preserved and housed in the stone structure. (Courtesy of the Harrison County Public Library.)

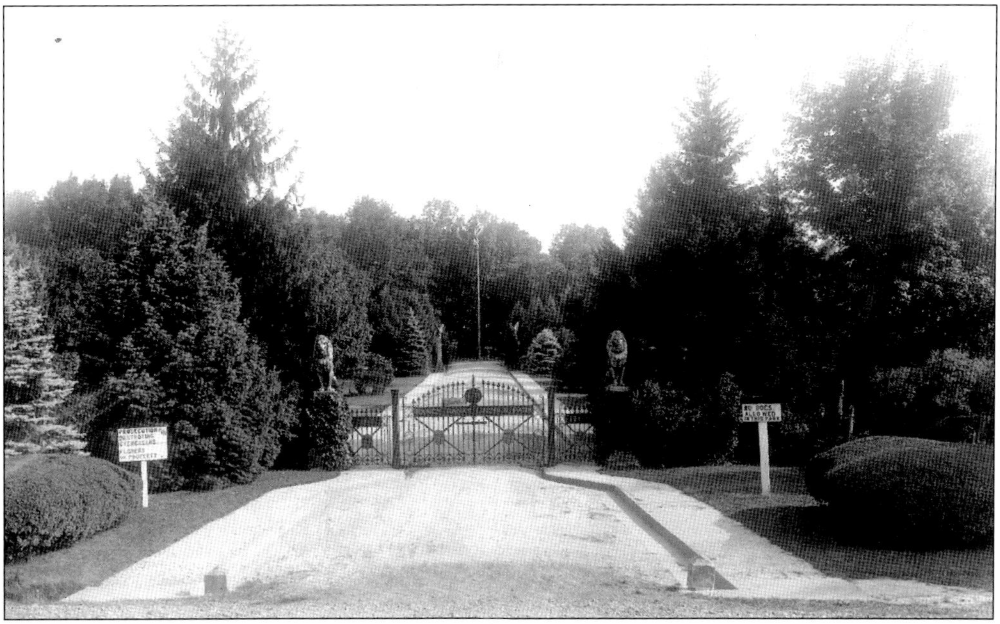

Abraham Lincoln and his family moved to Indiana from Kentucky in December 1816. He lived in Indiana, in what is now Spencer County, from the ages of 7 through 21. Lincoln's mother, Nancy Hanks Lincoln, died of milk sickness in 1818. In 1907, an effort was made to preserve and mark her grave. The commissioners of the Nancy Hanks Lincoln Burial Grounds fenced off 16 acres surrounding the grave. The area was secured by an iron gate that was flanked by sandstone lions. (Courtesy the Indiana Department of Natural Resources, Division of Forestry Archives.)

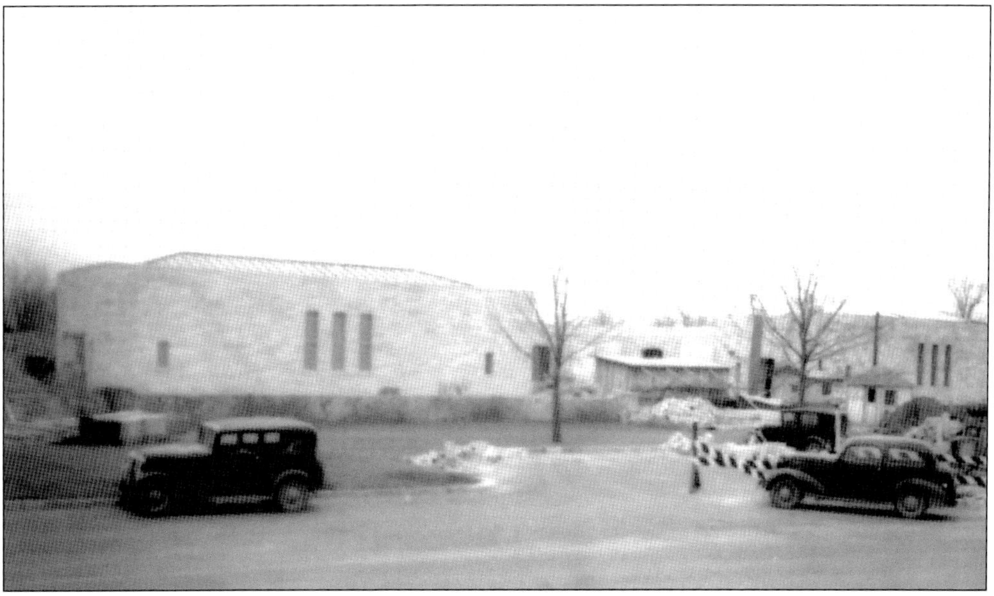

For over 30 years, the State of Indiana administered and operated the memorial to Lincoln and his mother. This photograph shows the construction of the Memorial Building which opened in 1943. In 1962, the site became part of the National Park Service and is now known as Lincoln Boyhood National Memorial. This building is now the Visitors Center. (Courtesy of USI Special Collections.)

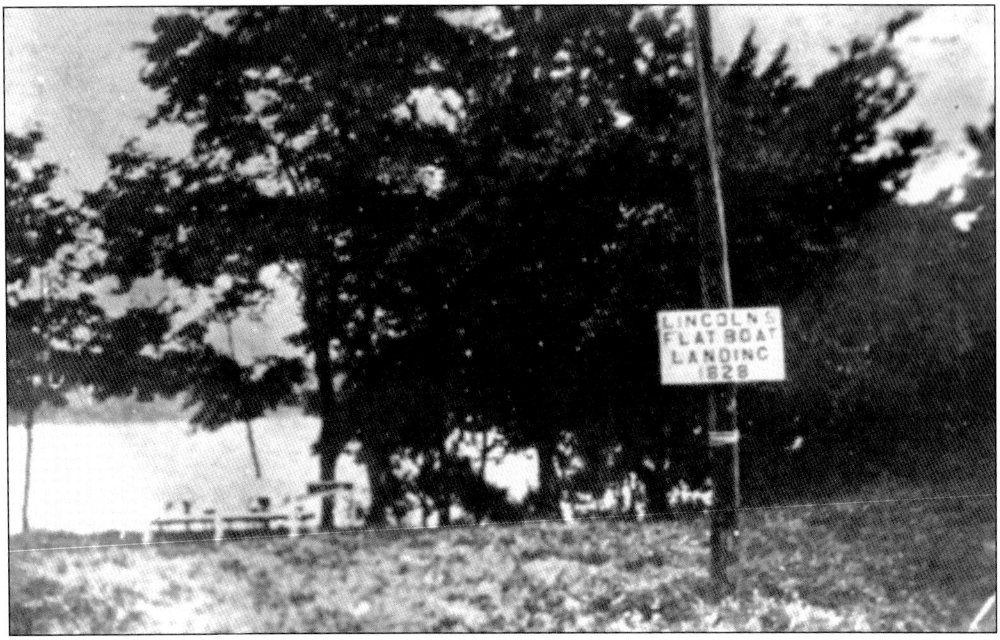

In April 1828, Abraham Lincoln took a flat boat trip to New Orleans for his employer William Gentry. The purpose of the trip was to sell produce and other goods. The trip exposed Lincoln to the world outside his Indiana home. He witnessed his first slave auction on this trip. The sign commemorates the landing spot of the Lincoln flatboat trip in Rockport. (Courtesy of Willard Library.)

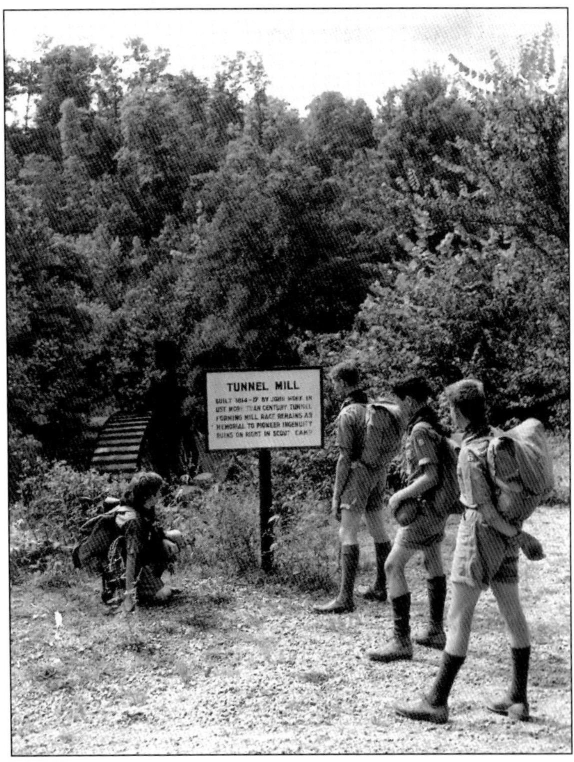

There are many interpretive signs and historical markers across the Ohio River Scenic Byway. Here, Boy Scouts read about the Tunnel Mill at the Scout Reservation in Charlestown. A tunnel was carved so that water could flow through it for a new mill. The process took nearly three years to complete. (Courtesy of the Harrison County Public Library.)

The town of Santa Claus is located just a few miles east of Lincoln Boyhood National Memorial. Legend surrounds as to how the town took the name Santa Claus, but local businessmen saw the potential in attracting tourists. Carl Barrett built this stone Santa Claus statue and opened Santa Claus Park in 1935. The statue is still standing today. Although Santa Claus is not directly on the Ohio River Scenic Byway, many people take a side trip to visit it and nearby Lincoln City. (Courtesy of USI Special Collections.)

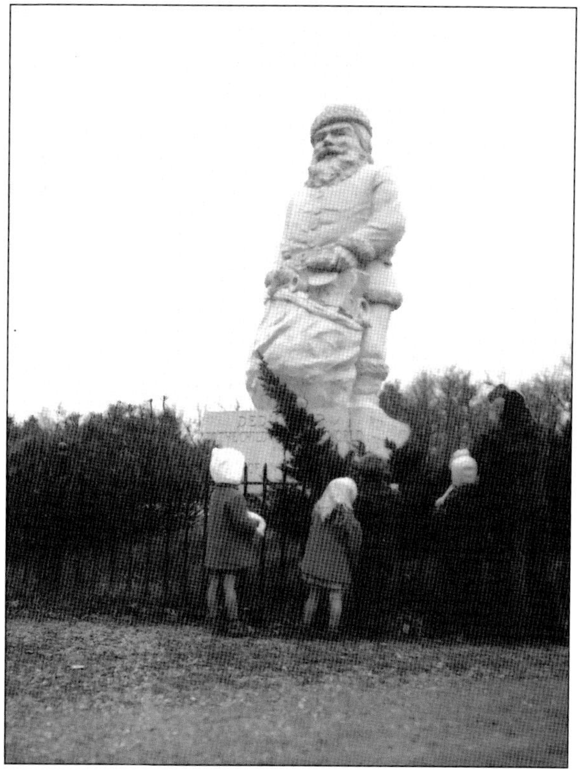

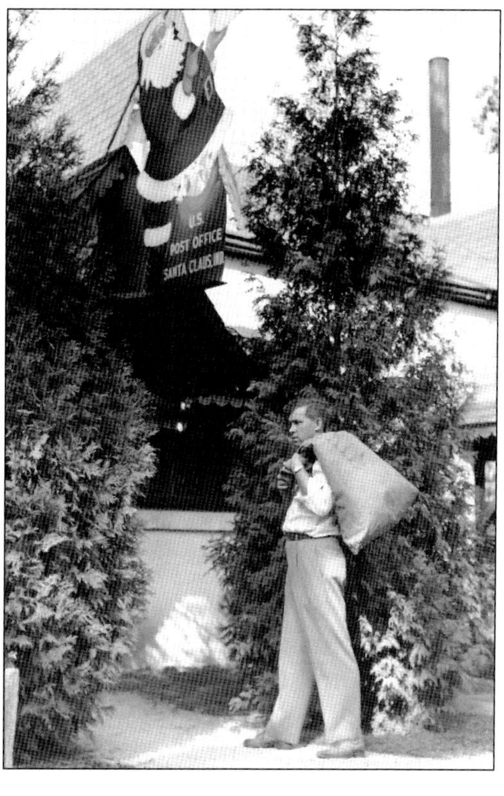

On May 21, 1856, Santa Claus was accepted as a United States Post Office. It was not until the late 1920s, when Postmaster James Martin began promoting the Santa Claus postmark, that it became a popular spot for Christmas letters and cards. A group of local volunteers called Santa's Elves make sure each child receives a reply from Santa Claus; this tradition has been traced back as far as 1914. (Courtesy of the Harrison County Public Library.)

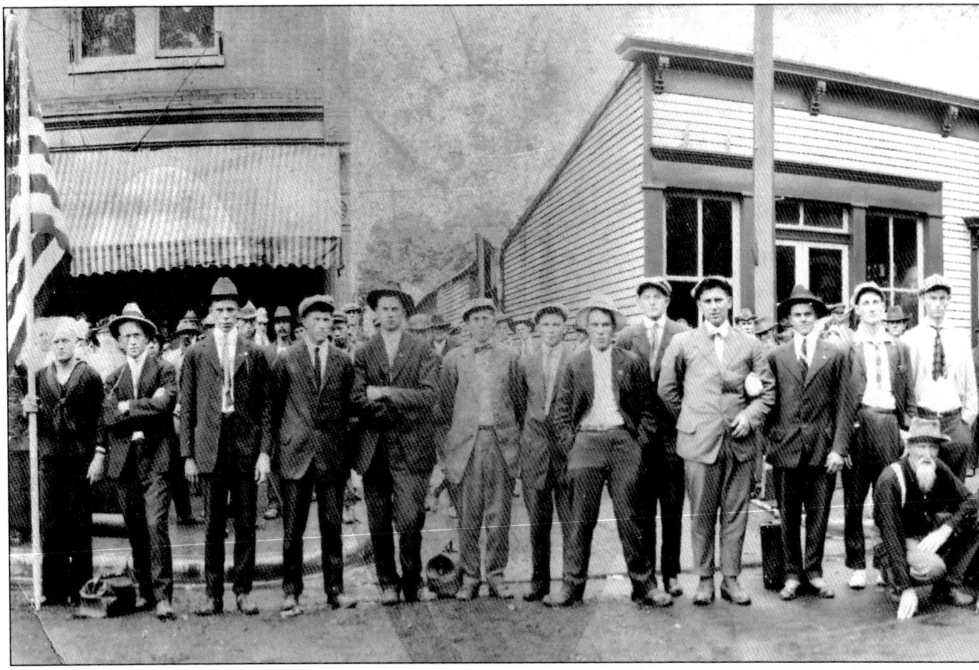

World War I greatly impacted southern Indiana. Evansville's James Bethel Gresham was the first American soldier killed in the war. Here, recruits from Corydon prepare to leave for World War I. (Courtesy of the Harrison County Public Library.)

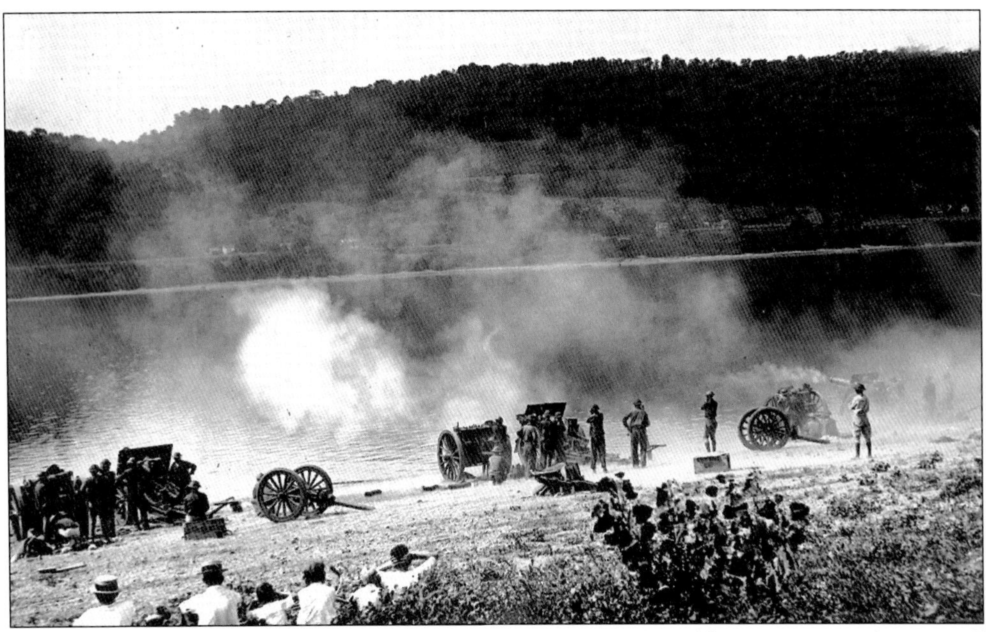

Several places along the Ohio River served as encampments for soldiers getting ready to go off to war. In Madison, soldiers practice artillery fire over the Ohio River. (Courtesy of the Jefferson County Historical Society.)

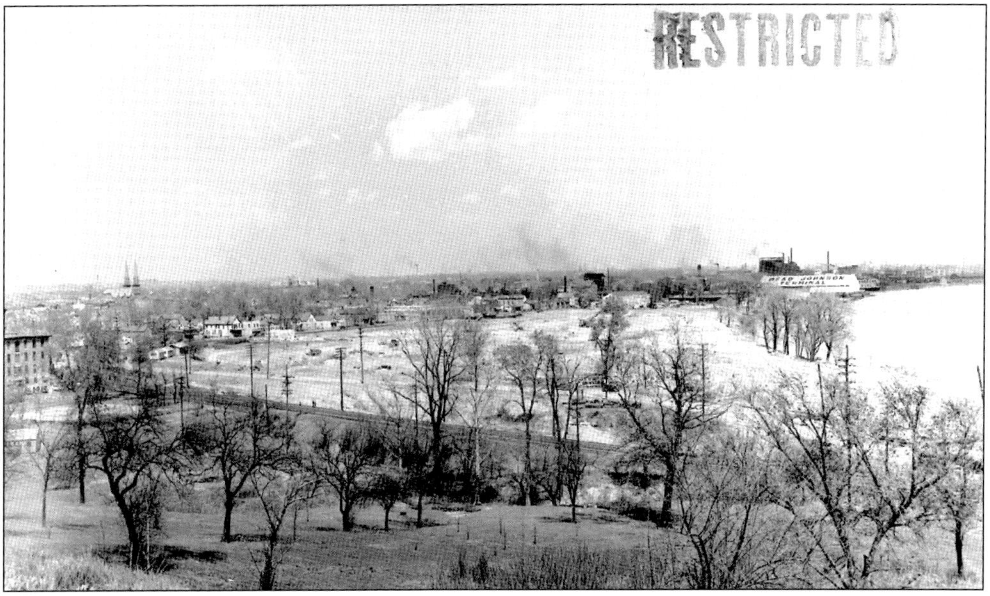

Construction of the Evansville Shipyard was documented in this photograph taken in the spring of 1942. (Courtesy of EMAHS.)

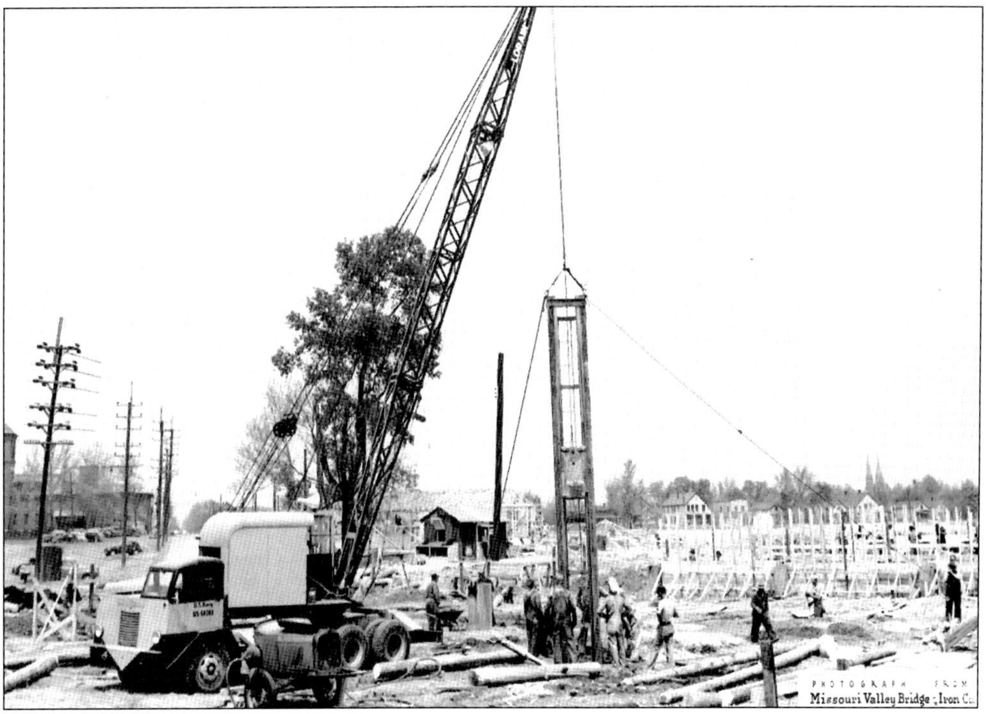

Communities along the Ohio River mobilized a huge effort for World War II. The location of the river was perfect for shipbuilding and for transporting goods. This photograph shows the ground that has been cleared to make way for the Evansville Shipyard. From the launching of the first ship on October 31, 1942, to the final ship on December 12, 1945, the Evansville Shipyard produced 166 Landing Ship Tanks or LSTs. Additional LSTs were produced at the Jeffersonville Shipyards in Jeffersonville. (Courtesy of EMAHS.)

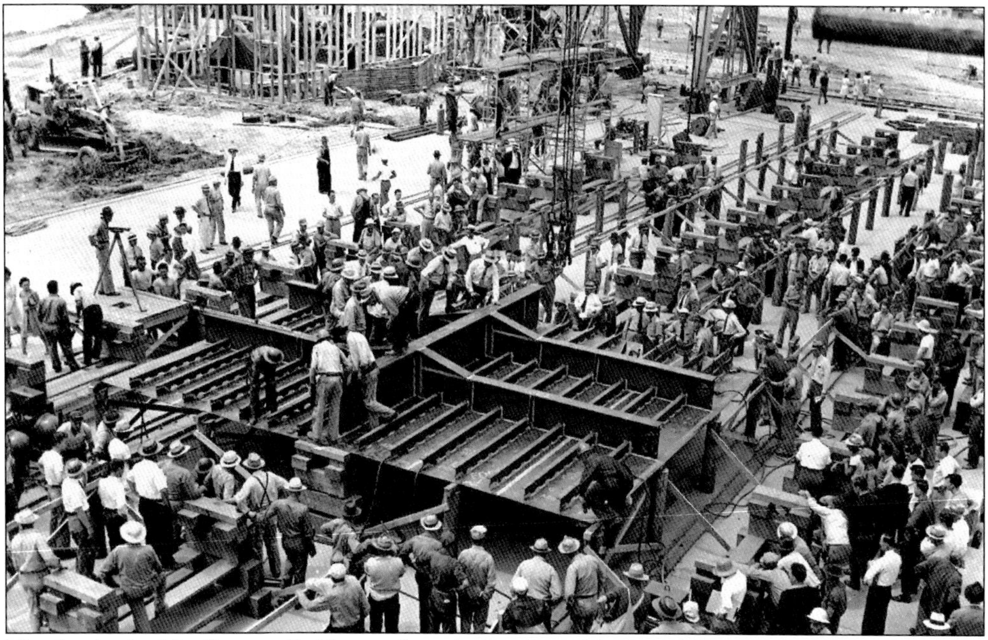

The first keel of the Evansville Shipyard was laid on June 25, 1942. After 129 days in construction, LST 157 was launched on October 31. It was then prepared for commissioning. After being checked out by the Navy officials and deemed acceptable, a broom was hoisted in the mast, signifying a clean sweep. Then the shipyard sold the ship to the Navy in a commissioning ceremony. (Courtesy of EMAHS.)

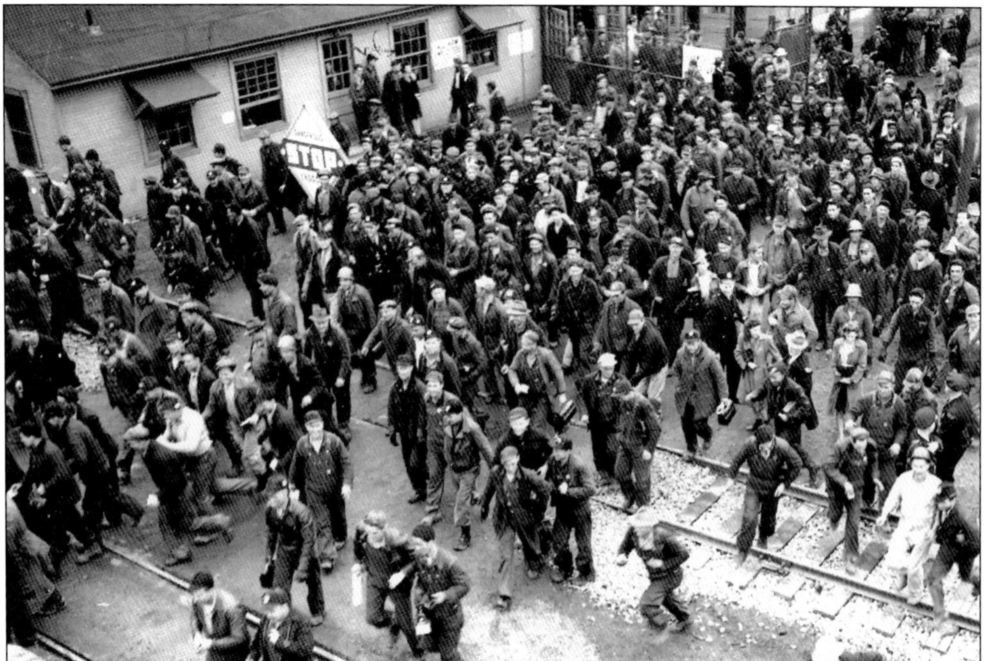

Men employed at the shipyard were photographed crossing the tracks of Alley No. 1 on February 1, 1943. There were three eight-hour shifts—graveyard, swing, and day. (Courtesy of EMAHS.)

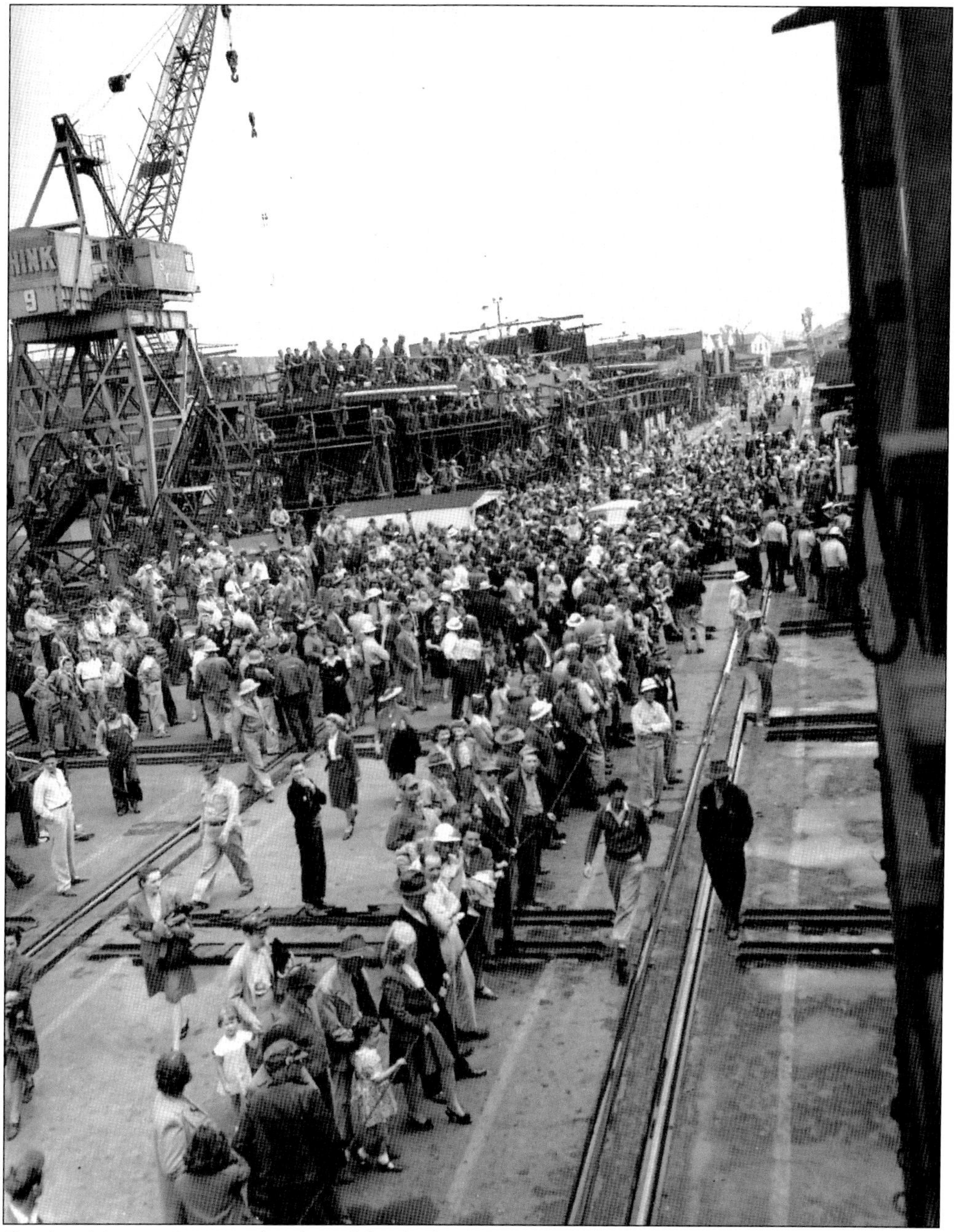

On April 20, 1945, a crowd gathered for the launching of APB 48, the USS *Vanderburgh*, named after the county in which Evansville is located. An APB was a self-propelled barrack ship. (Courtesy of EMAHS.)

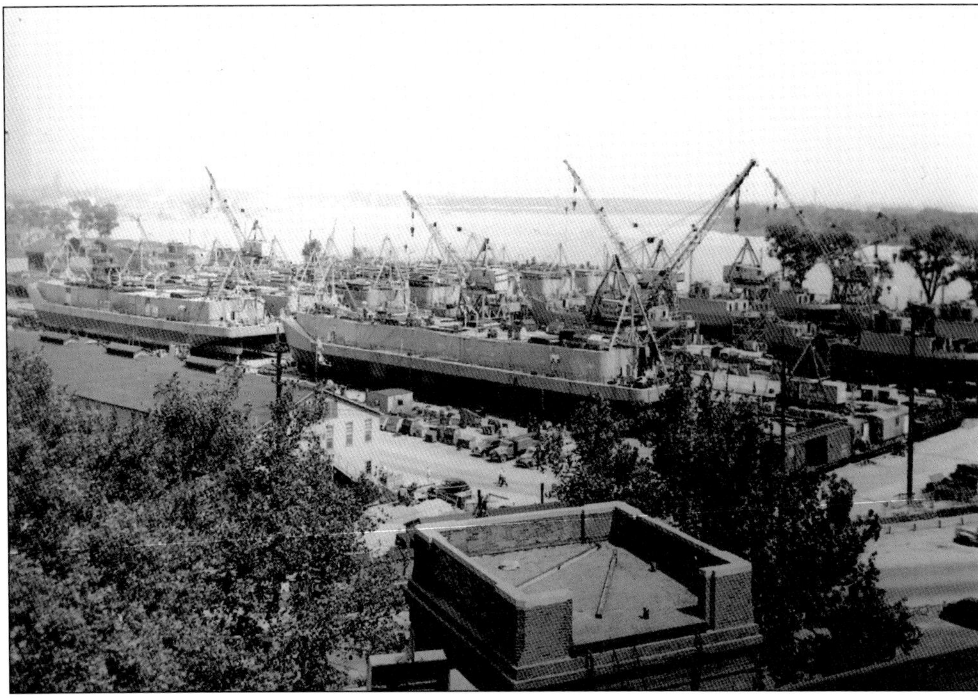

The Evansville Shipyard was photographed from Mead Johnson and Company on July 17, 1945, shortly before the war ended. (Courtesy of EMAHS.)

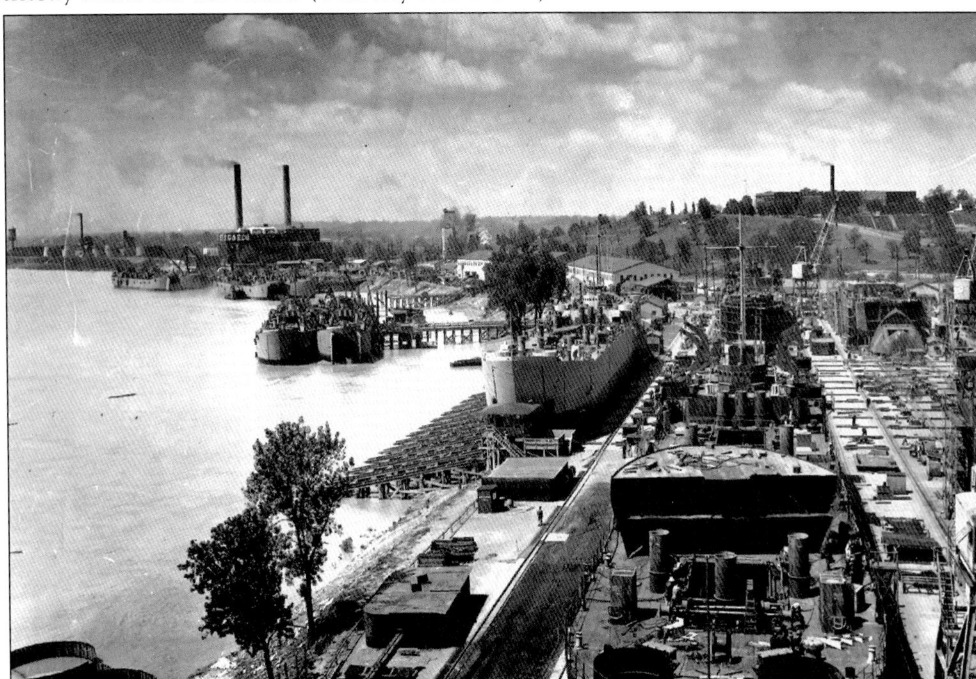

This general view of the shipyard, taken from the east and showing Reitz Hill and the SIGECO power plant, was taken May 22, 1943. It documents the huge scale of LST production. The shipyard was the largest employer in Evansville's history. (Courtesy of EMAHS.)

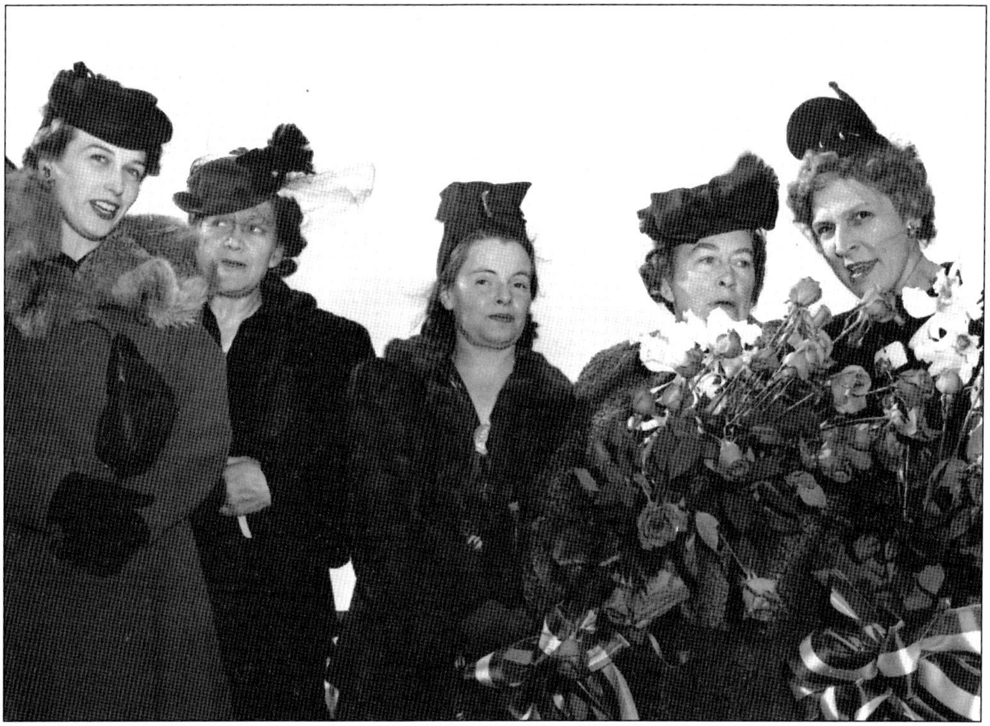

Women are decked out in their finery for the christening of an LST. (Courtesy of Willard Library.)

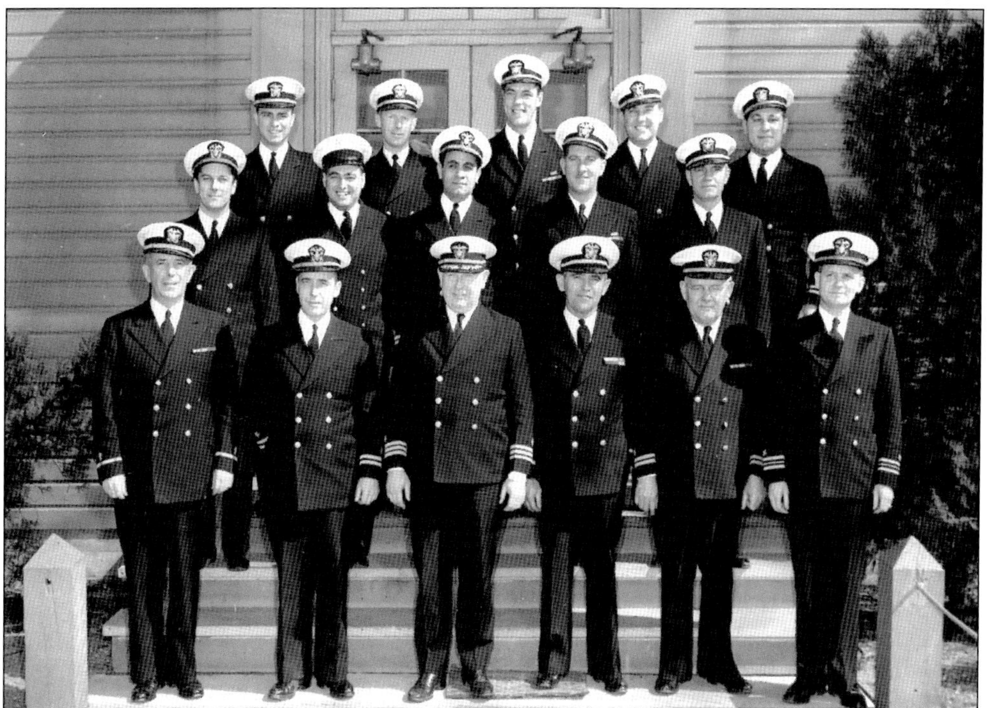

In this photograph, 16 navy officers pose at the Evansville Shipyard on March 10, 1945. (Courtesy of EMAHS.)

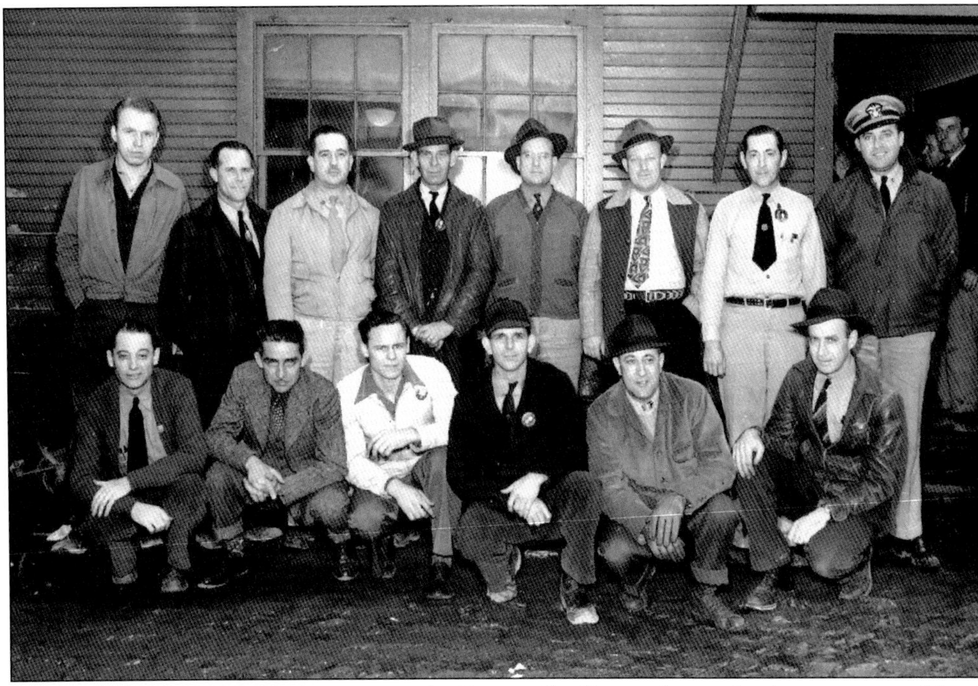

Inspectors for the Navy Department at the Evansville Shipyard pose for this picture on March 3, 1945. (Courtesy of EMAHS.)

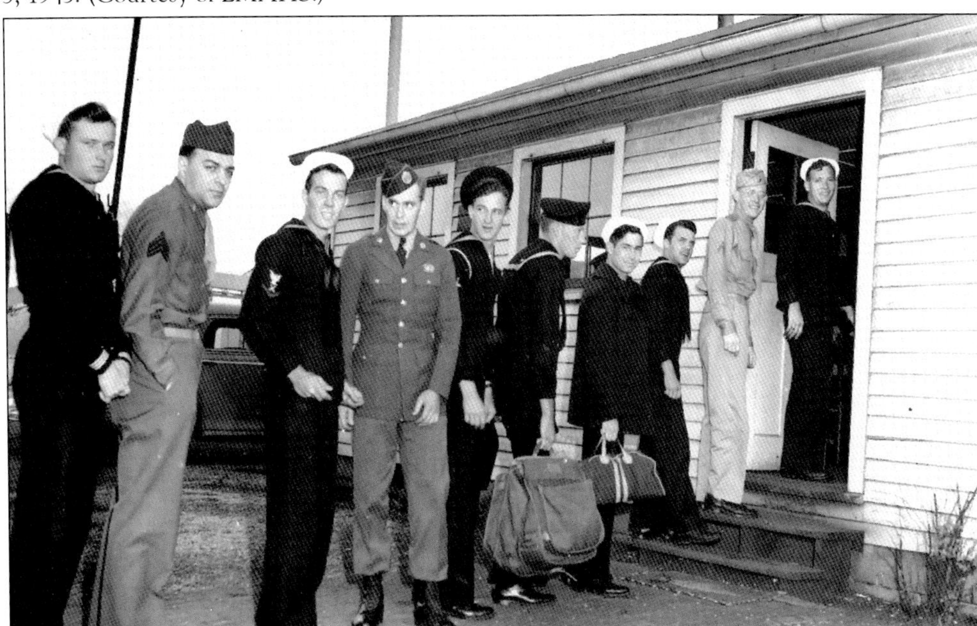

The Red Cross Canteen, across the street from the Louisville and Nashville Railroad terminal in Evansville, was one of the busiest spots in the city. Thousands of servicemen were served free coffee and donuts. The city gained national fame for its generosity to men and women in uniform. The Rotary Club of Evansville gave its 1944 Civic Award to the volunteers who worked at the canteen. (Courtesy of EMAHS.)

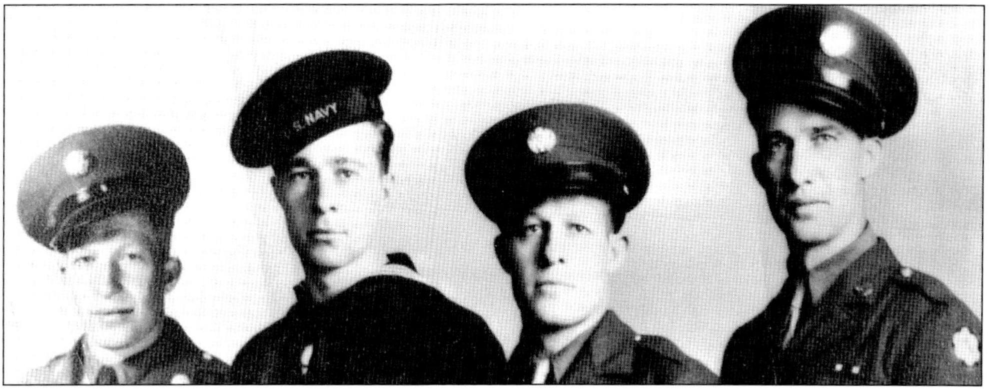

Corydon servicemen from various branches of the military pose for this photograph. The servicemen are, from left to right, ? Dewey, ? Orlan, Everett Rissler, and Charles Bube. (Courtesy of the Harrison County Public Library.)

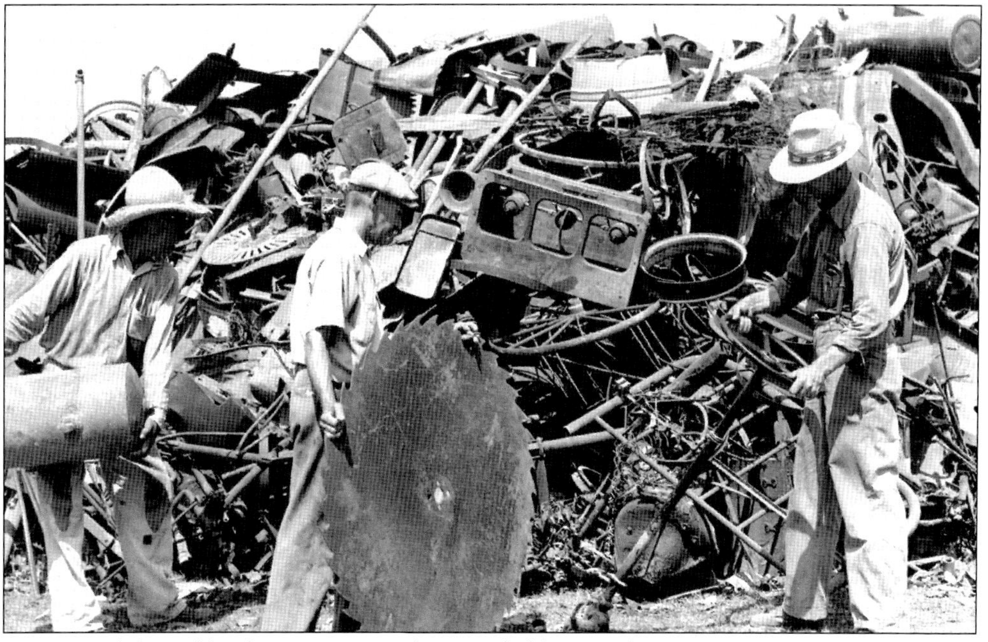

Scrap metal drives like this one in Corydon were held across the country. By the war's end, scrap drives had accounted for a large proportion of the steel, tin, and other metals that were used in defense industries. (Courtesy of the Harrison County Public Library.)

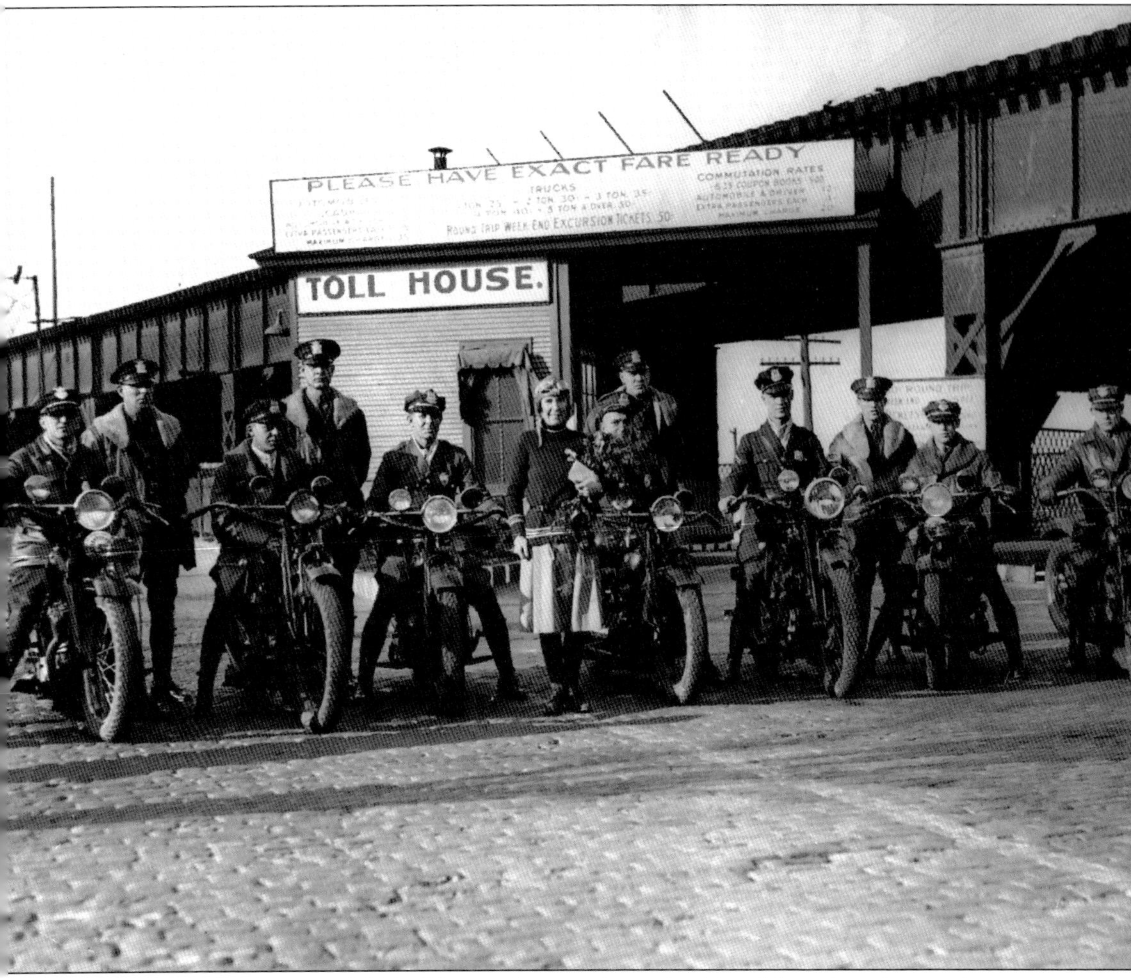

The famed female aviator Mildred Bruce is being welcomed to New Albany by police on the entrance to the Kentucky and Indiana Bridge. (Courtesy of the New Albany-Floyd County Library.)

Two

NATURAL
GEOLOGICAL FEATURES AND FORCES OF NATURE

Like historic qualities, natural qualities are a big part of the Ohio River Scenic Byway. They include geological features, like the limestone bluffs and waterfalls at Clifty Falls State Park in Madison and the fossil beds at the Falls of the Ohio State Park in Clarksville. They include the heavily forested hills of the Harrison-Crawford State Forest and the Hoosier National Forest, as well as the vast river bottoms and the cypress sloughs found on the far western edge of the state.

Natural qualities can also mean the forces of nature that impact the communities and people along the byway. The winter of 1918 was unusually cold, and huge ice gorges formed as the Ohio River froze.

The Ohio River has seen many devastating floods, most notably in 1884, 1913, 1937, and 1997. The flood of 1937 was documented in many photographs. Millions of people along the entire Ohio River were affected in some way. Major reconstruction took place following the flood and in some cases, places were lost forever. The entire town of Leavenworth was even moved to higher ground as a result.

People in the communities along the Ohio River Scenic Byway enjoy the many natural qualities found in this part of the state and also live with the consequences that nature can impart.

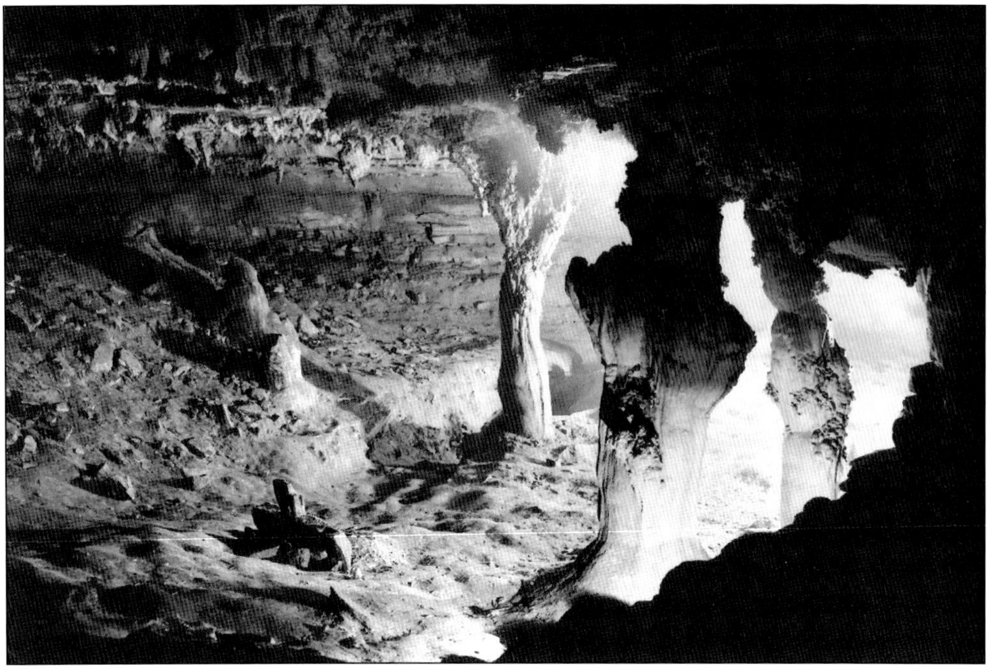

Due to the abundance of limestone in the region, southern Indiana has many caves. This area is known as the Pillard Palace at Wyandotte Cave located in the Harrison-Crawford State Forest between Corydon and Leavenworth. (Courtesy of USI Special Collections.)

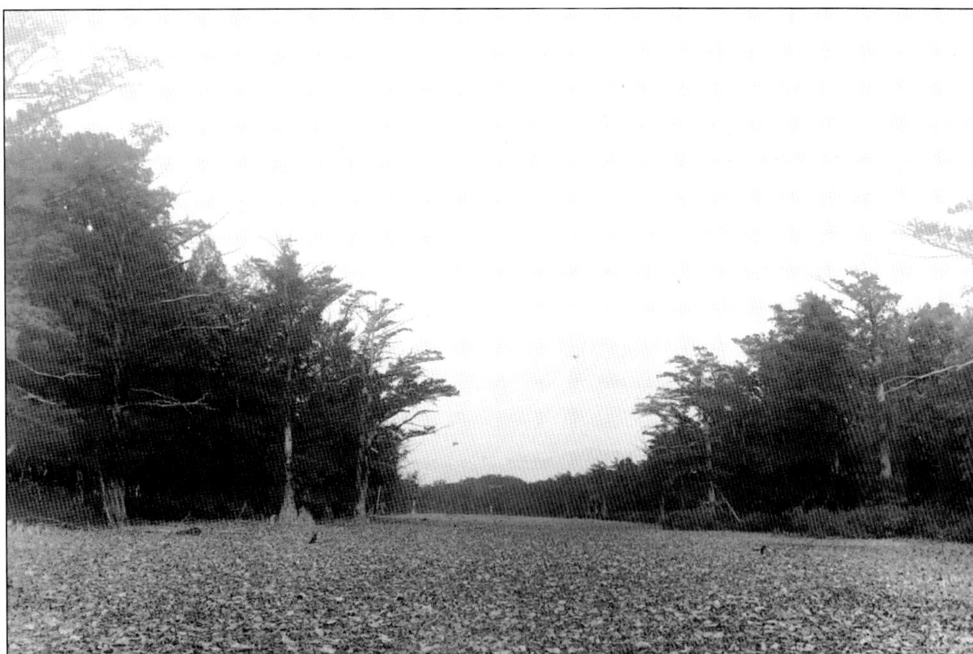

This cypress slough located three miles east of Mount Vernon was dry at the time this photograph was taken in October 1917. Now a nature preserve, it is believed to be the northernmost stand of bald cypress trees in North America. (Courtesy the Indiana Department of Natural Resources, Division of Forestry Archives.)

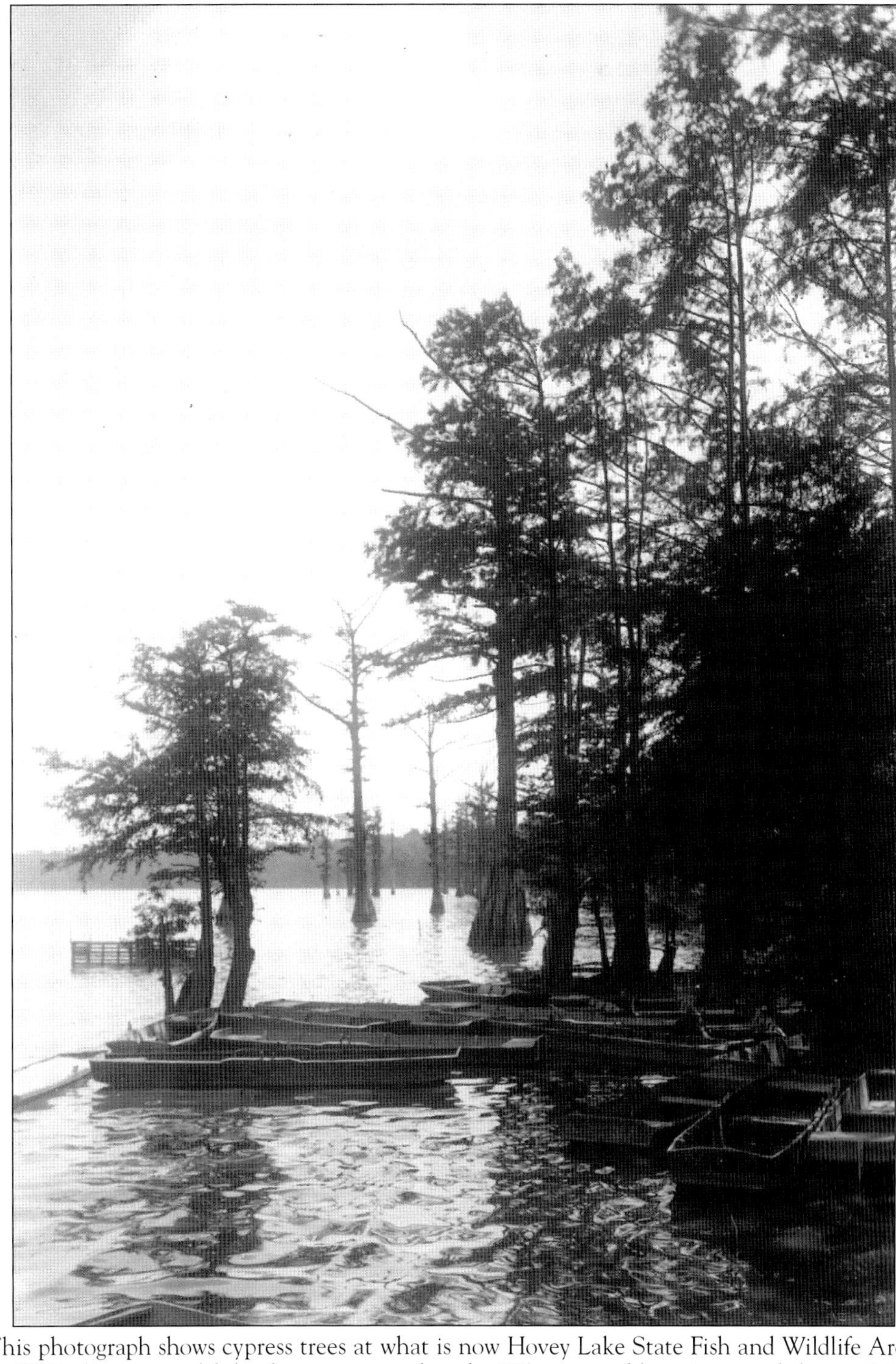

This photograph shows cypress trees at what is now Hovey Lake State Fish and Wildlife Area. In 1940, the state and federal governments bought 885 acres and later increased that to 4,298; much of this is underwater. The lake and wetlands are a stopover for migratory birds, and a haven for many types of fish and wildlife. (Courtesy the Indiana Department of Natural Resources, Division of Forestry Archives.)

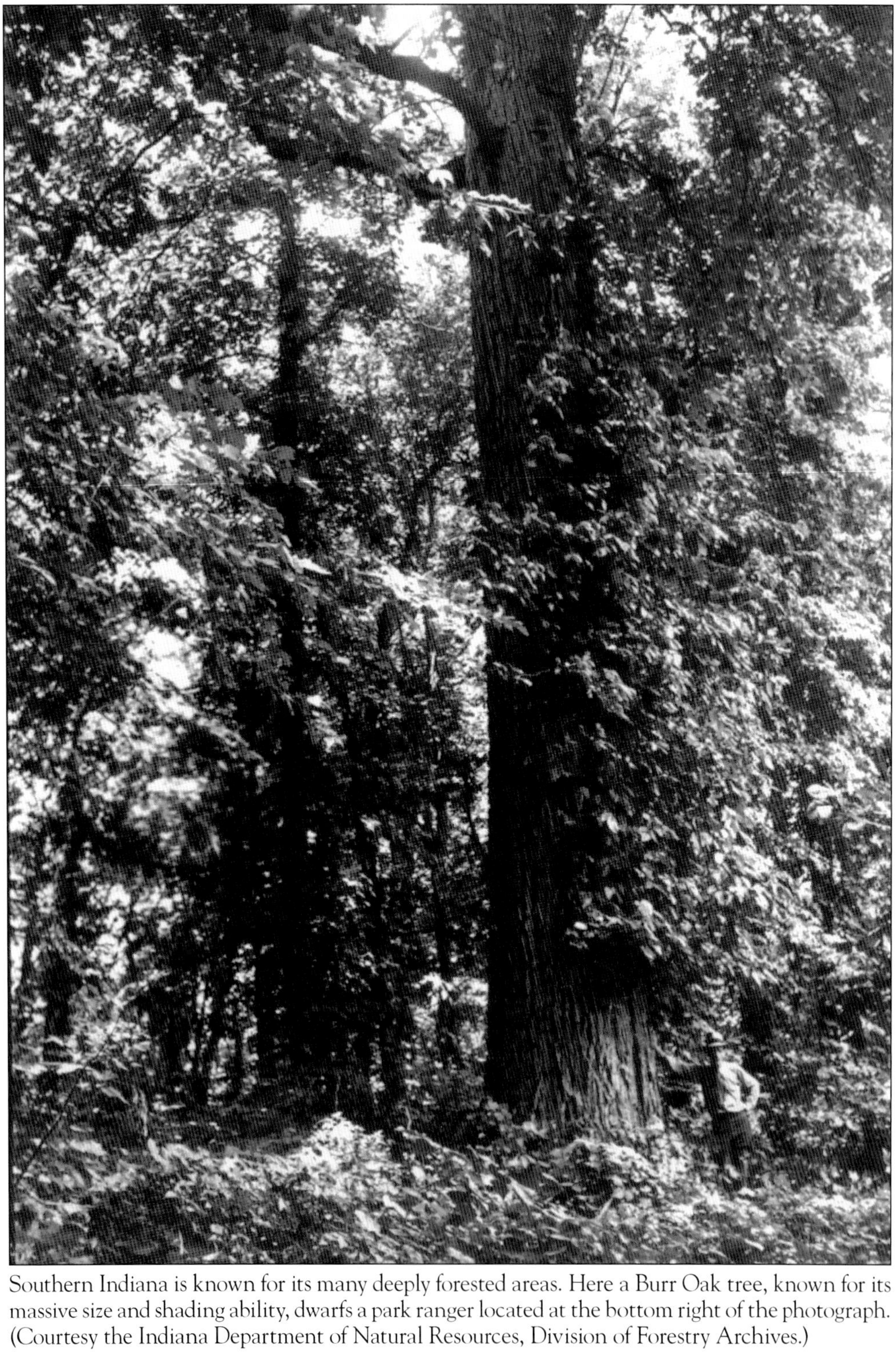

Southern Indiana is known for its many deeply forested areas. Here a Burr Oak tree, known for its massive size and shading ability, dwarfs a park ranger located at the bottom right of the photograph. (Courtesy the Indiana Department of Natural Resources, Division of Forestry Archives.)

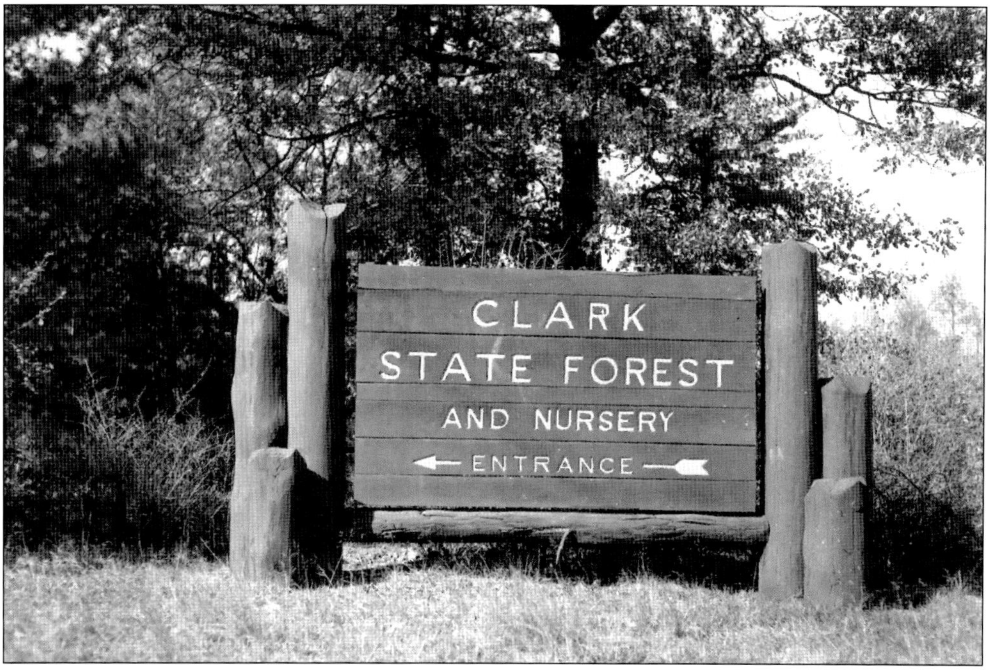

The sign marks the entrance to Clark State Forest and Nursery. In 1903, it became the first Indiana State Forest and was one of the earliest in the country. (Courtesy the Indiana Department of Natural Resources, Division of Forestry Archives.)

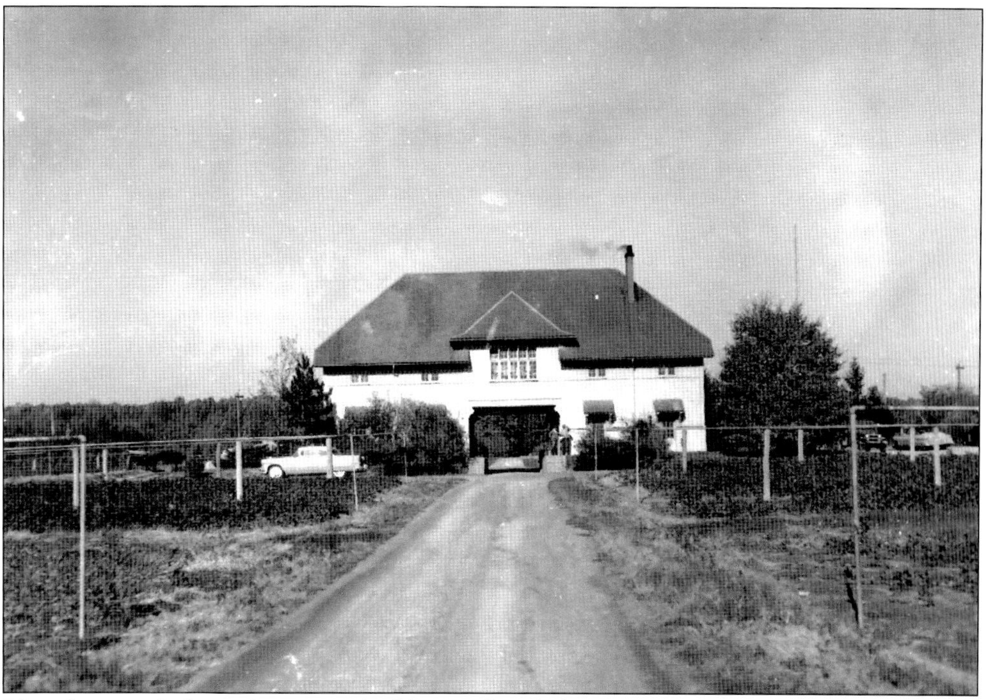

This photograph shows the nursery building at the Clark State Forest. It was originally a research forest and also served as a seedling tree nursery. (Courtesy the Indiana Department of Natural Resources, Division of Forestry Archives.)

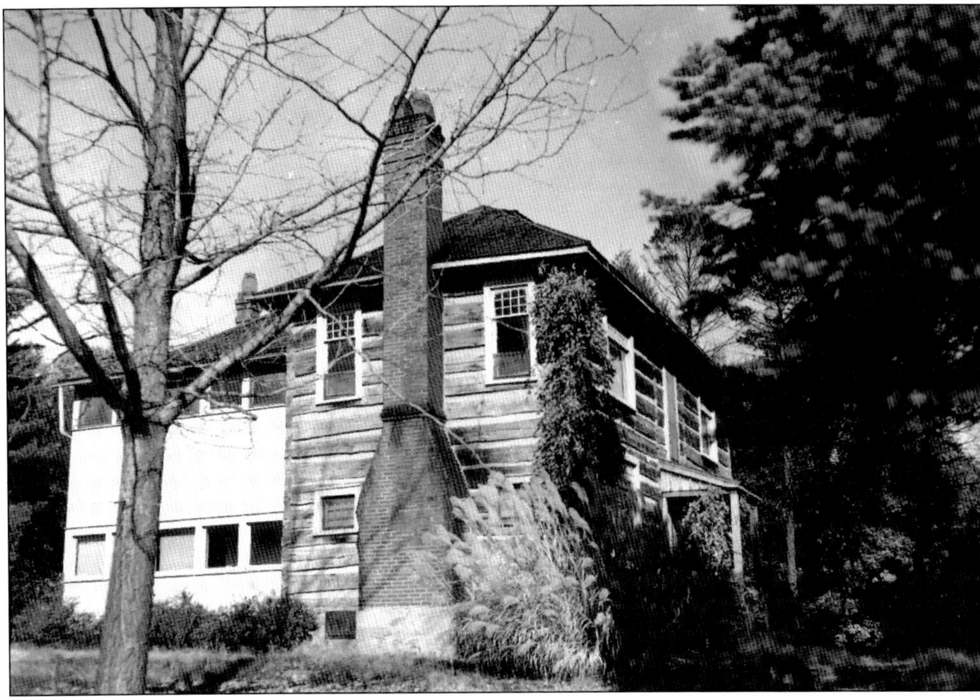

The log house at the Clark State Forest was the original administration building and also served as the residence for the park's manager. (Courtesy the Indiana Department of Natural Resources, Division of Forestry Archives.)

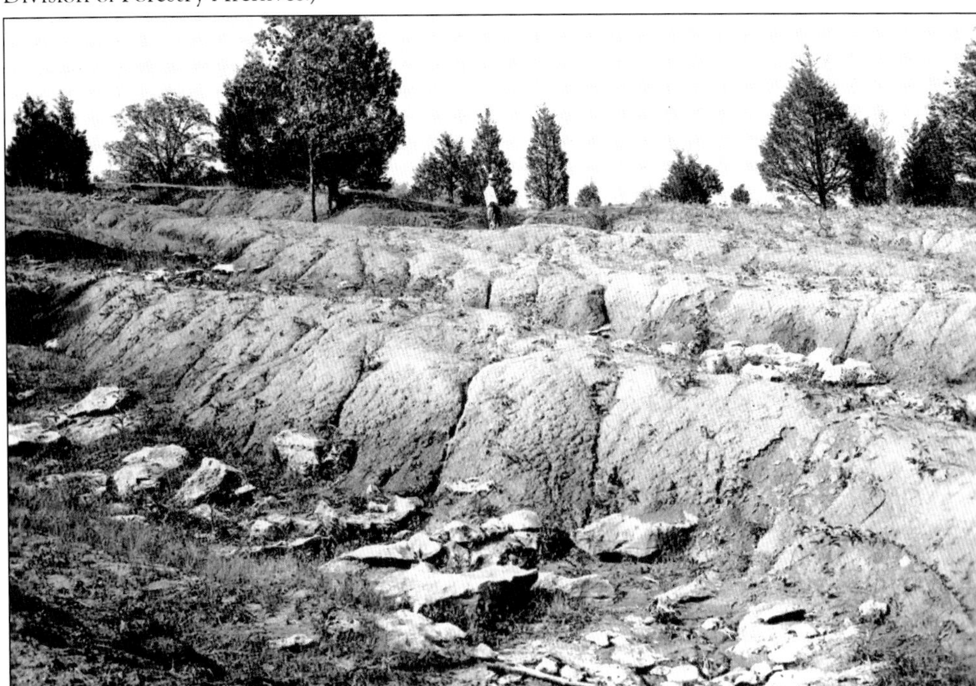

As trees were heavily forested in southern Indiana, erosion became a common problem. (Courtesy the Indiana Department of Natural Resources, Division of Forestry Archives.)

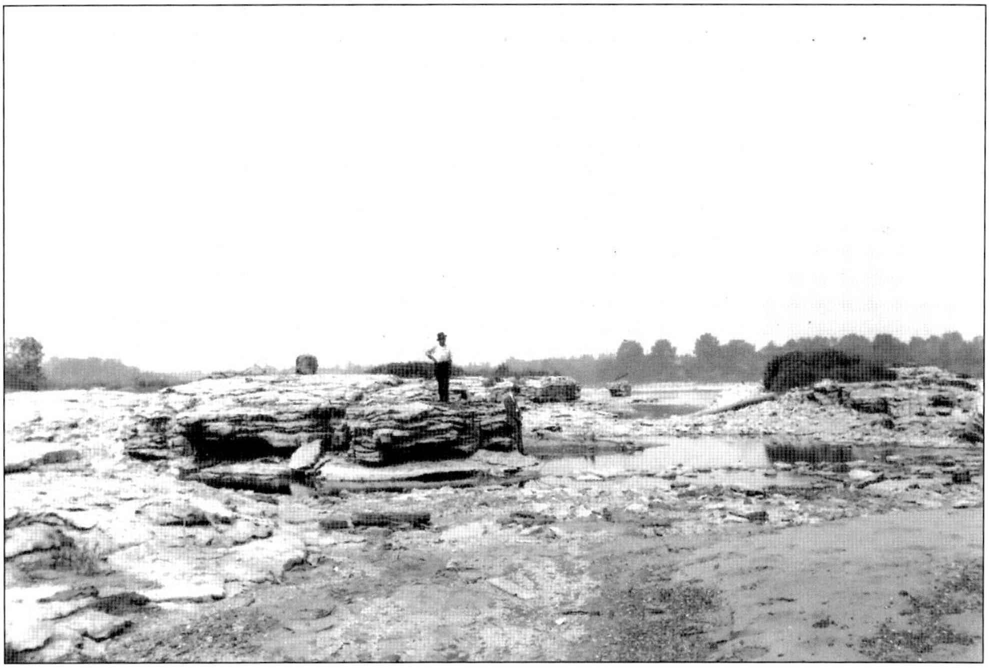

The Falls of the Ohio is the only natural obstruction in the Ohio River. It is located by Louisville and the Indiana cities known as the Falls Cities—Jeffersonville, Clarksville, and New Albany. The Falls of the Ohio are actually cascading rapids that cause the Ohio River to drop 26 feet in elevation over a two-mile stretch. During low water, people can walk out on this area and see fossils from 400 million year old Devonian fossil beds. (Courtesy of the Jeffersonville Township Public Library.)

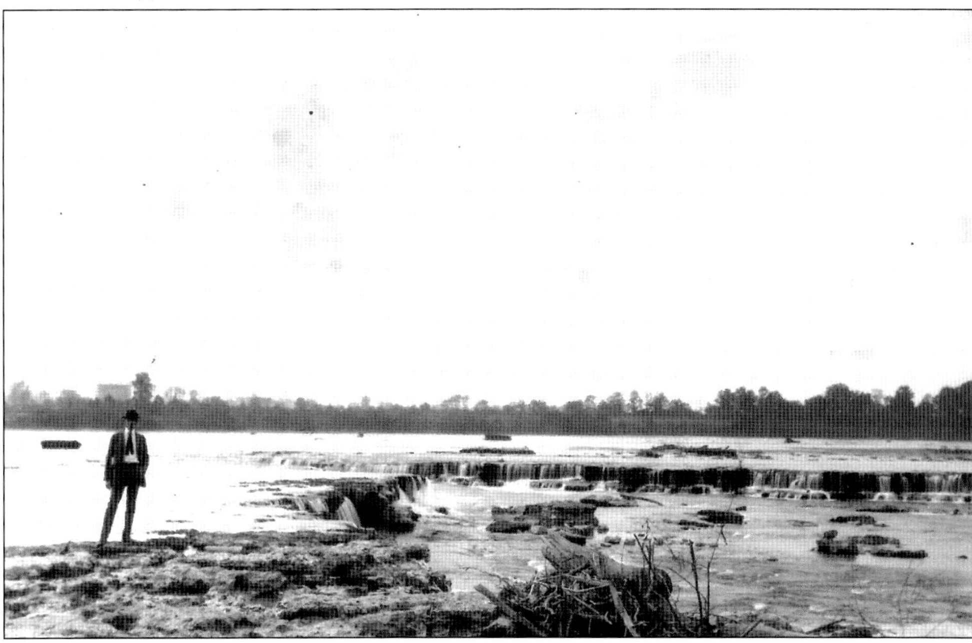

This photograph, taken on October 6, 1922, shows a four-foot drop at the head of the Big Slough. (Courtesy of the Jeffersonville Township Public Library.)

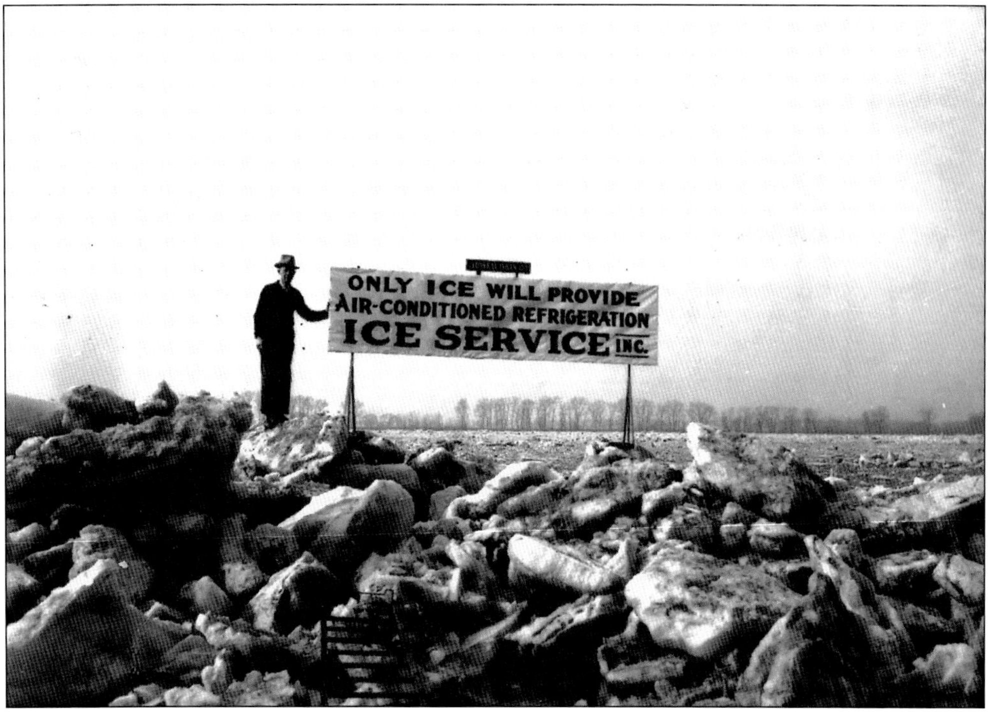

A severe cold spell afflicted southern Indiana during the winter of 1918. The Ohio River froze over. This sign's advertisement shows a use for the ice gorges. (Courtesy of USI Special Collections.)

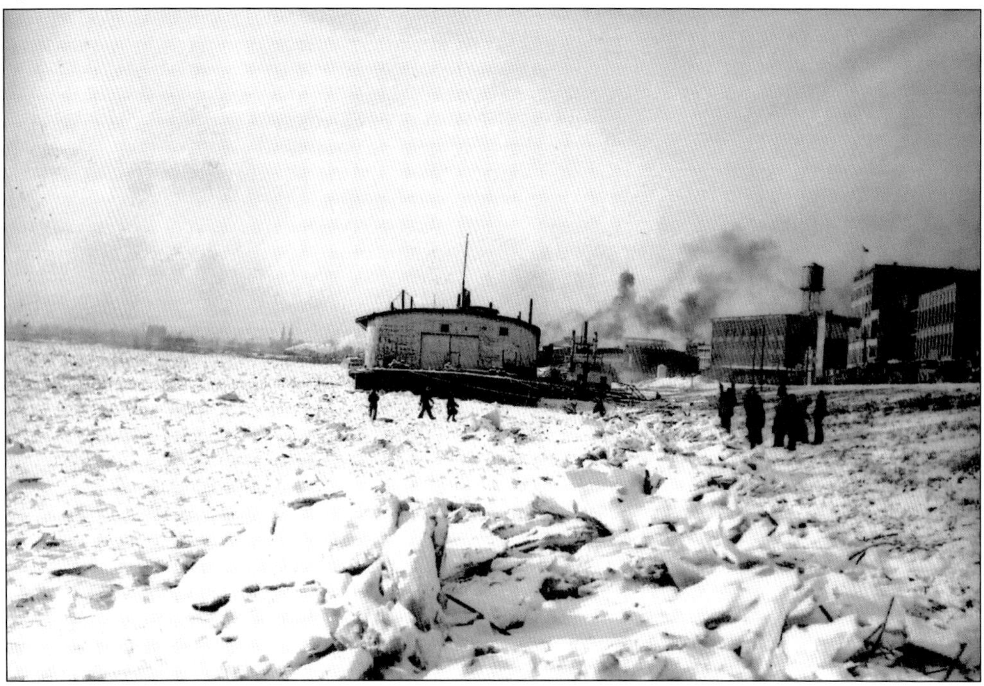

Many boats were damaged or destroyed from the ice gorges of 1918. This photograph shows the Evansville Wharf. (Courtesy of USI Special Collections.)

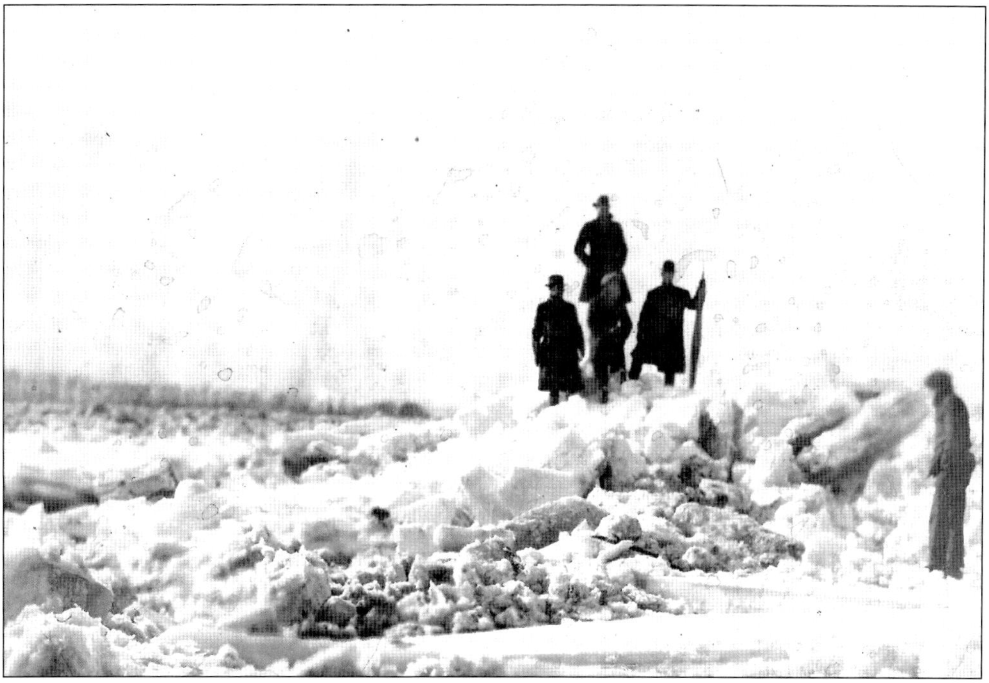

People took advantage of this rare condition to have their pictures taken on the ice gorges on the Ohio River. This one stood at the end of Main Street in Evansville. (Courtesy of Willard Library.)

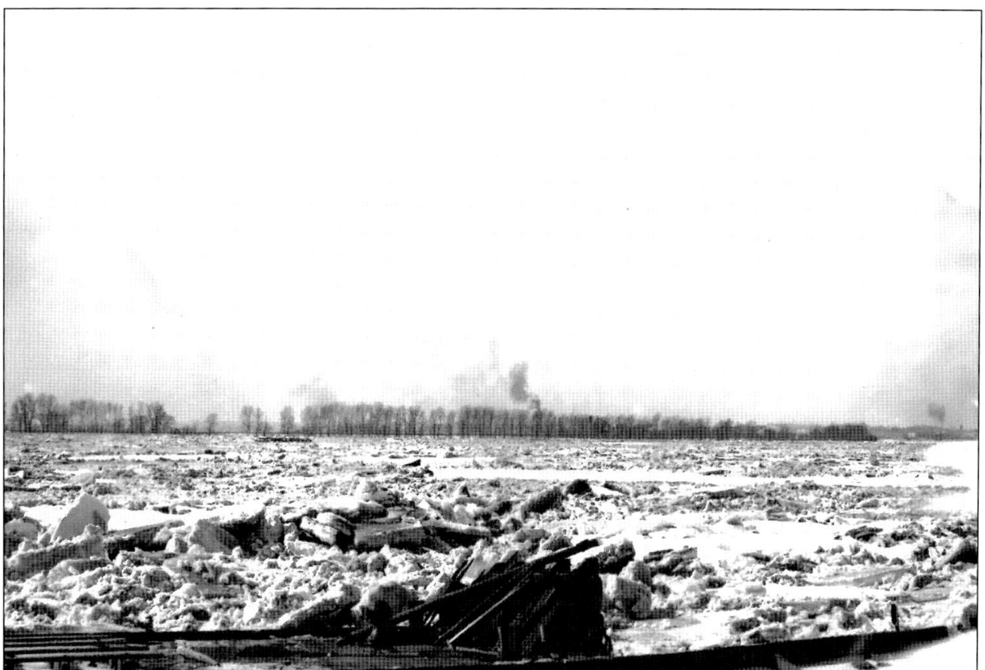

Evansville Courier photographer Karl Kae Knecht took this photograph of the Ohio River upstream from Evansville to document the severity of the conditions. (Courtesy of USI Special Collections.)

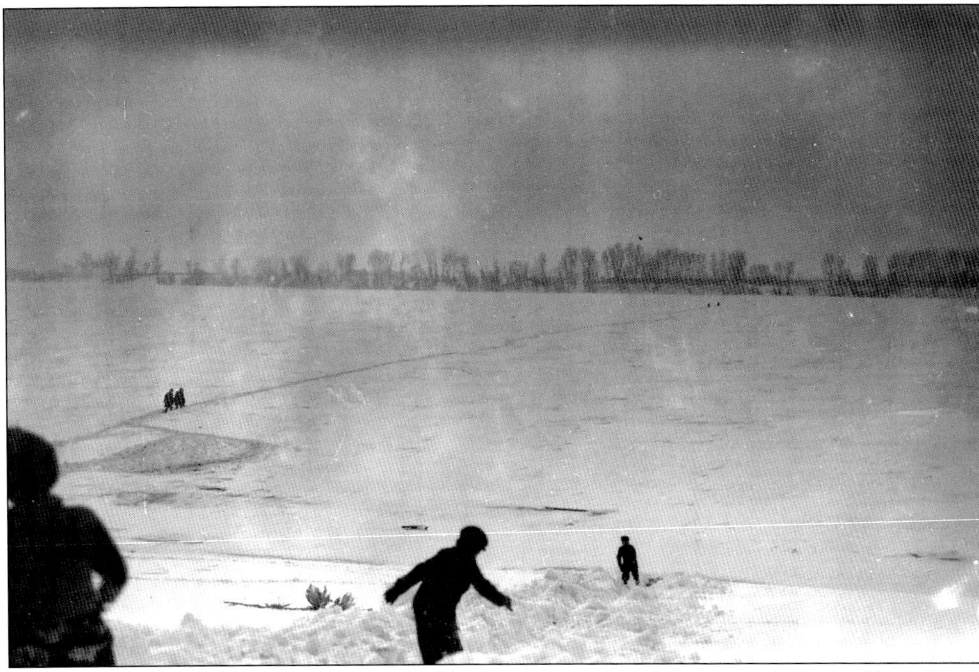

While the snow and frozen river wreaked havoc on travel and shipping along the Ohio River, it provided amusement for children who could walk across the frozen river. (Courtesy of USI Special Collections.)

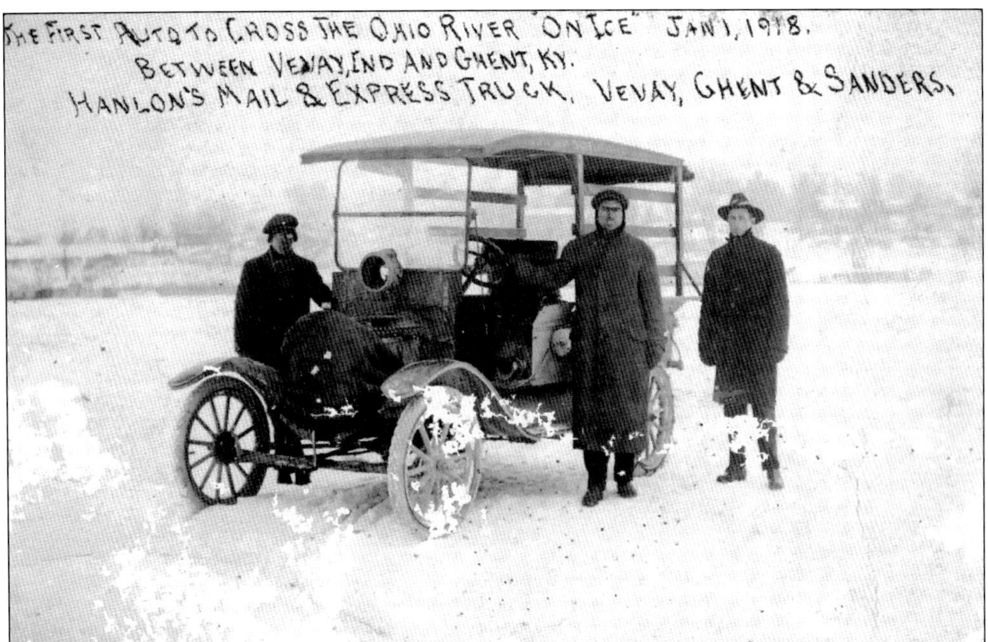

This photograph commemorates the first car to cross the Ohio River on ice. Hanlon's Mail and Express Truck made the trip on January 1, 1918, between Vevay, Indiana, and Ghent, Kentucky. (Courtesy of the Switzerland County Historical Society and Museum.)

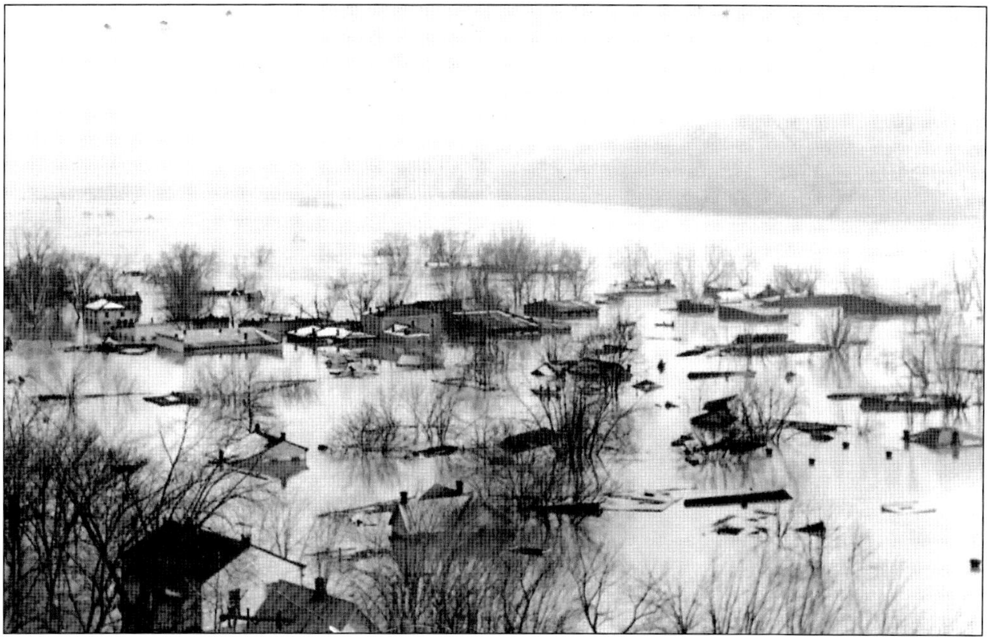

The Ohio River has experienced many great floods, most notably in 1884, 1913, 1937, and 1997. The tops of houses are barely visible at the town of Leavenworth during the flood of 1937. The town moved to higher ground the following year. (Courtesy of the Harrison County Public Library.)

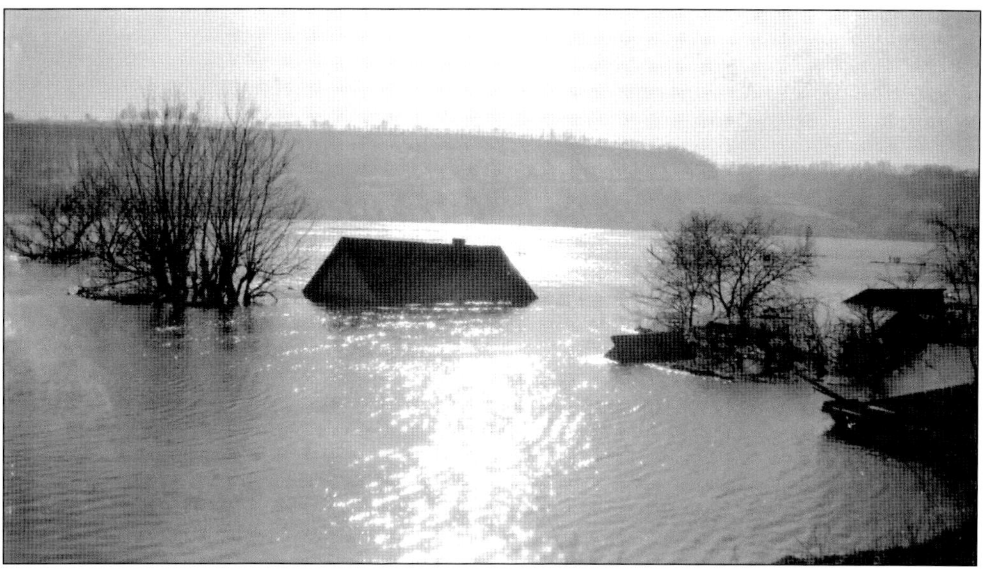

A house floats near Madison during the 1937 flood. (Courtesy of the Jefferson County Historical Society.)

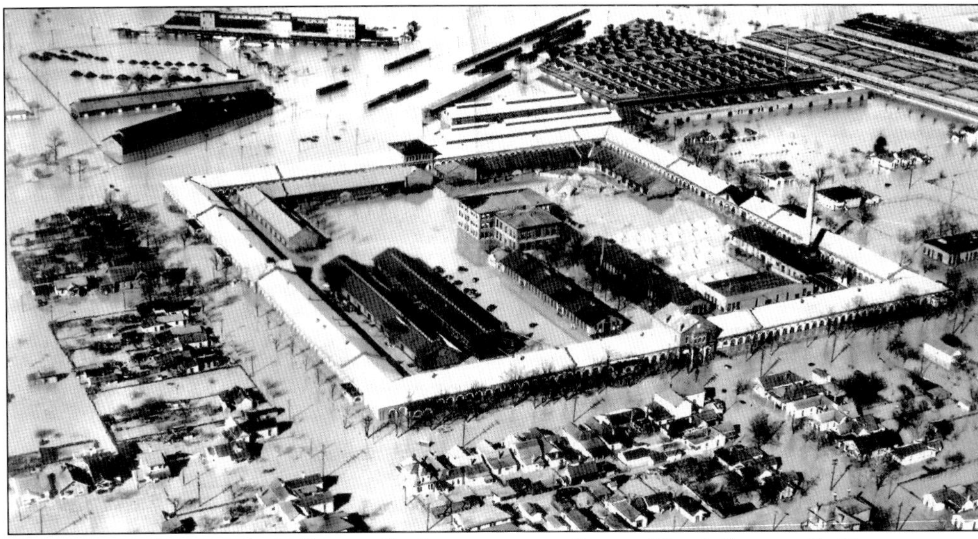

Floodwaters take over the Jeffersonville Quartermaster Depot. The Jeffersonville Quartermaster Depot was a military warehouse that served through several wars including the Spanish American War, World Wars I and II, and the Korean War. It closed in 1958. (Courtesy of the Jeffersonville Township Public Library.)

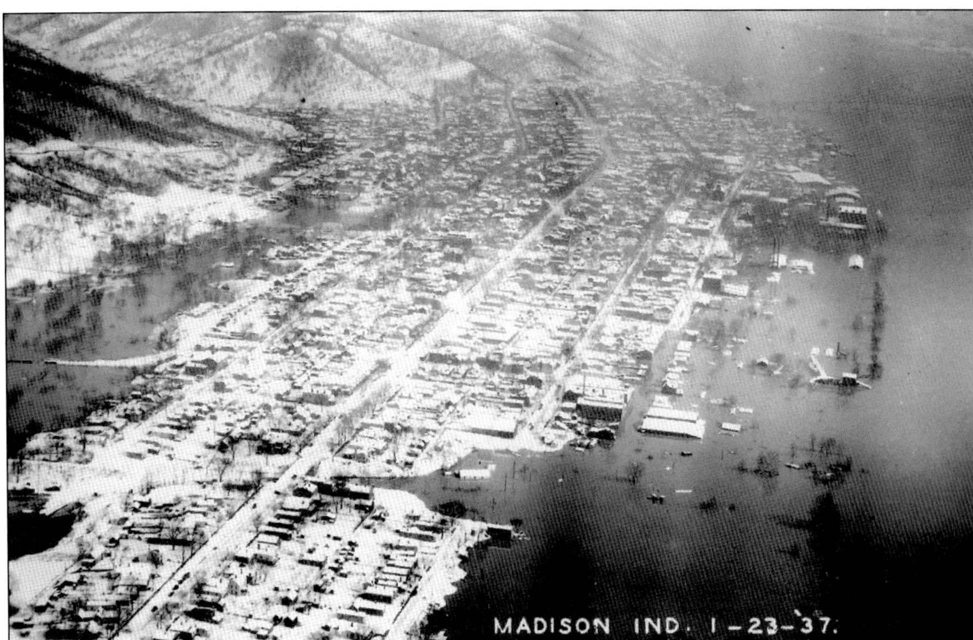

An aerial view of Madison shows the extent of flooding in this photograph taken on January 23, 1937. (Courtesy of the Jefferson County Historical Society.)

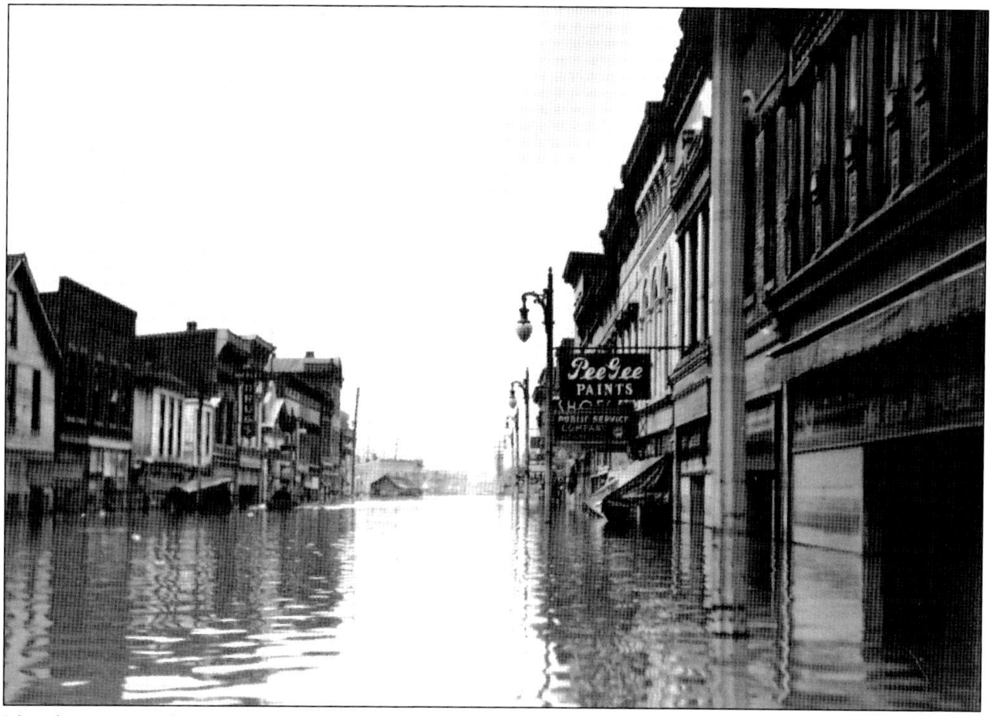

Floodwaters are beginning to recede on Spring Street in downtown Jeffersonville. (Courtesy of the Jeffersonville Township Public Library.)

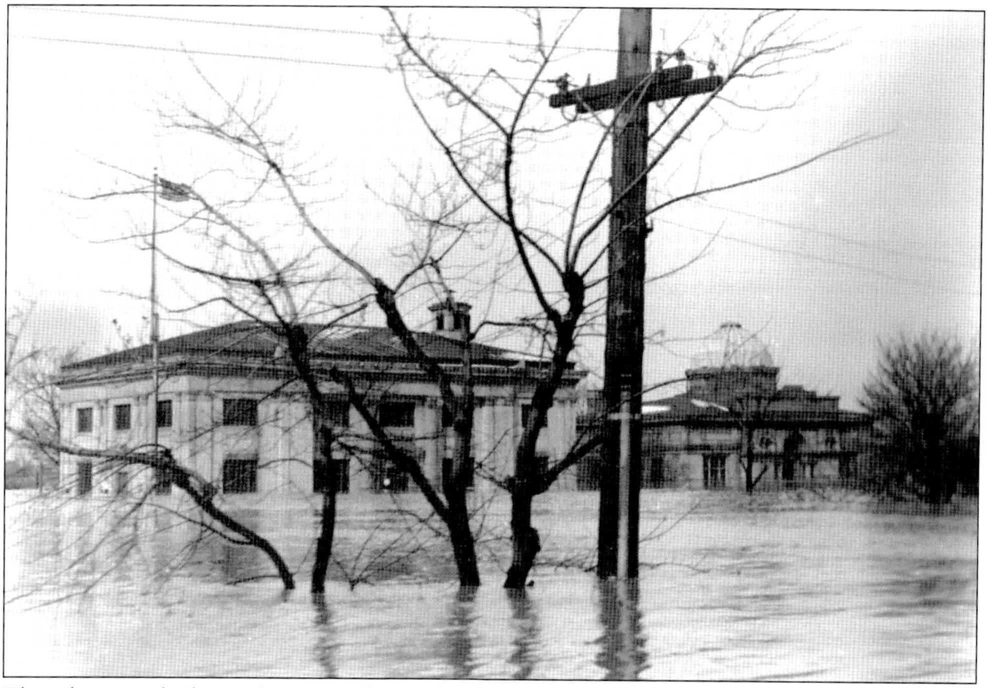

This photograph shows the post office and Jeffersonville Township Library during the flood of 1937. All of the books in the library were damaged beyond salvation and were dumped into the mud. (Courtesy of the Jeffersonville Township Public Library.)

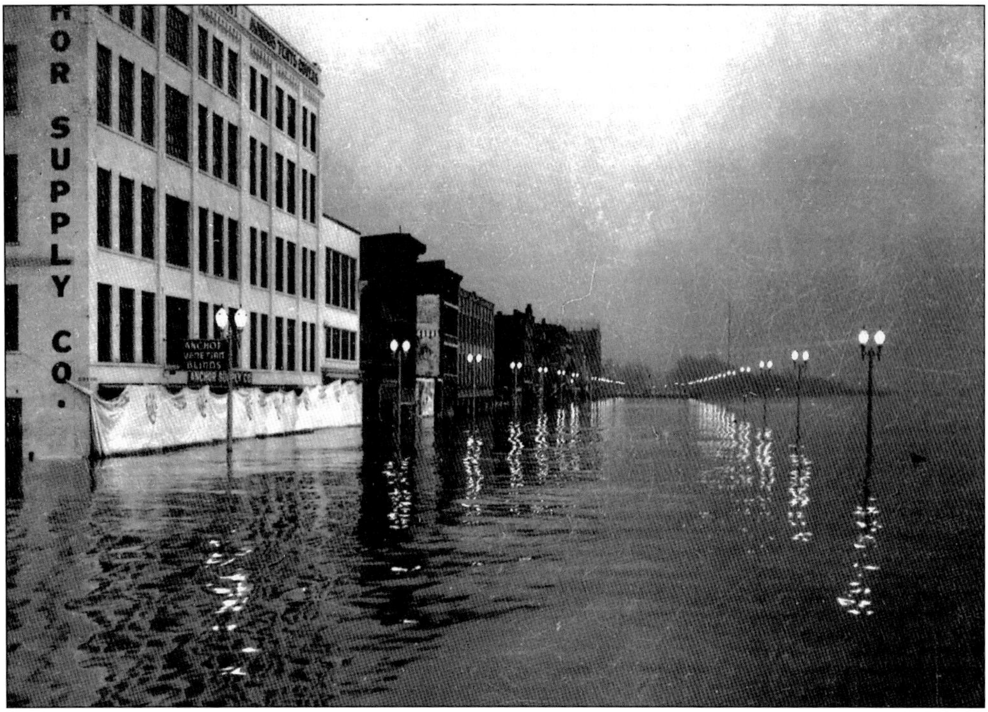

Street lights cast an eerie glow over the floodwaters on Evansville's Riverside Drive. (Courtesy of USI Special Collections.)

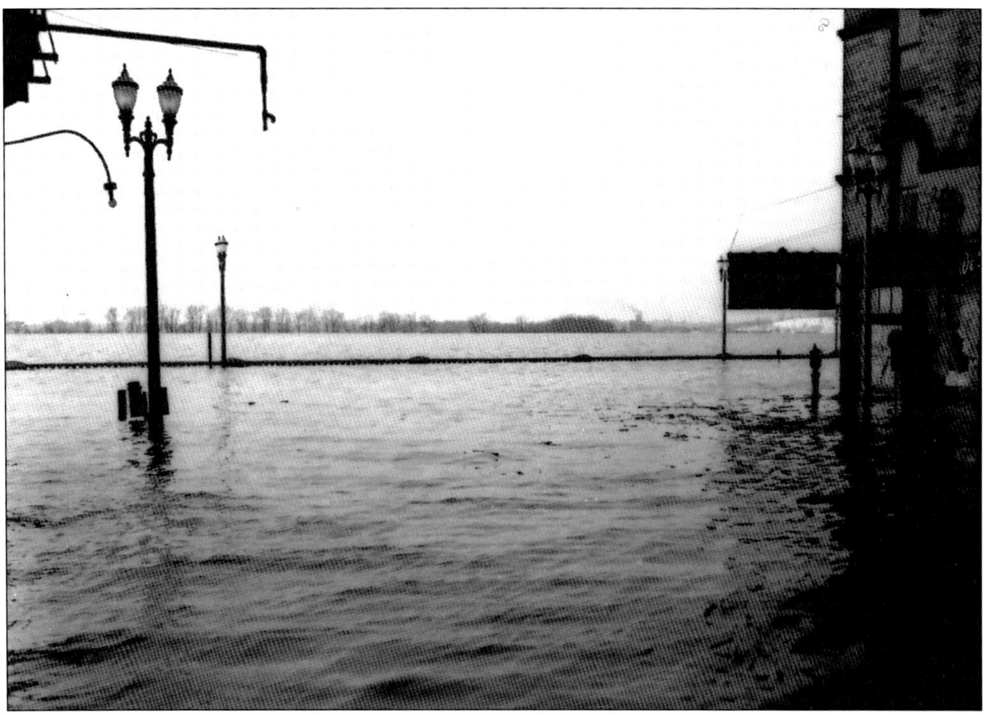

Another view of the flood of 1937 shows the water covering the waterfront downtown. The tree line in the back of the photograph is Kentucky. (Courtesy of USI Special Collections.)

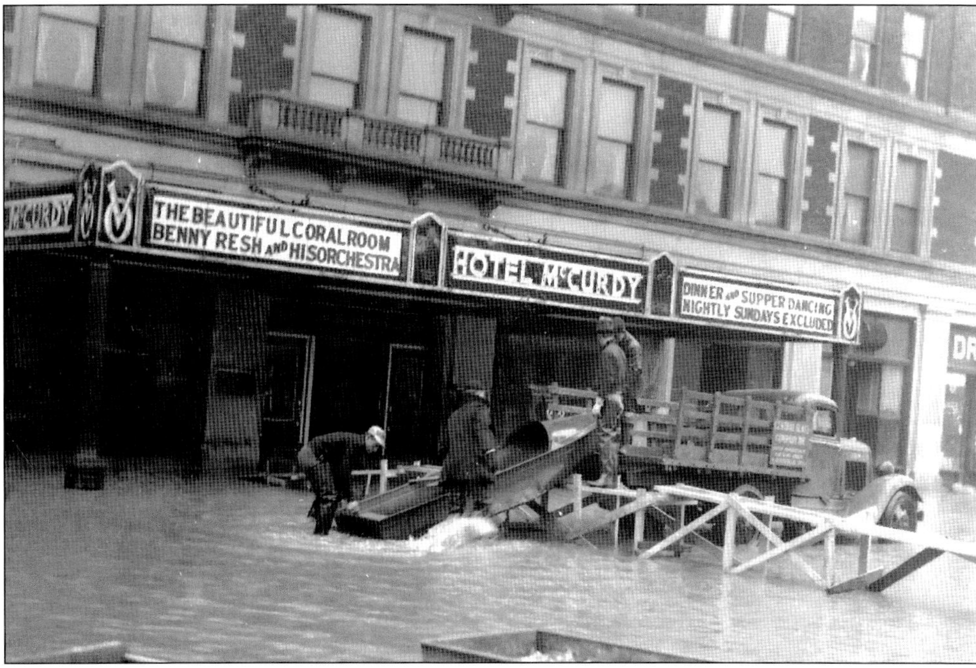

A rescue boat is lowered into the floodwaters in front of Evansville's Hotel McCurdy. Named after the prominent industrialist William McCurdy, it was the most elegant hotel on either side of the river below Louisville. (Courtesy of USI Special Collections.)

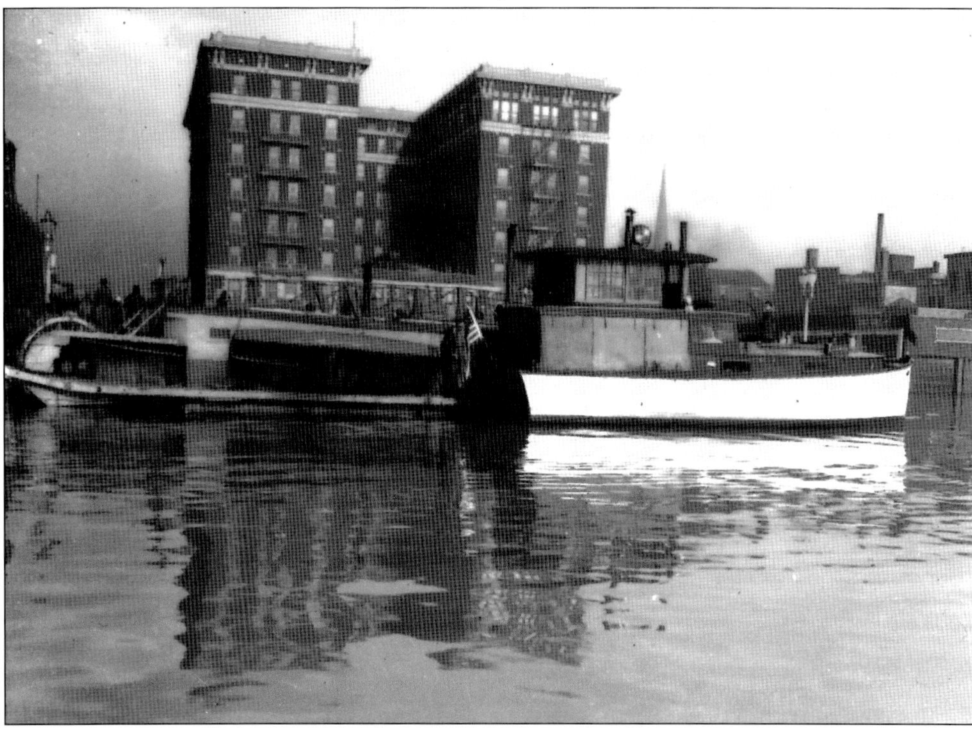

A boat is shown on the high water in front of the Hotel McCurdy. (Courtesy of USI Special Collections.)

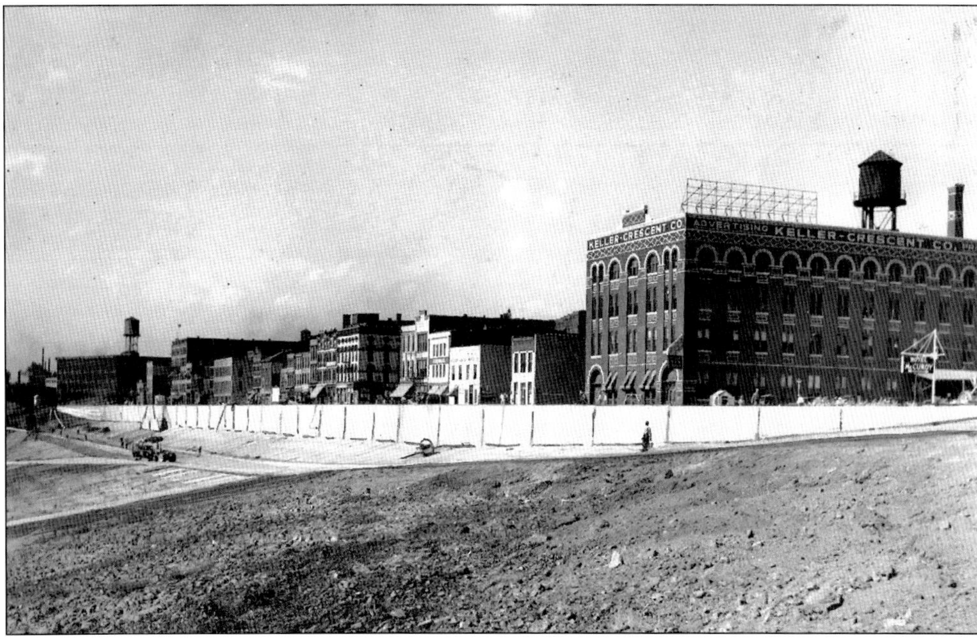

Dress Plaza, named for Evansville mayor William H. Dress, was a New Deal construction project. The half-million dollar riverfront improvement plan was completed in 1936. This photograph shows the plaza under construction. A few months later, this entire area would be under water. (Courtesy of Willard Library.)

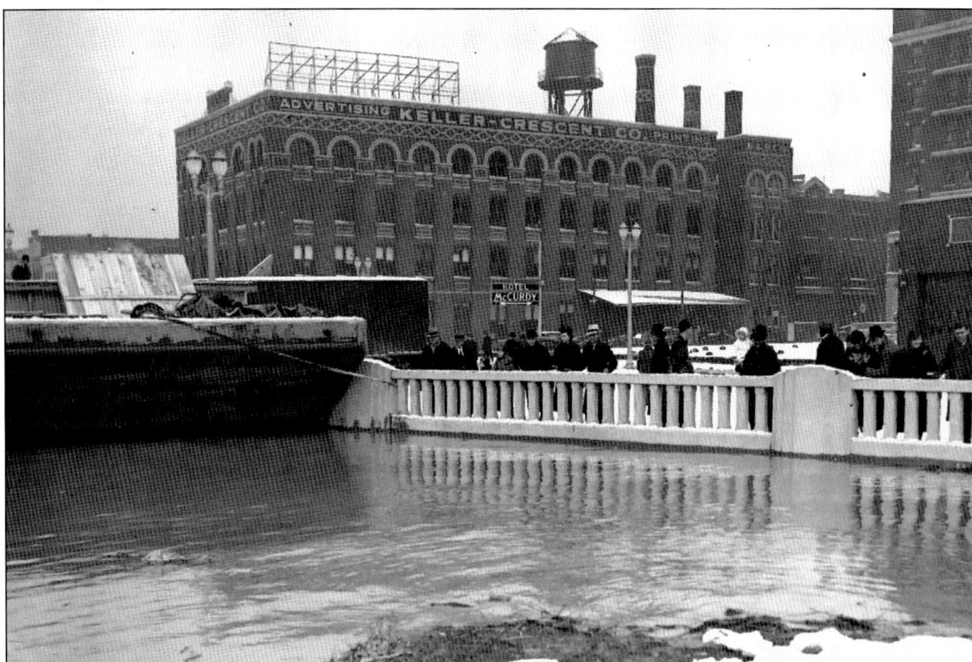

Taken from nearly the same vantage point with the Keller-Crescent building in the background, this photograph shows the height the flood water reached. A boat is anchored to the railing along the pedestrian sidewalk. (Courtesy of Willard Library.)

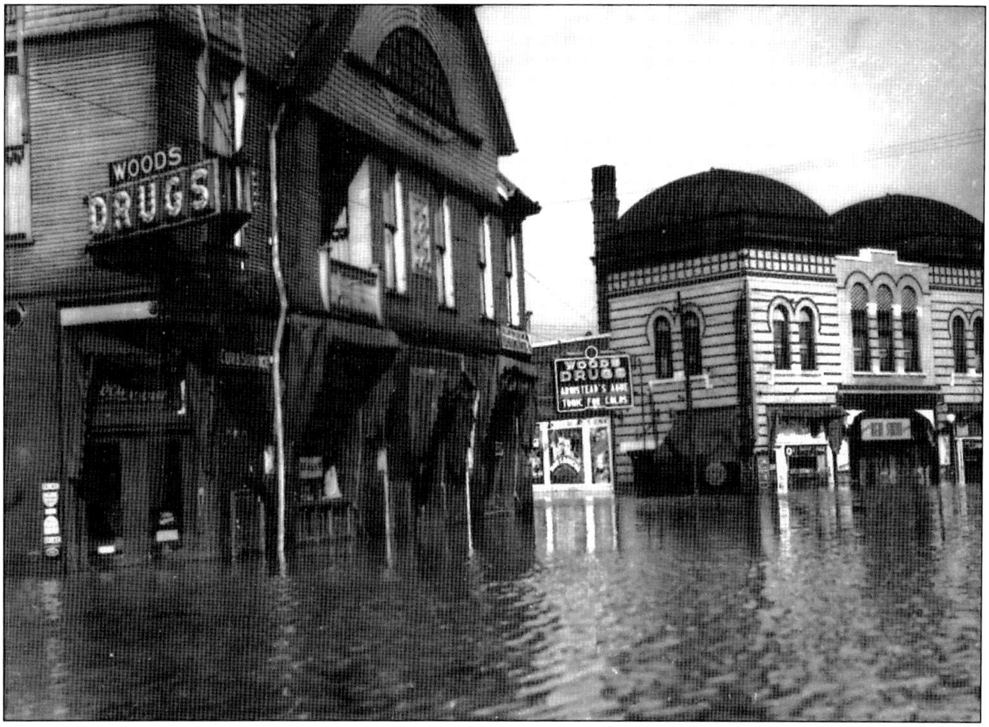

Two photographs taken from the same vantage point show the flood waters in the Haynie's Corner district in downtown Evansville. The first photograph shows the Alhambra Theater in the back and the original Woods Drugs in the front. After the flooding, a new Woods Drugs replaced the old, damaged building. (Courtesy of USI Special Collections.)

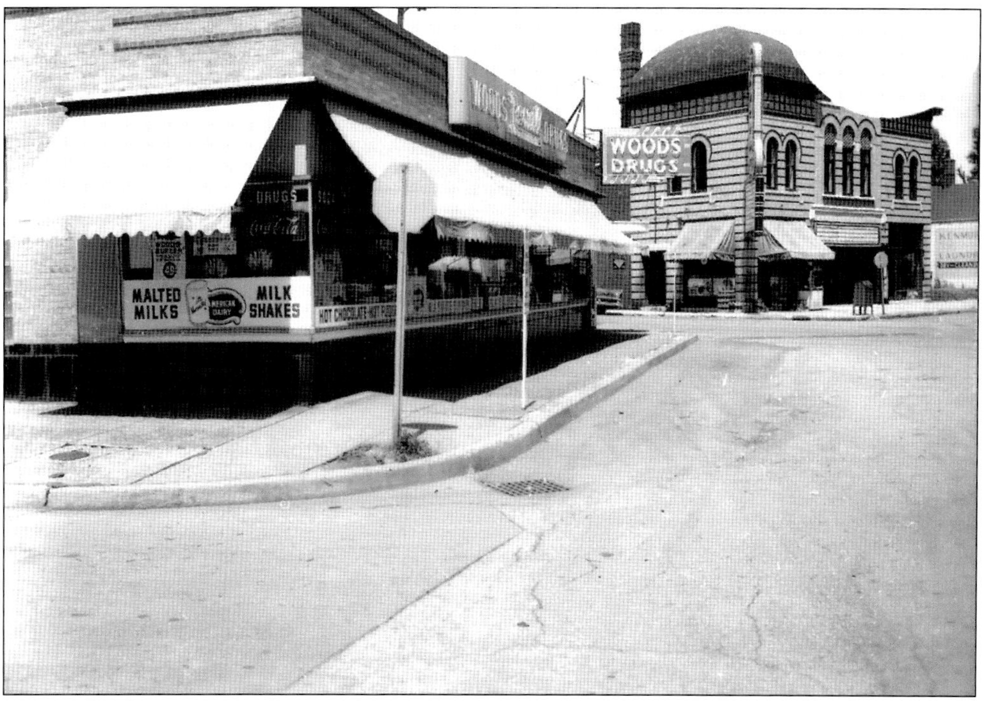

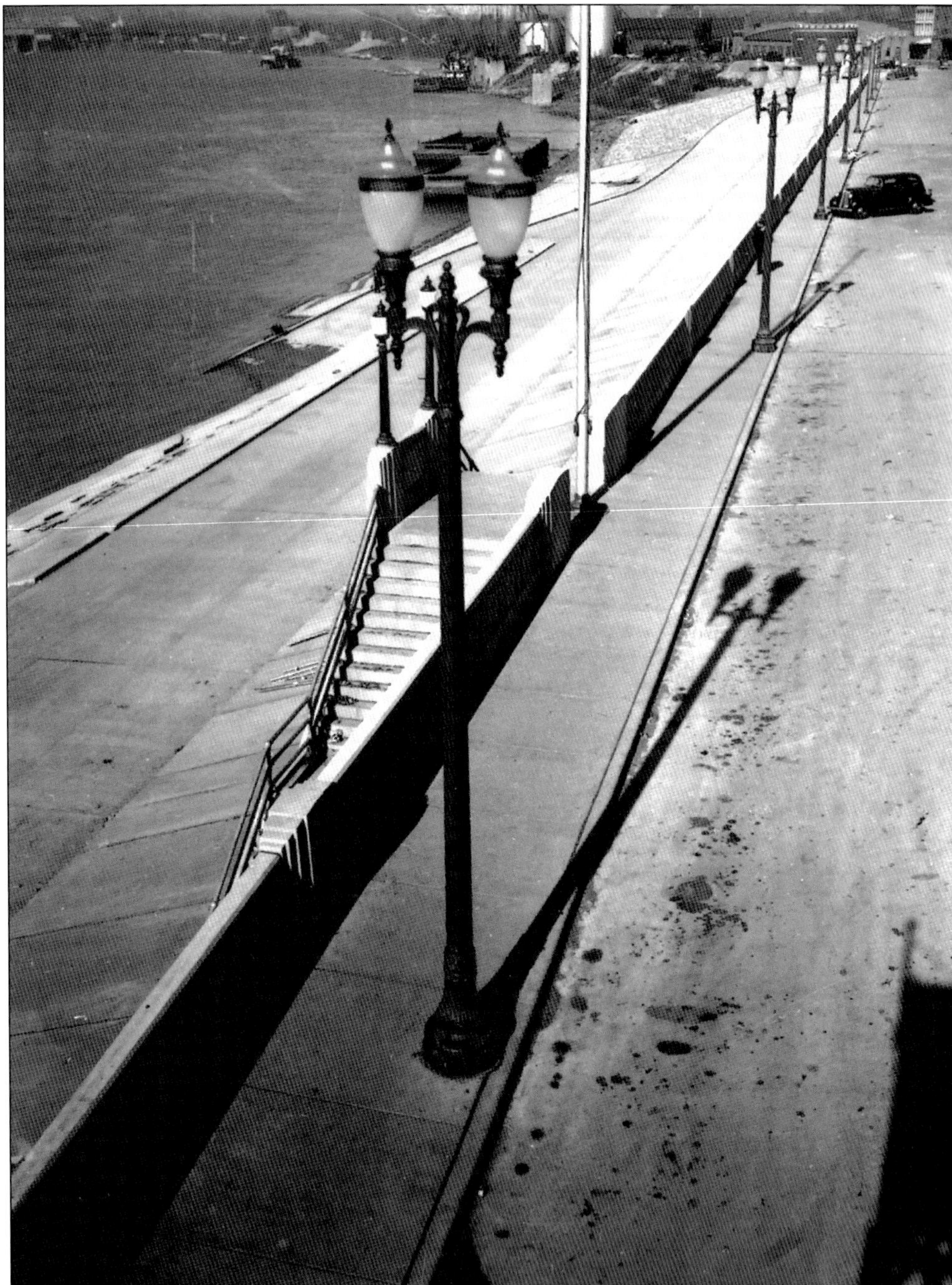

After the completion of Dress Plaza, the downtown area now had a buffer from the riverfront. A pedestrian esplanade provided an area to walk and view the river and boat ramps gave access to the river below. (Courtesy of USI Special Collections.)

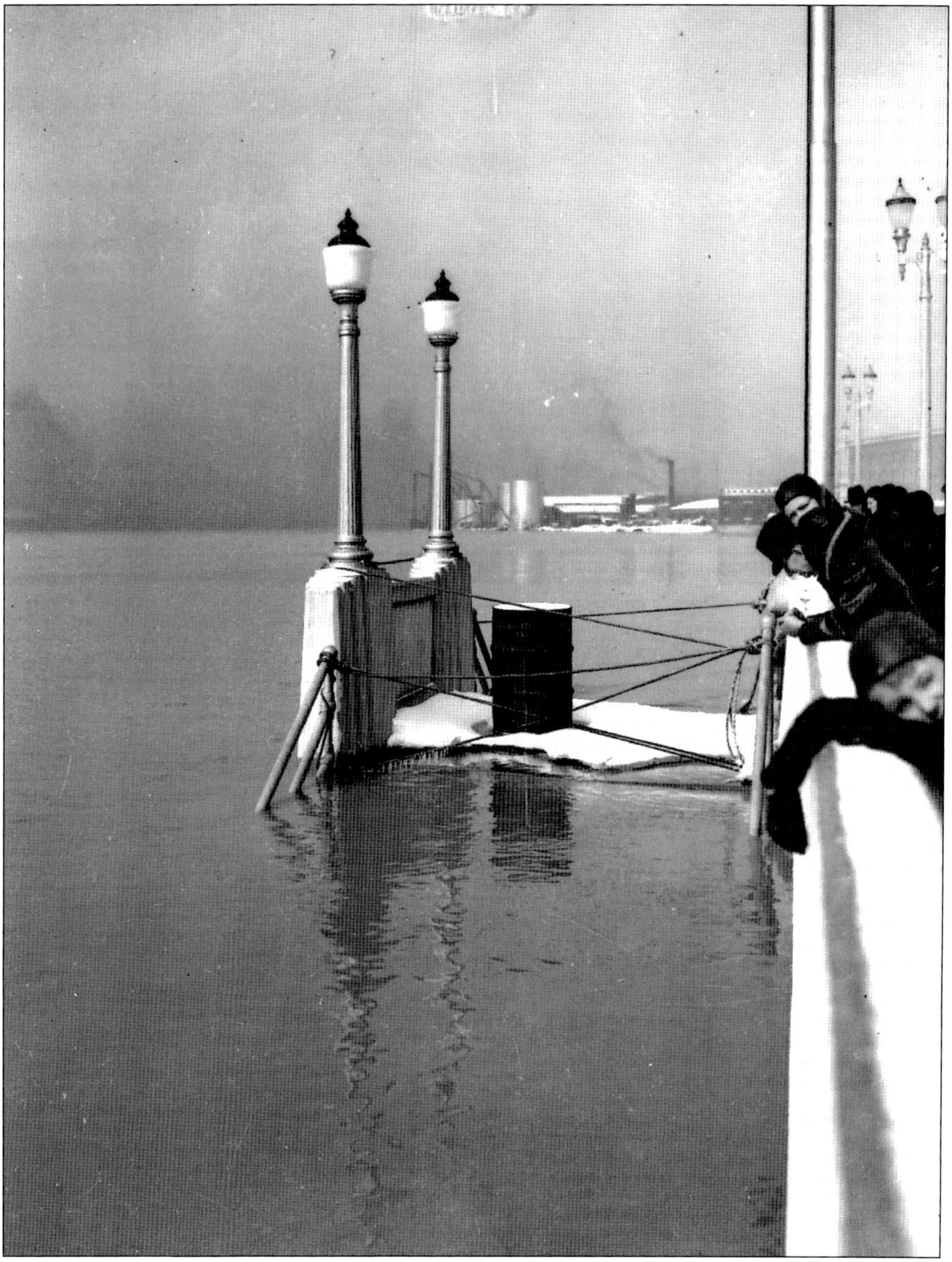

Taken from a similar angle, this photograph is another testament to the height that the water reached in the 1937 flood. (Courtesy of USI Special Collections.)

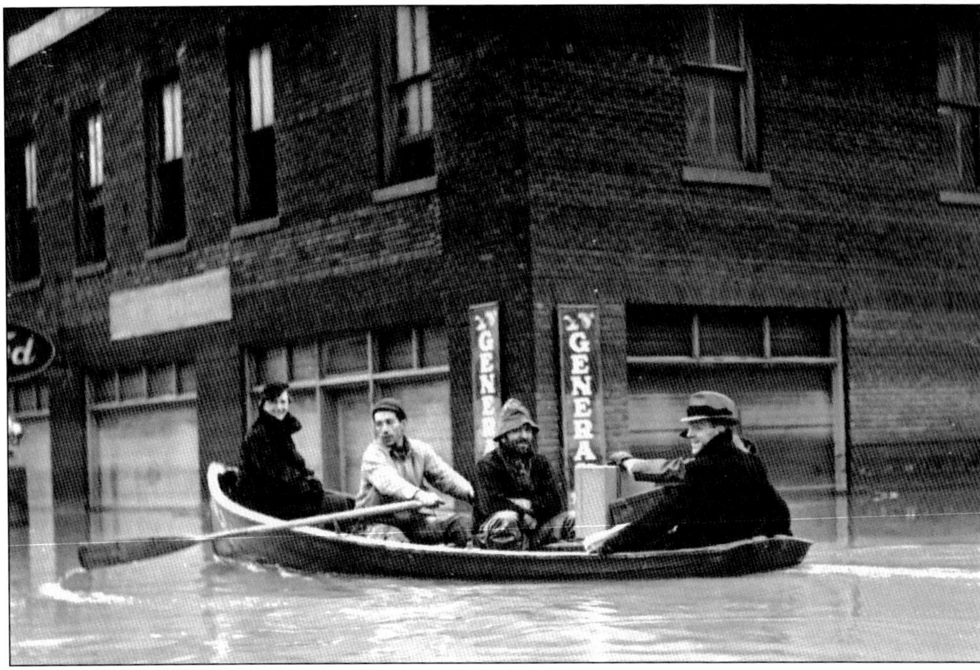

Men row a boat in front of the Ford Agency in Jeffersonville. The water level had already dropped by six feet when this photograph was taken. Once the water went down, the real work began to salvage buildings and possessions. (Courtesy of the Jeffersonville Township Public Library.)

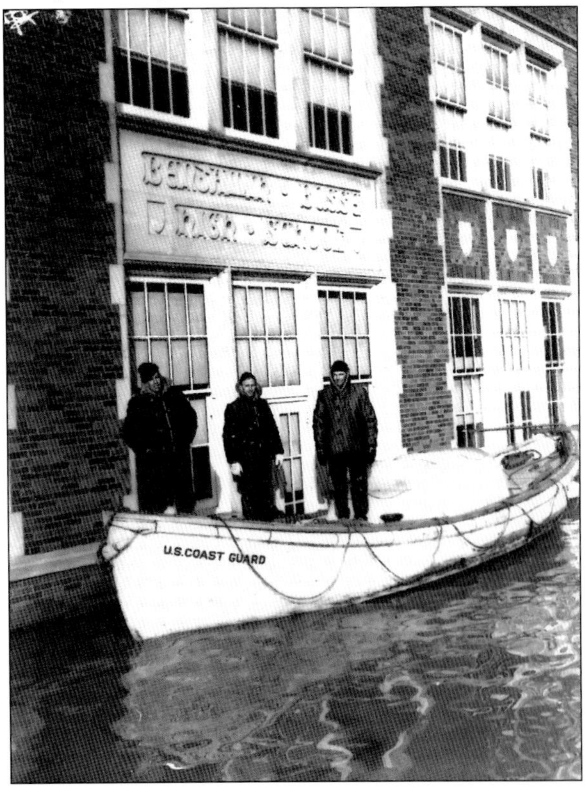

A United States Coast Guard boat sits in front of Bosse High School in Evansville. The school is located several miles from the river. Former students recounted how the flood line could be seen on the velvet stage curtains in the auditorium even in the late 1940s. (Courtesy of USI Special Collections.)

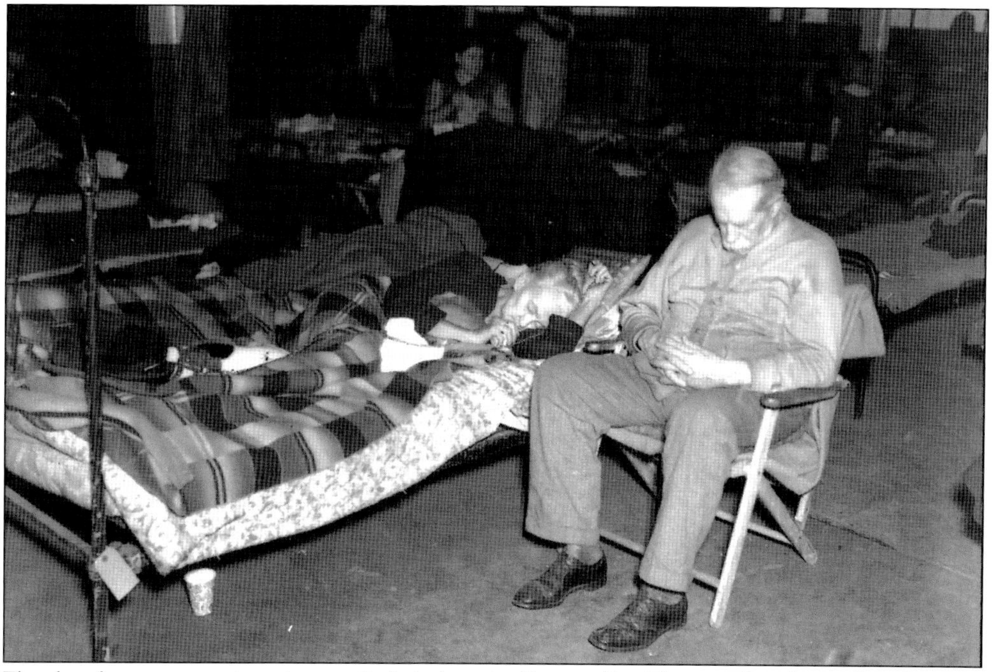

Flood refugees pass time in a relief shelter in Evansville. Thousands of people all along the Ohio River were displaced from their homes and had to seek shelter. (Courtesy of USI Special Collections.)

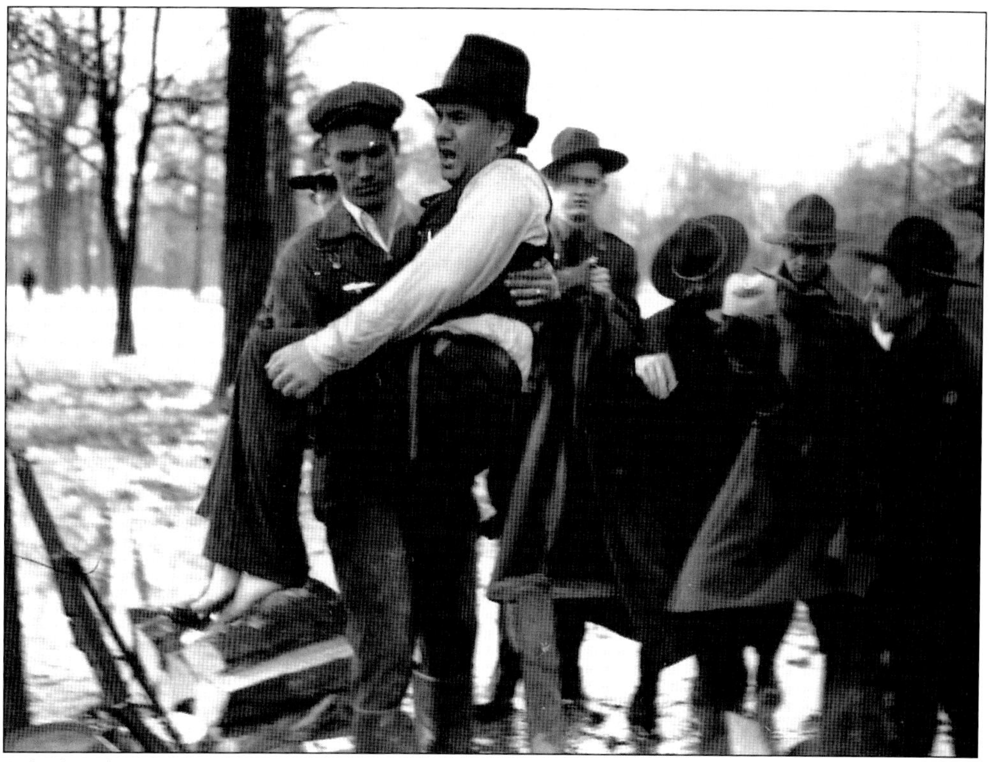

Relief workers evacuate a man from the 1937 flood waters. (Courtesy of USI Special Collections.)

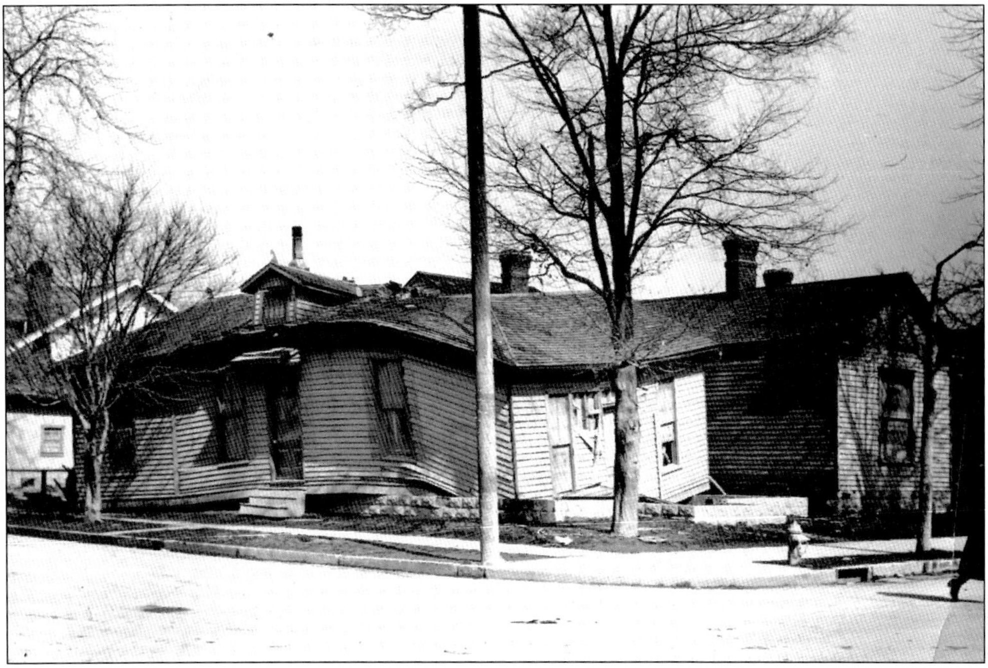

A house in Jeffersonville exhibits damage from the 1937 flood. It has come off its foundation, and the wood siding is bowed and warped. Many houses and businesses were completely destroyed in the flood. Others were salvageable and remain standing today. (Courtesy of the Jeffersonville Township Public Library.)

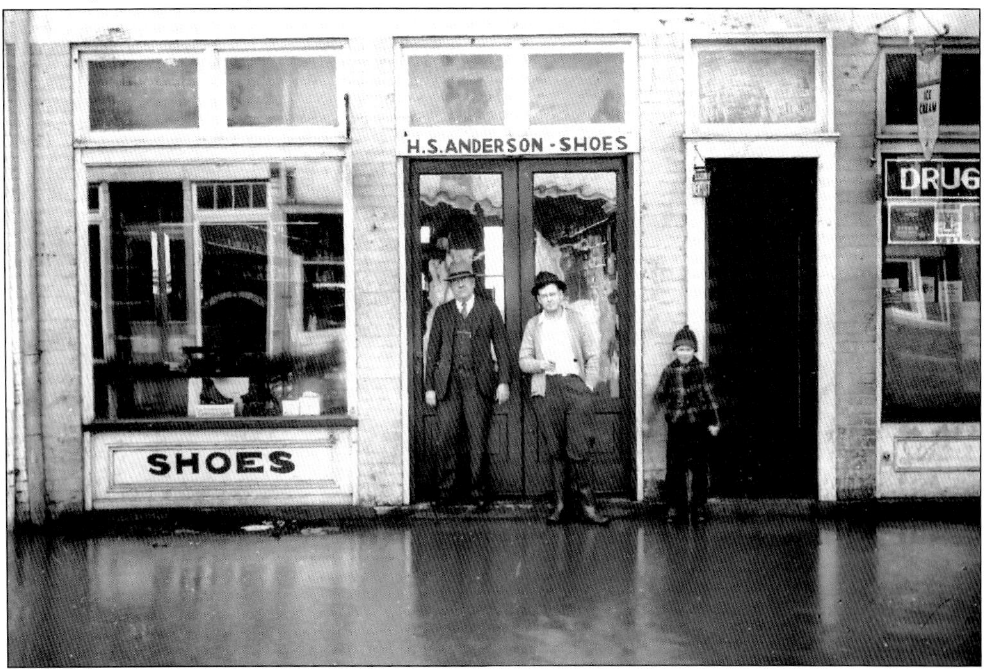

Two men and a boy stand among the receding floodwaters in front of the H. S. Anderson Shoe store in Rising Sun. The flood lasted from January through February 1937. (Courtesy of the Ohio County Indiana Historical Society and Museum.)

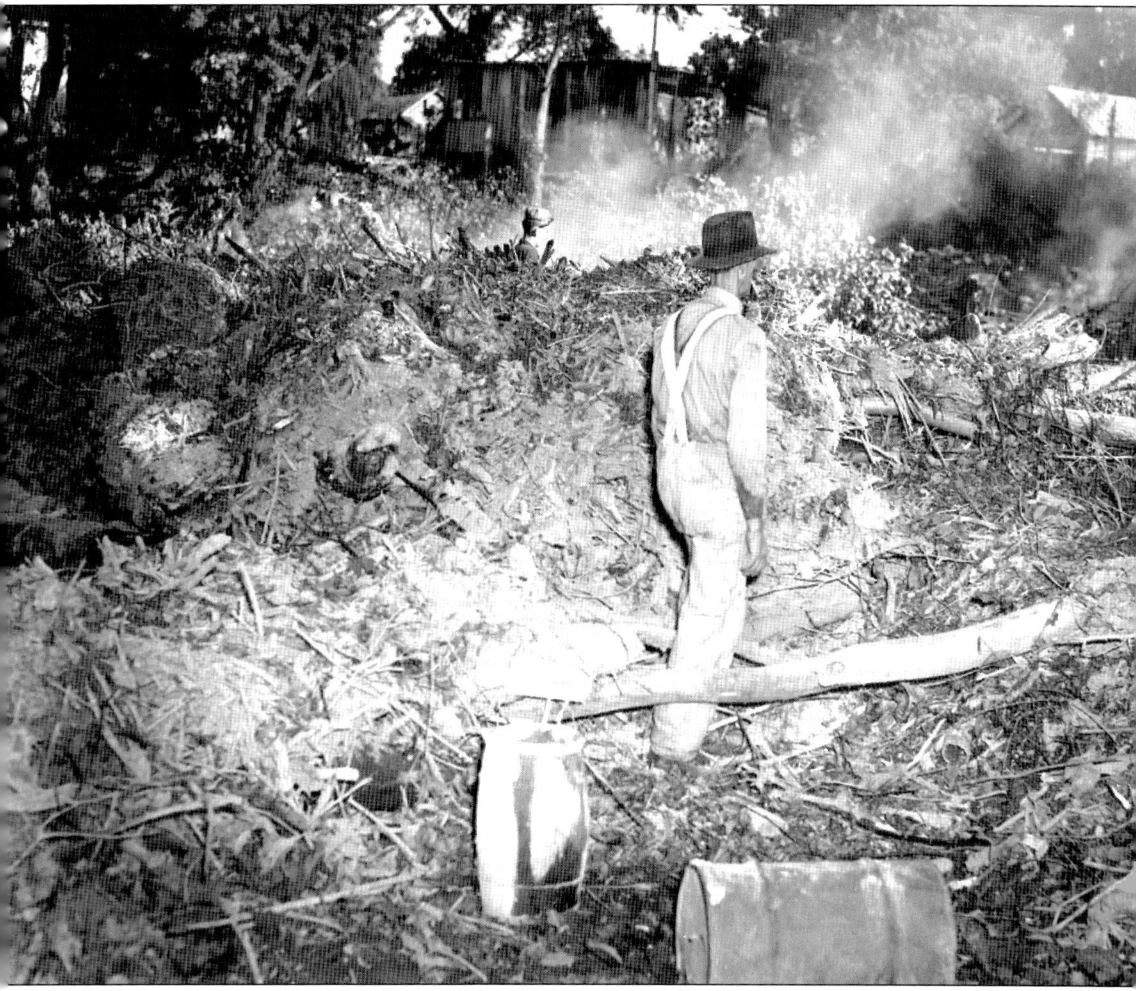

After the 1937 flood subsided, much work remained to clear the debris left by the high water. Here Mr. Crecelius of Harrison County clears flood debris. (Courtesy of the Harrison County Public Library.)

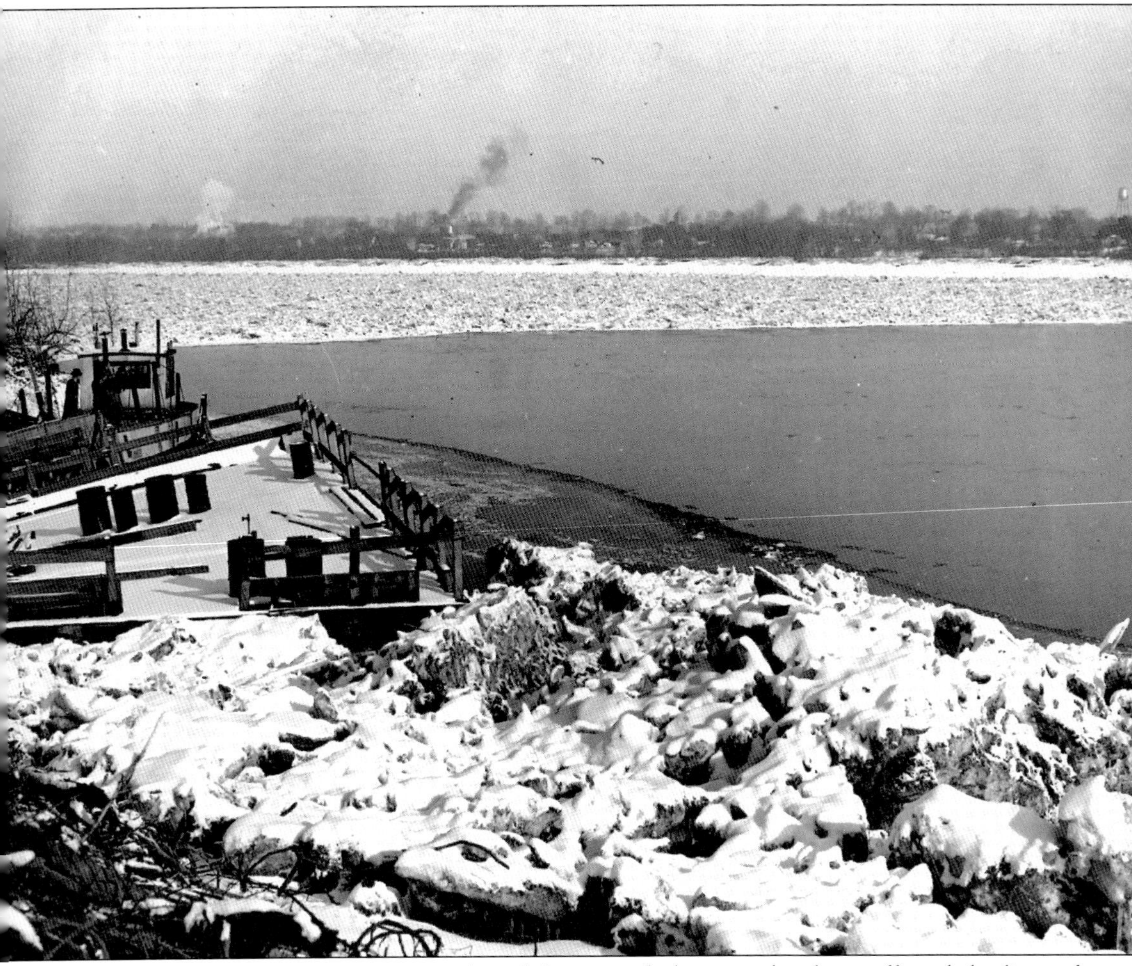

Flooding and ice gorges are just a few of the natural elements that have affected the lives of people in Ohio River Scenic Byway communities. This photograph shows the impact of nature along the Ohio River. (Courtesy of Willard Library.)

Three

Recreational
Fun and Play Along the Byway

Recreational activities abound along the Ohio River Scenic Byway. This is as true today as it was in the past. Hiking, camping, fishing, picnicking, biking, and swimming are just a few examples of things people have enjoyed over the years.

As automobiles became more prevalent, and roads and highways crisscrossed the countryside, it was not uncommon for the family to take to the road on a weekend afternoon for a leisurely drive. In fact, the term Sunday drive is part of the contemporary lexicon. Hotels and motels, restaurants, and other roadside attractions sprung up to accommodate the automobile traveler.

The Ohio River is a virtual playground for those who enjoy the water. Marinas and boat clubs attract those who enjoy boating for pleasure. The river and its tributaries, as well as the many lakes and streams in southern Indiana, offer ample opportunities for fishing. Evansville and Madison are known for their hydroplane boat races.

Today as the country's interstates become congested with traffic, many people look for opportunities to take the road less traveled and see the real America. Scenic byways offer that experience.

Visitors are not the only ones to benefit from and enjoy recreational activities. They are just as important to the citizens who live in the communities along the byway. Festivals, county fairs, parades, summer concerts in the bandstands, and other special events are part of the fabric of life for a community and provide a link to that city or town's heritage.

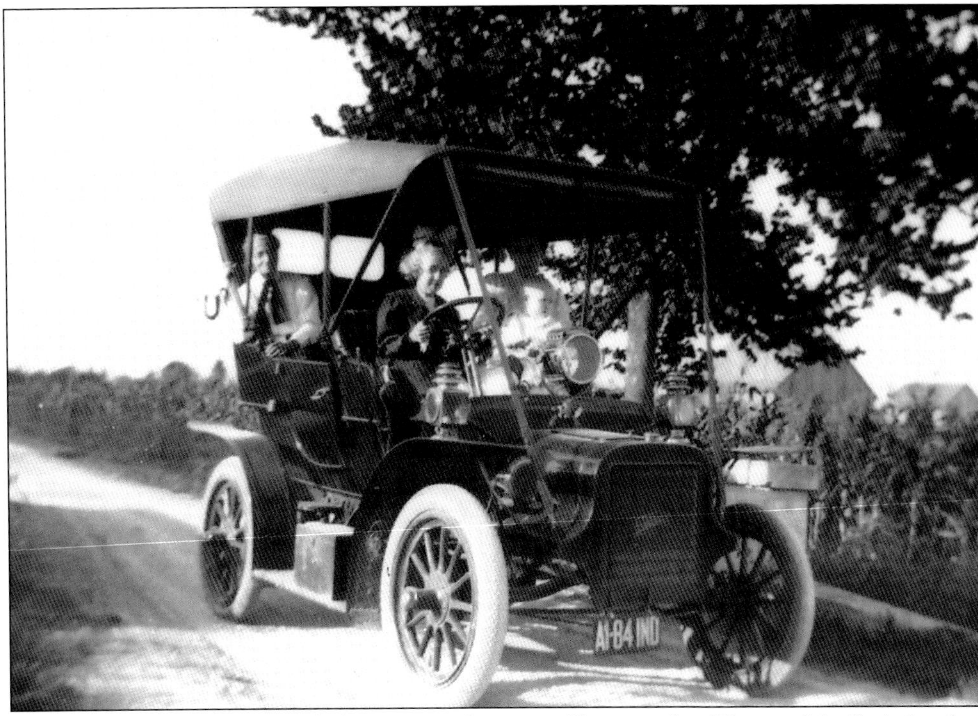

Early automobile travel provided recreation for many. Photographer Thomas Mueller's family is shown in their new 1914 Hupmobile, near Evansville. (Courtesy of USI Special Collections.)

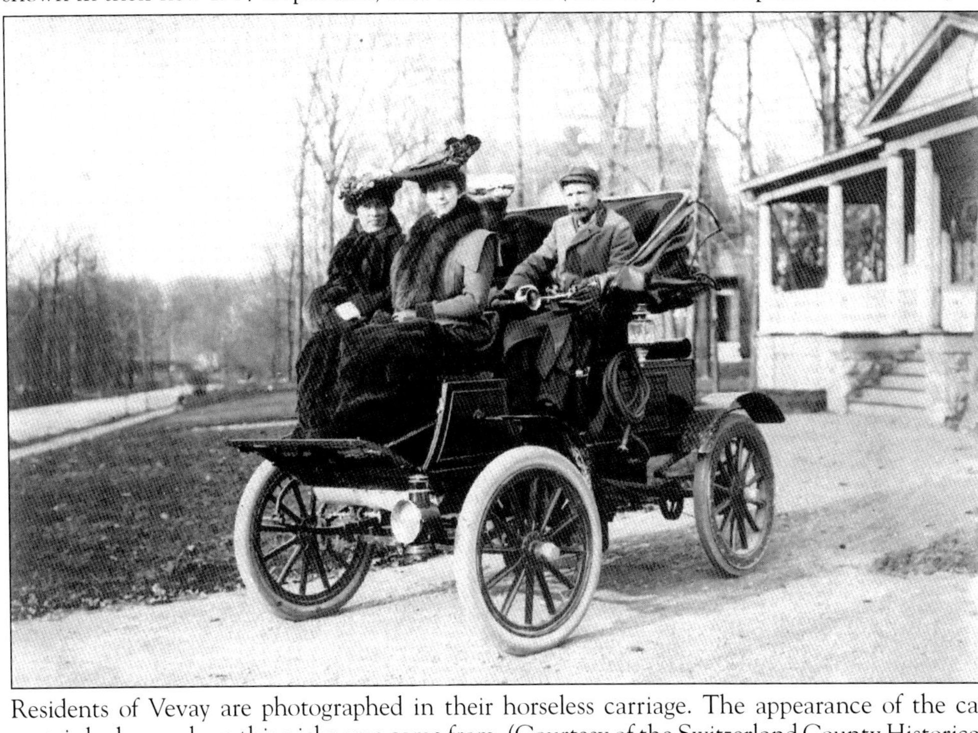

Residents of Vevay are photographed in their horseless carriage. The appearance of the car certainly shows where this nickname came from. (Courtesy of the Switzerland County Historical Society and Museum.)

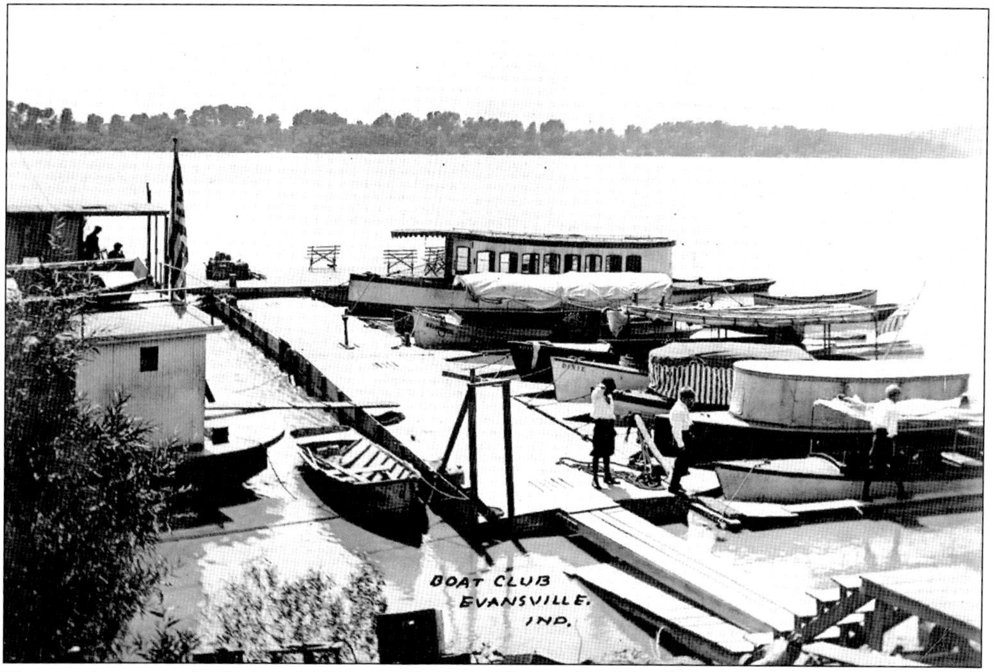

Pleasure boats are docked at the Evansville Boat Club at the foot of Main Street. This photograph was taken during the 1920s. Although the river was an economic resource used to transport goods, it still offered recreational opportunities for people in cities and towns along its banks. Today speed boats and jet skis are as abundant on warm summer days as barges. (Courtesy of Willard Library.)

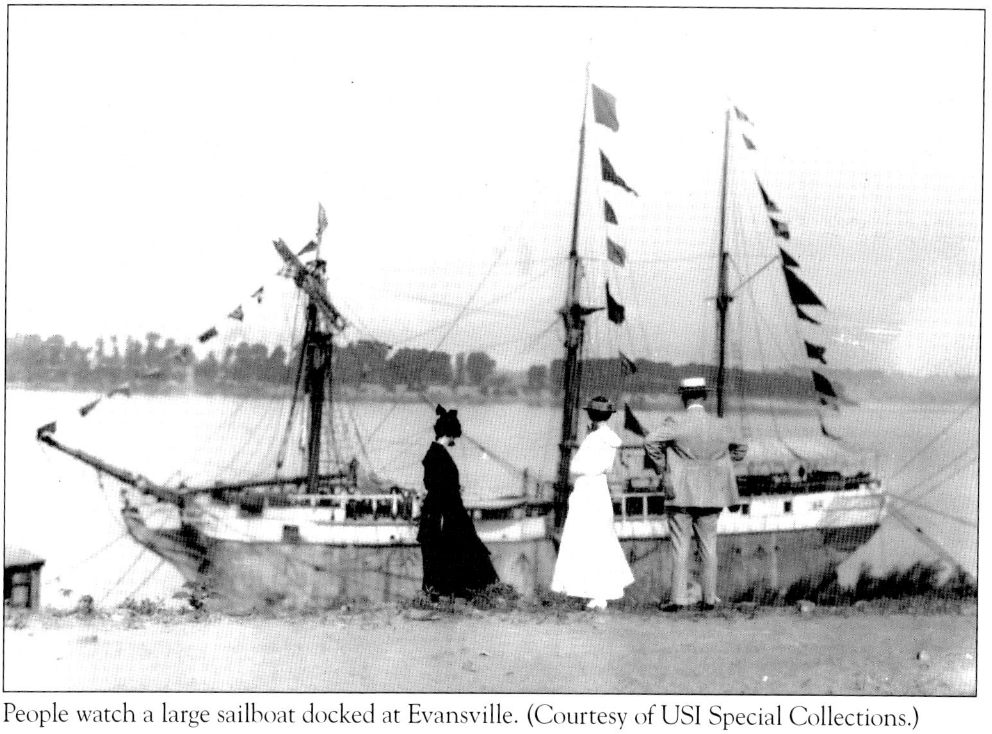

People watch a large sailboat docked at Evansville. (Courtesy of USI Special Collections.)

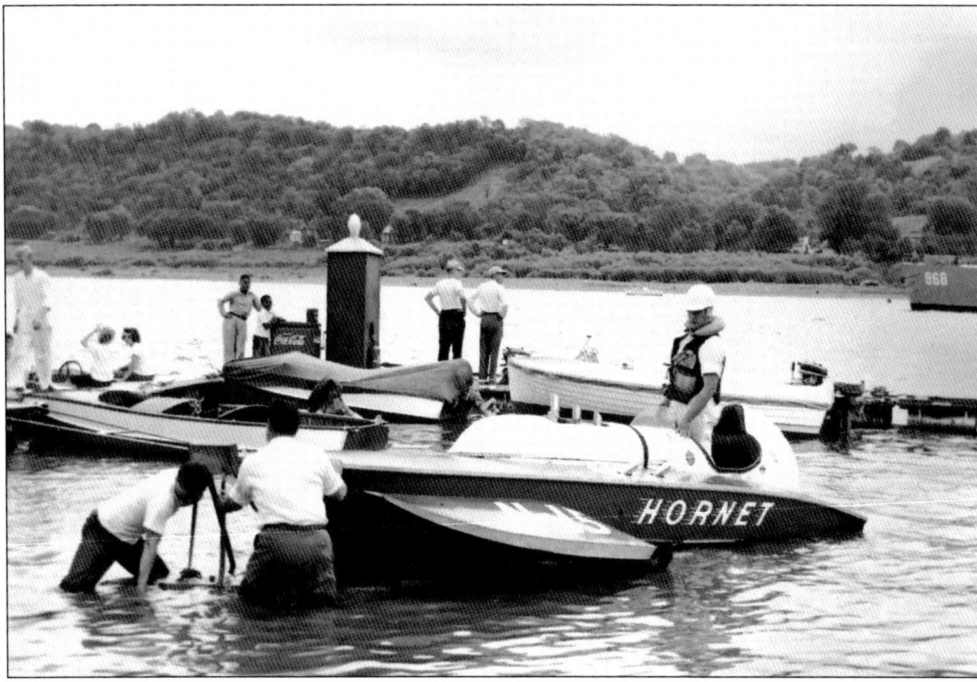

Men work on Marion Cooper's *Hornet* during the Rising Sun Regatta in 1950. The boat would win the first Indiana Governor's Cup at the 1951 Madison Regatta. (Courtesy of the Ohio County Historical Society.)

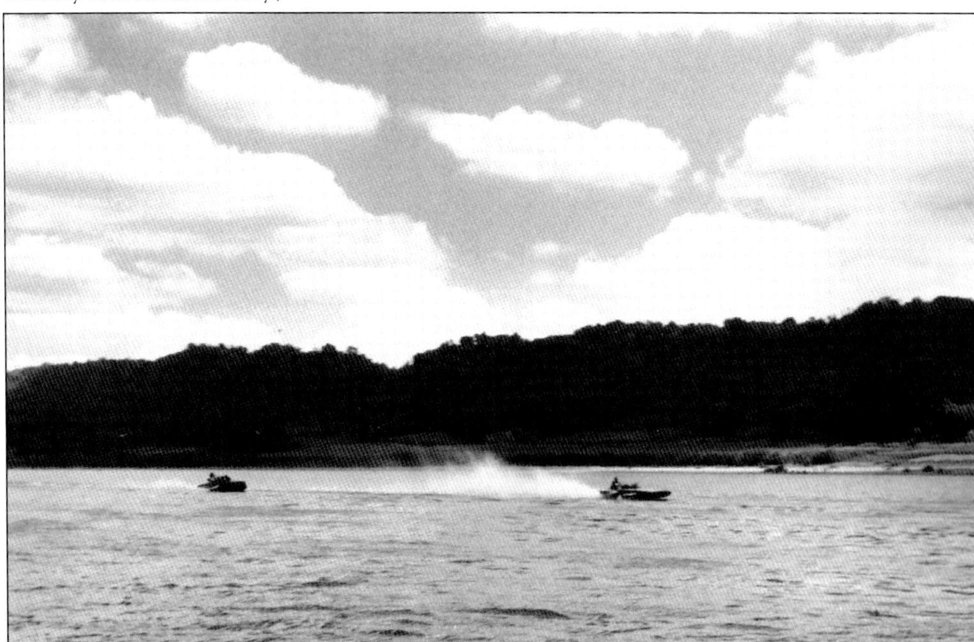

The Rising Sun boat races were only held from 1948 to 1951. They were resurrected for a brief time in the 1980s and again in 2000. Hydroplane racing has been a popular sport on the Ohio River. Both Madison and Evansville are known for their races, which continue today. (Courtesy of the Ohio County Historical Society.)

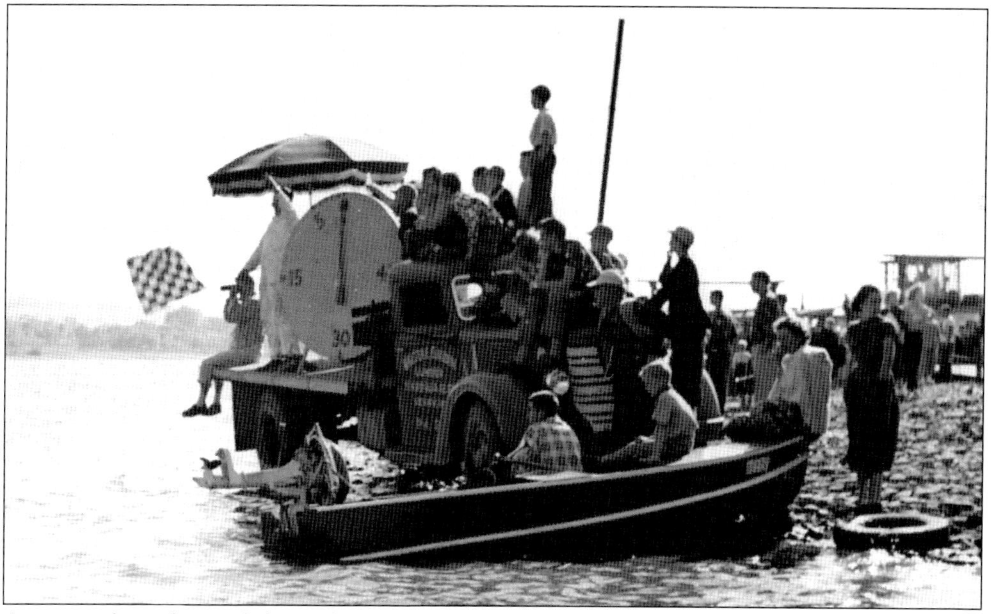

A group of people watch boats from the landing in Vevay. This photograph was taken in 1951. (Courtesy of the Switzerland County Historical Society.)

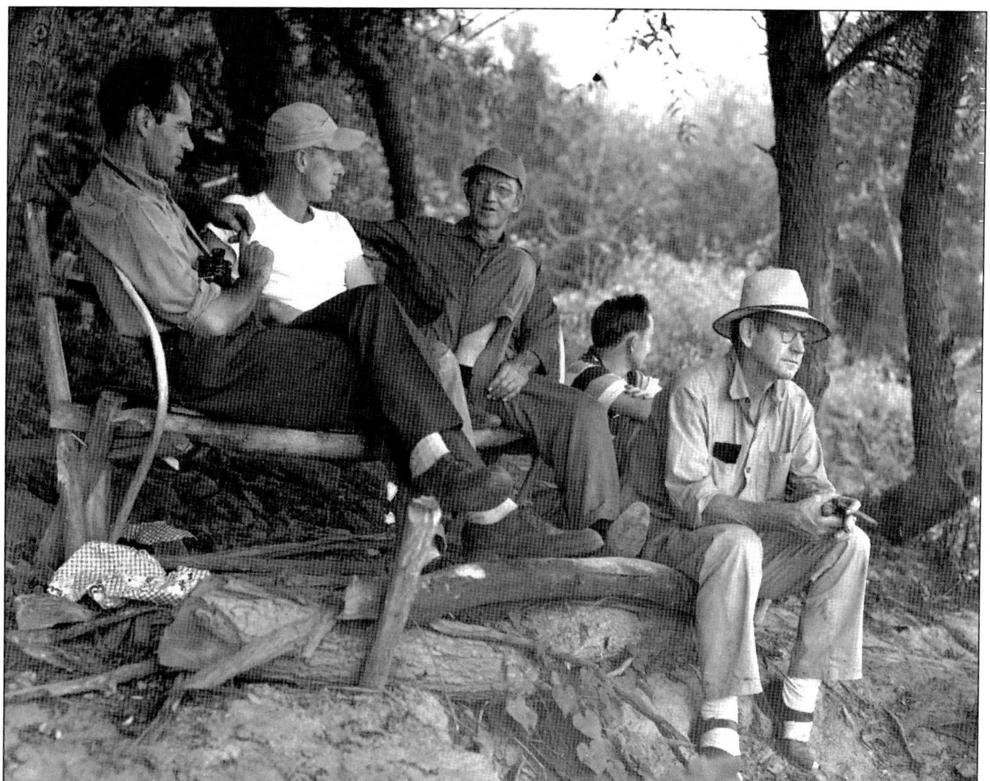

A group of men from Vevay pass the time by watching boats on the Ohio River. (Courtesy of the Switzerland County Historical Society and Museum.)

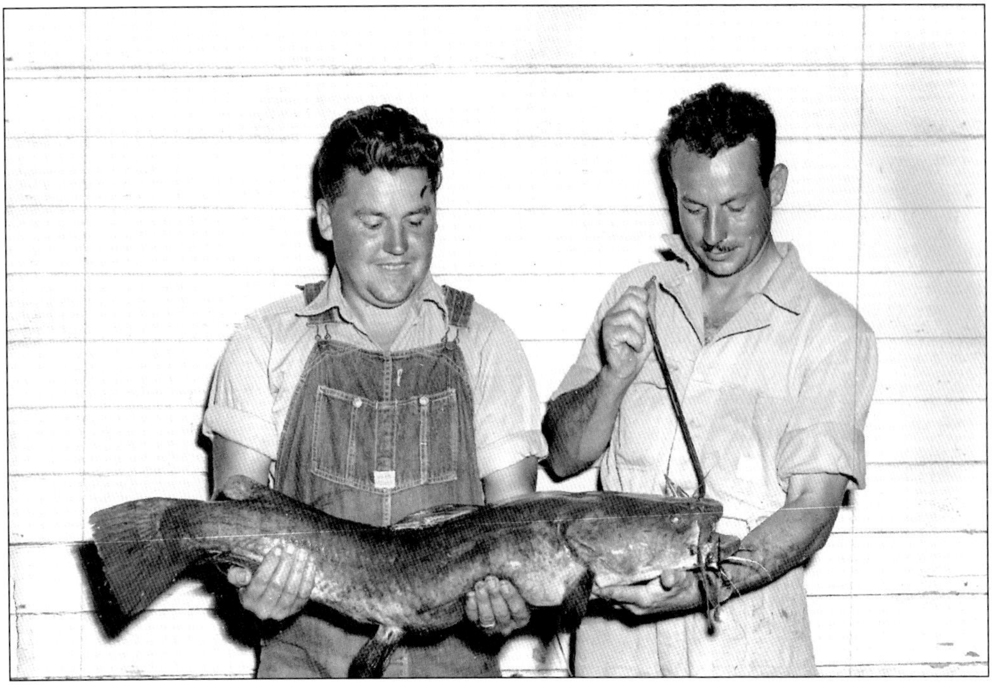

Fishing on the Ohio River provided an enjoyable pastime for many people over the years. These men from Corydon display a catfish that was caught in the river. (Courtesy of the Harrison County Public Library.)

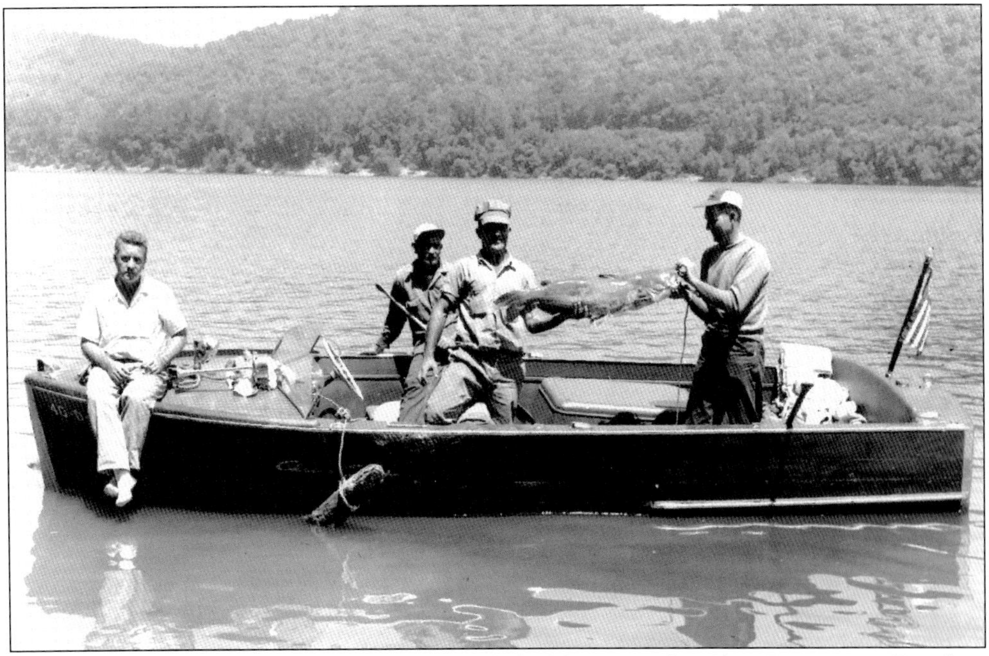

A group of men fishing display their catch while fishing on the Ohio River near Corydon. Fishing for catfish differs from other types of fishing due to the size of the fish. Catfish are often called bottom-feeders. Channel catfish can weigh 25 pounds or more, and flatheads and blues are regularly 30 to more than 50 pounds. (Courtesy of the Harrison County Public Library.)

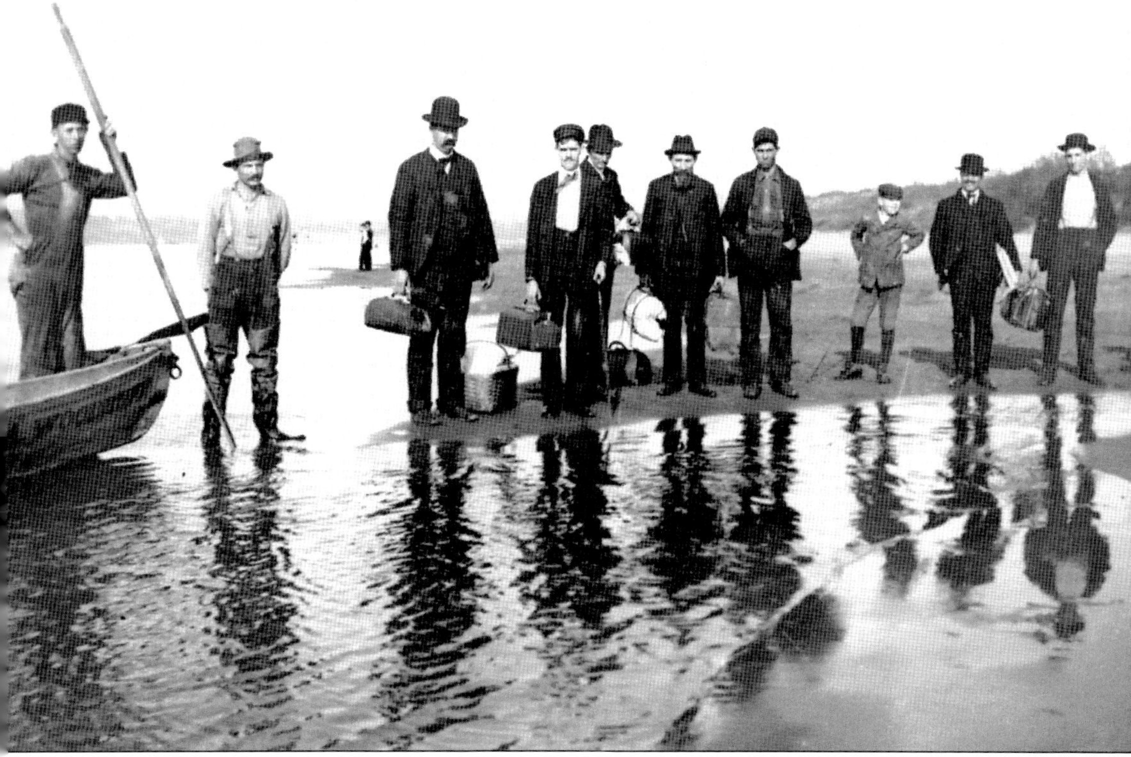

A group of fisherman stands on the banks of the Ohio River, near New Albany. (Courtesy of the New Albany-Floyd County Library.)

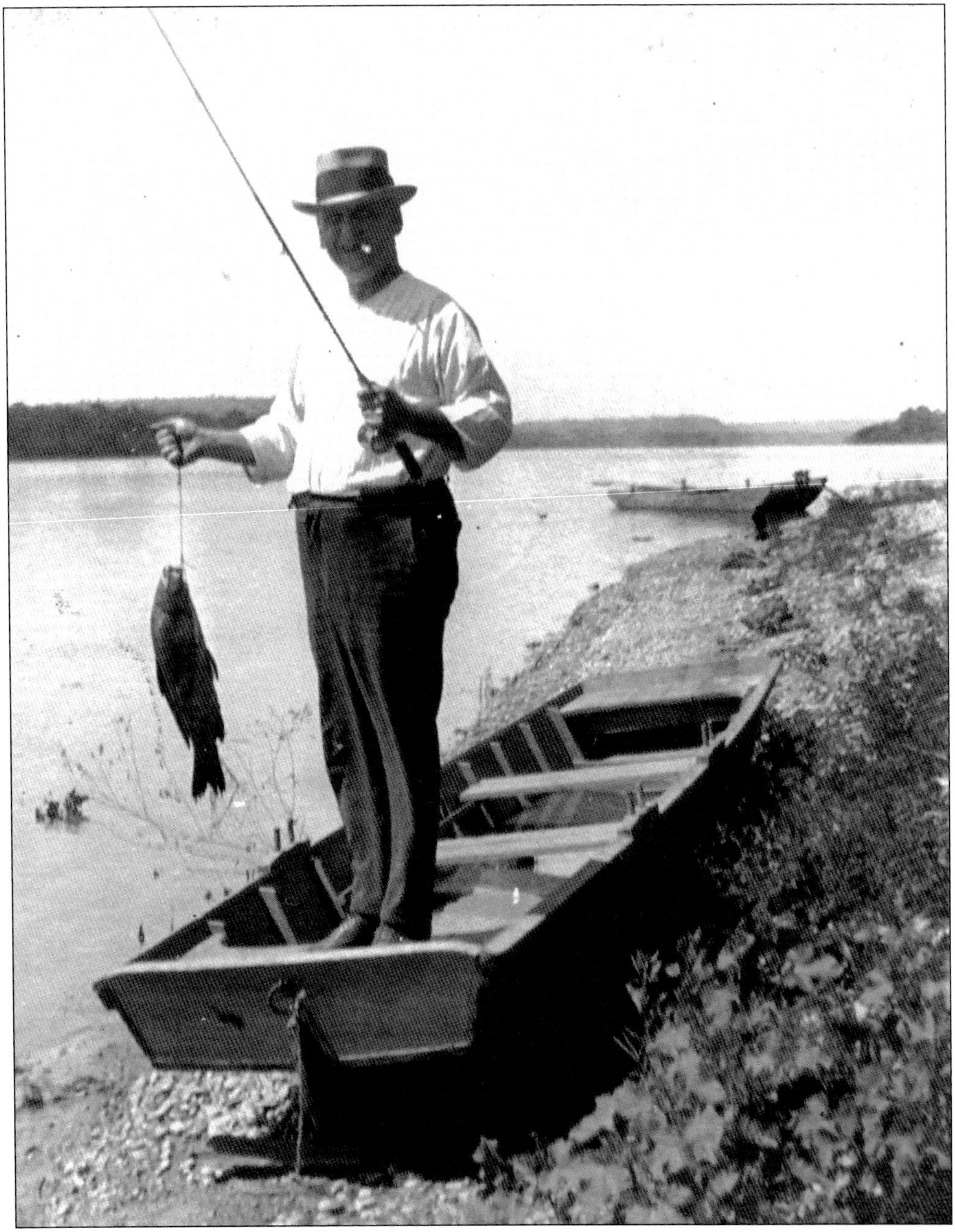

A Vevay resident proudly displays his catch. (Courtesy of the Switzerland County Historical Society and Museum.)

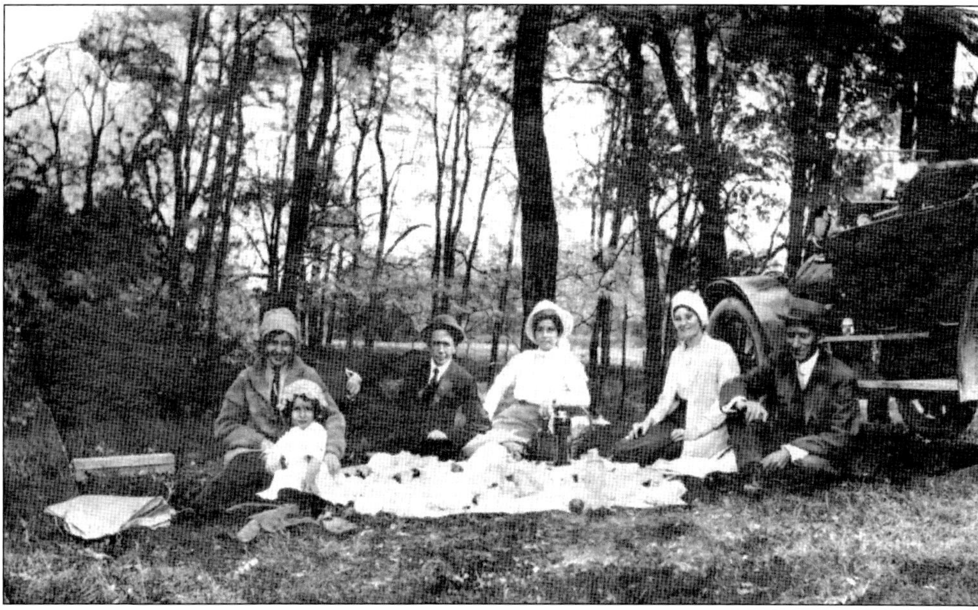

Clifty Falls State Park in Madison has attracted visitors to its scenic vistas, waterfalls, and geologic formations. A family enjoys a picnic in the early 1900s. (Courtesy of the Switzerland County Historical Society and Museum.)

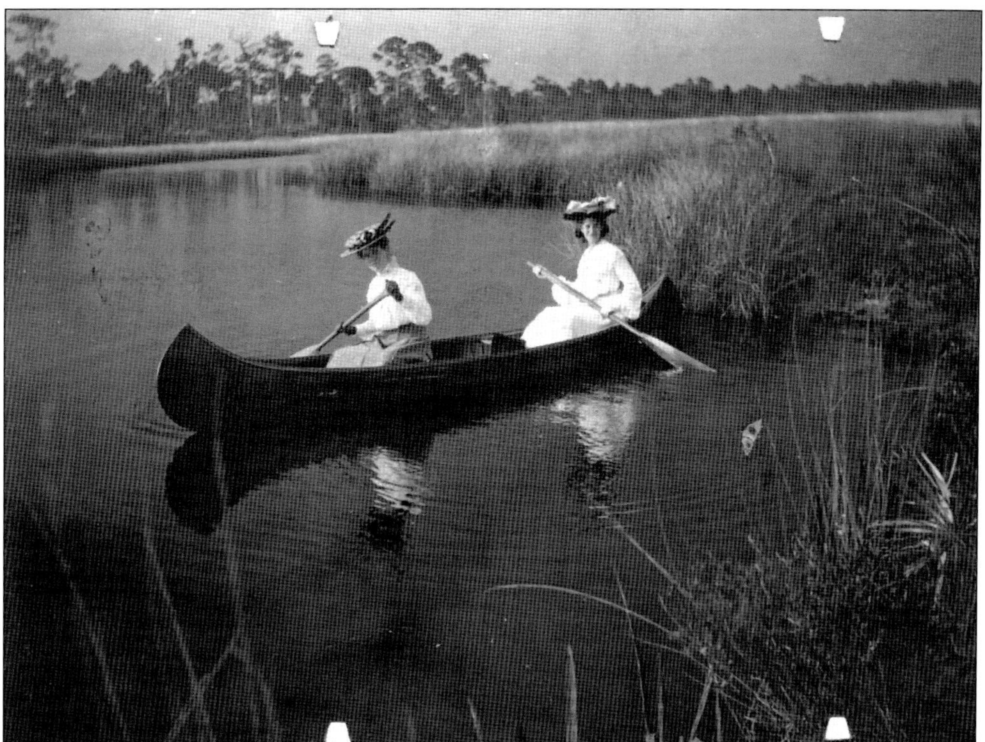

Two women paddle a canoe on a lake in Switzerland County. (Courtesy of the Switzerland County Historical Society and Museum.)

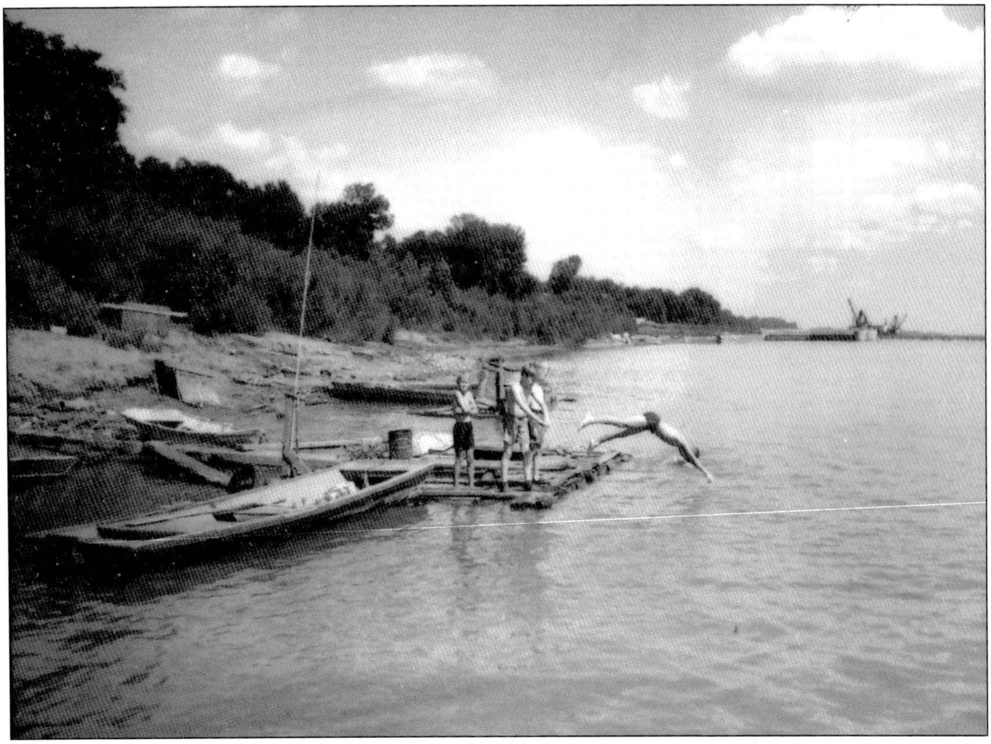

A group of boys enjoys diving into the Ohio River near Newburgh. The construction of the Newburgh Lock and Dam is visible in the background. (Courtesy of USI Special Collections.)

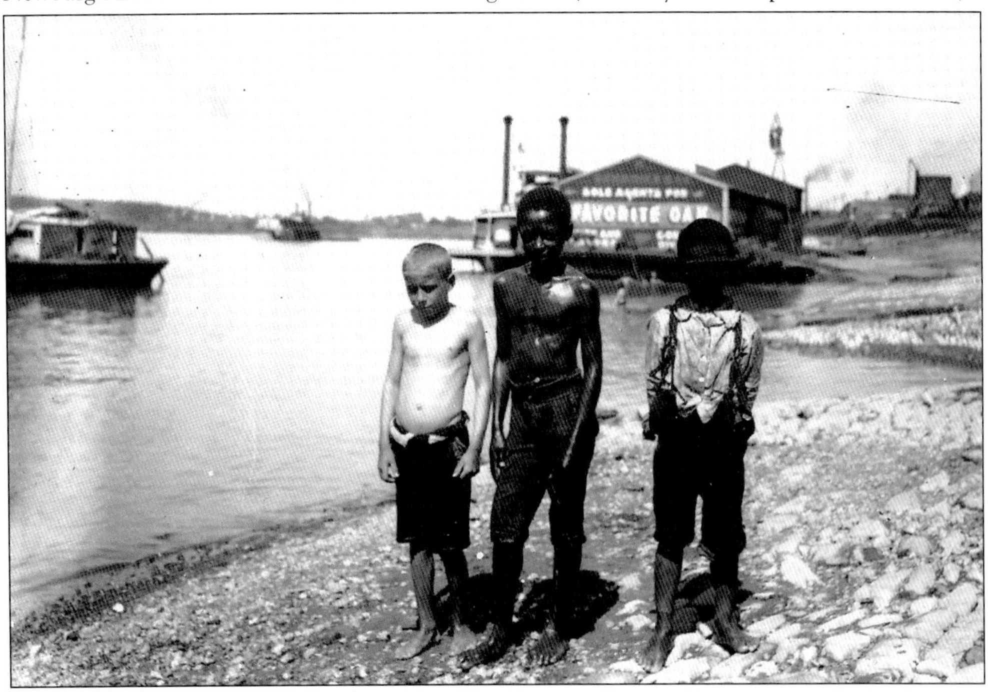

Children gathered along the banks of the Ohio River in Evansville to enjoy a dip in the river during the hot summer months. (Courtesy of USI Special Collections.)

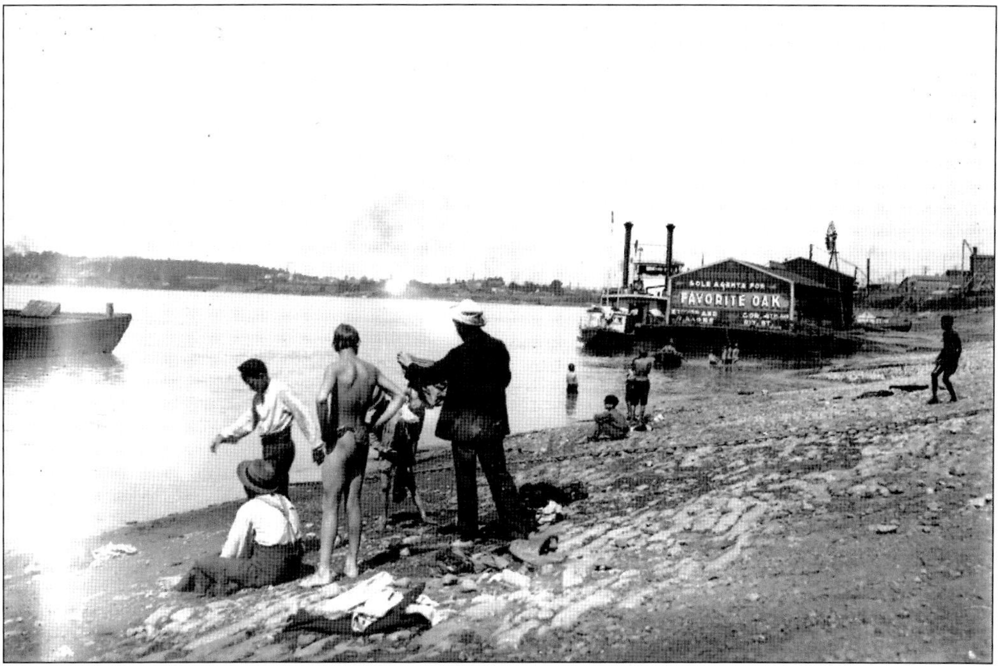

Swimming in the Ohio River offered summertime recreation for the adventuresome of all ages, despite threats posed by passing boats, floating debris, deep water, and swift currents. (Courtesy of USI Special Collections.)

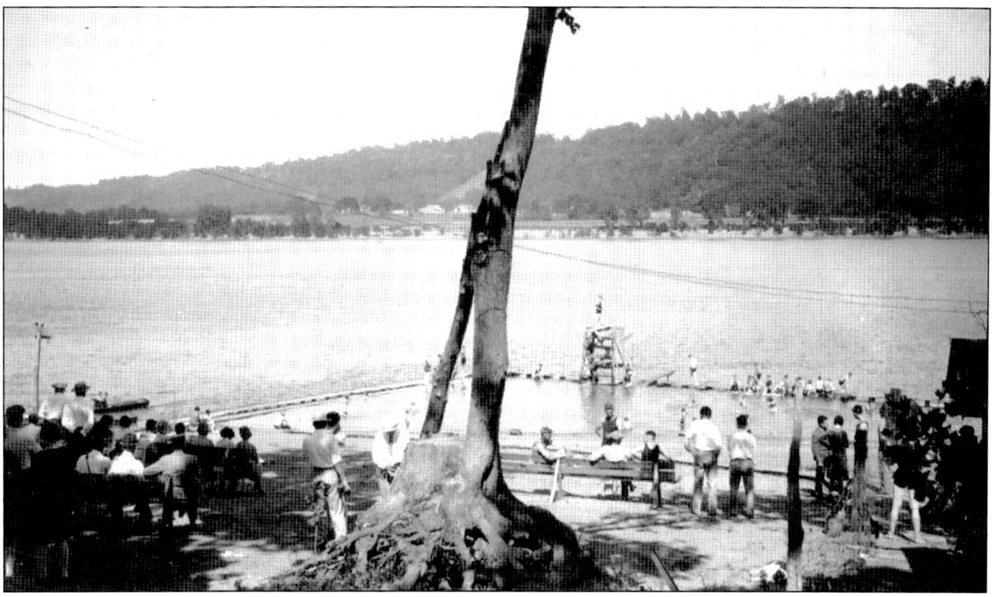

Hanover Beach was a popular spot on a hot summer day. Hanover is located just west of Madison and is the home of Hanover College. (Courtesy of the Jefferson County Historical Society.)

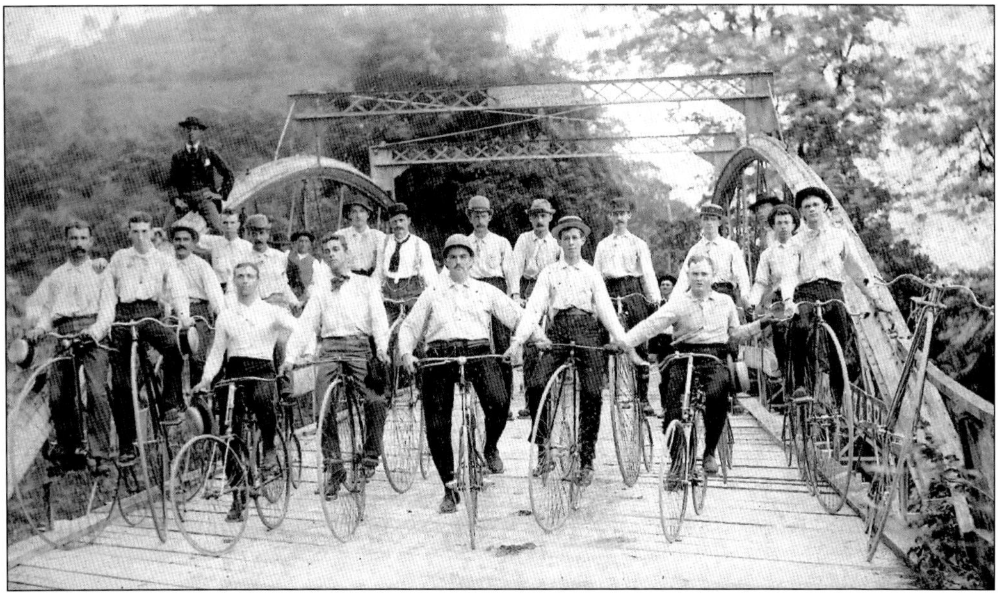

In the late 1800s and early 1900s, cycling became a fad in the United States and was a great source of recreation. Clubs were formed, like the Madison Bicycle Club pictured here on Eagle Hollow Bridge. Interest in cycling later declined with the introduction of automobiles. (Courtesy of the Jefferson County Historical Society.)

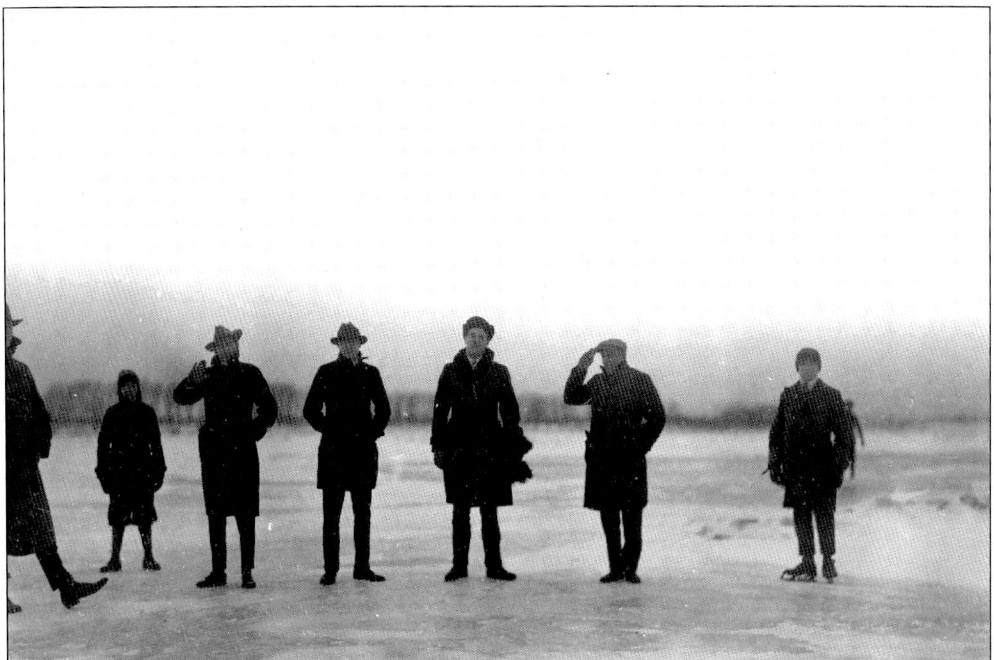

Seasonal recreation along the Ohio River took many forms. Here, a group of men take advantage of a cold winter, most likely in 1918 when the Ohio River froze, to ice skate or walk on the ice near Evansville. (Courtesy of Willard Library.)

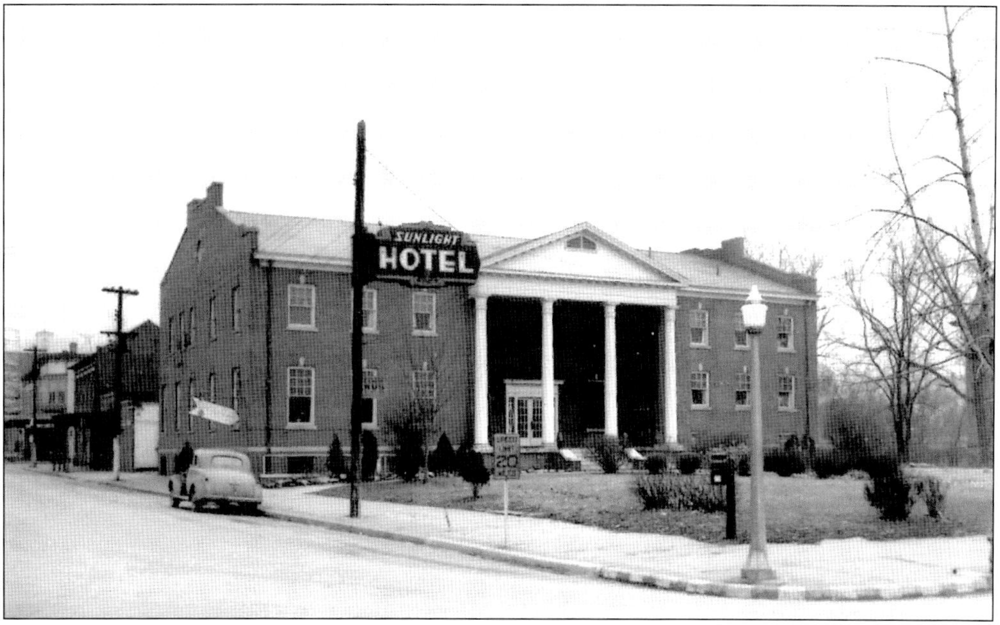

Hotels became more prevalent in small towns as travel increased due to the automobile. The Sunlight Hotel in Cannelton was located at First and Washington Streets rather than Fourth and Washington Streets because it offered a better view of the Ohio River, prior to the erection of the flood wall. It was built by Anton Hafel and was completed and dedicated on April 29, 1929. (Courtesy of USI Special Collections.)

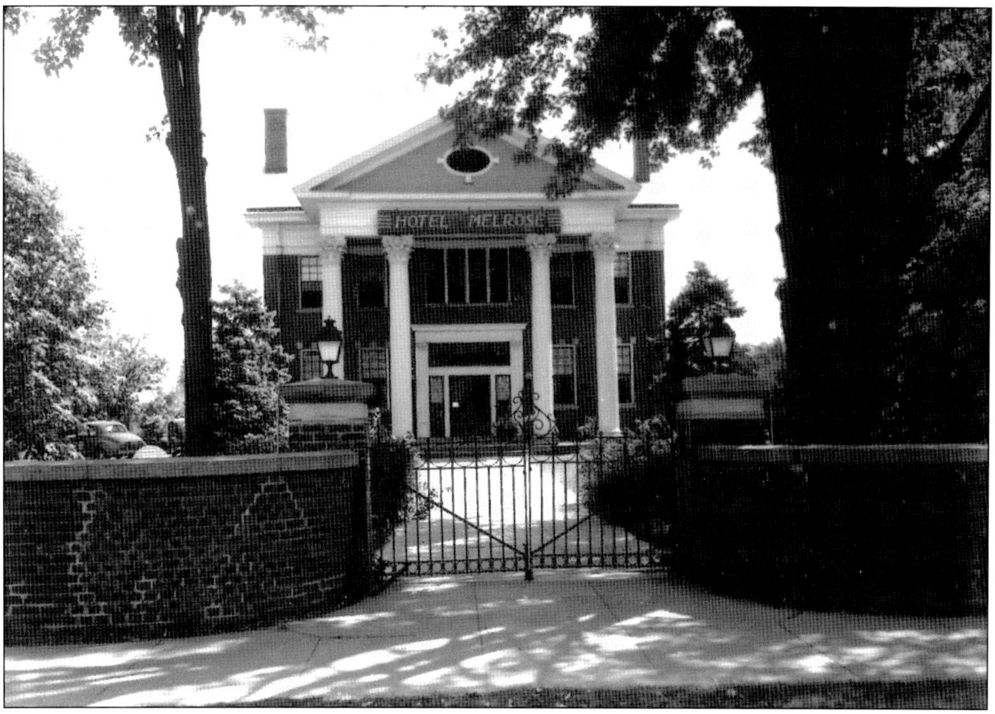

The Melrose Hotel in Rockport is housed in a stately old house. More modern motels soon began to dot the nation's highways. (Courtesy of USI Special Collections.)

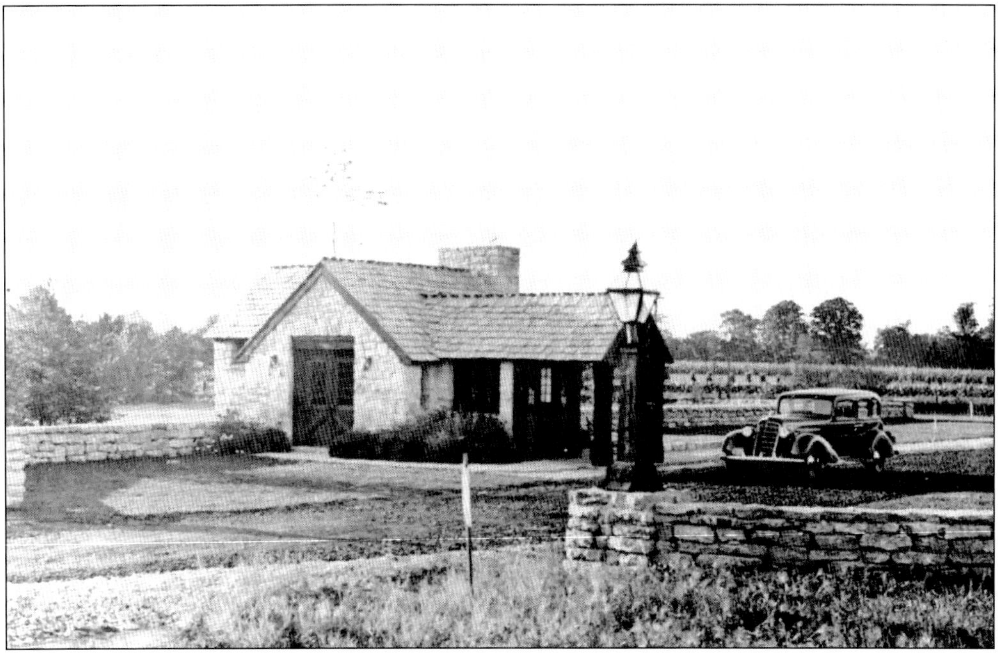

The north gate at Clifty Falls State Park, which is pictured here, sits on Indiana State Highway 62 on the upper portion of Madison. The south gate sits on lower Madison on Indiana State Highway 56. The gatehouses were constructed by the Civilian Conservation Corps, a New Deal program designed to combat poverty during the Great Depression. This photograph was taken in 1938.

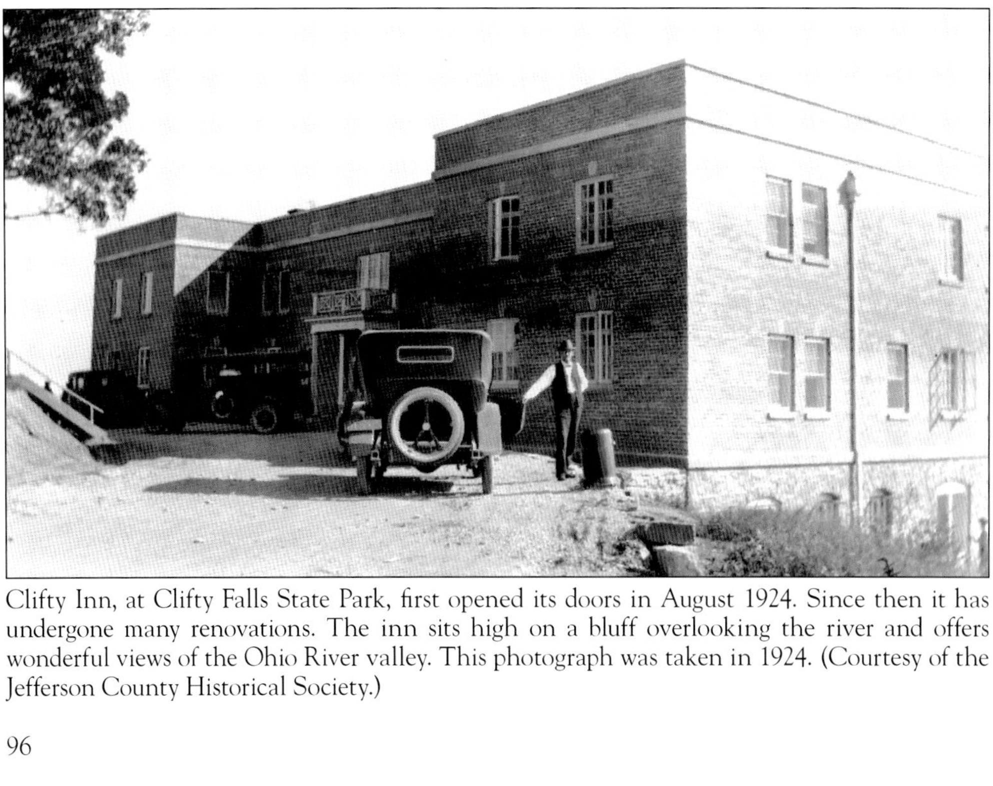

Clifty Inn, at Clifty Falls State Park, first opened its doors in August 1924. Since then it has undergone many renovations. The inn sits high on a bluff overlooking the river and offers wonderful views of the Ohio River valley. This photograph was taken in 1924. (Courtesy of the Jefferson County Historical Society.)

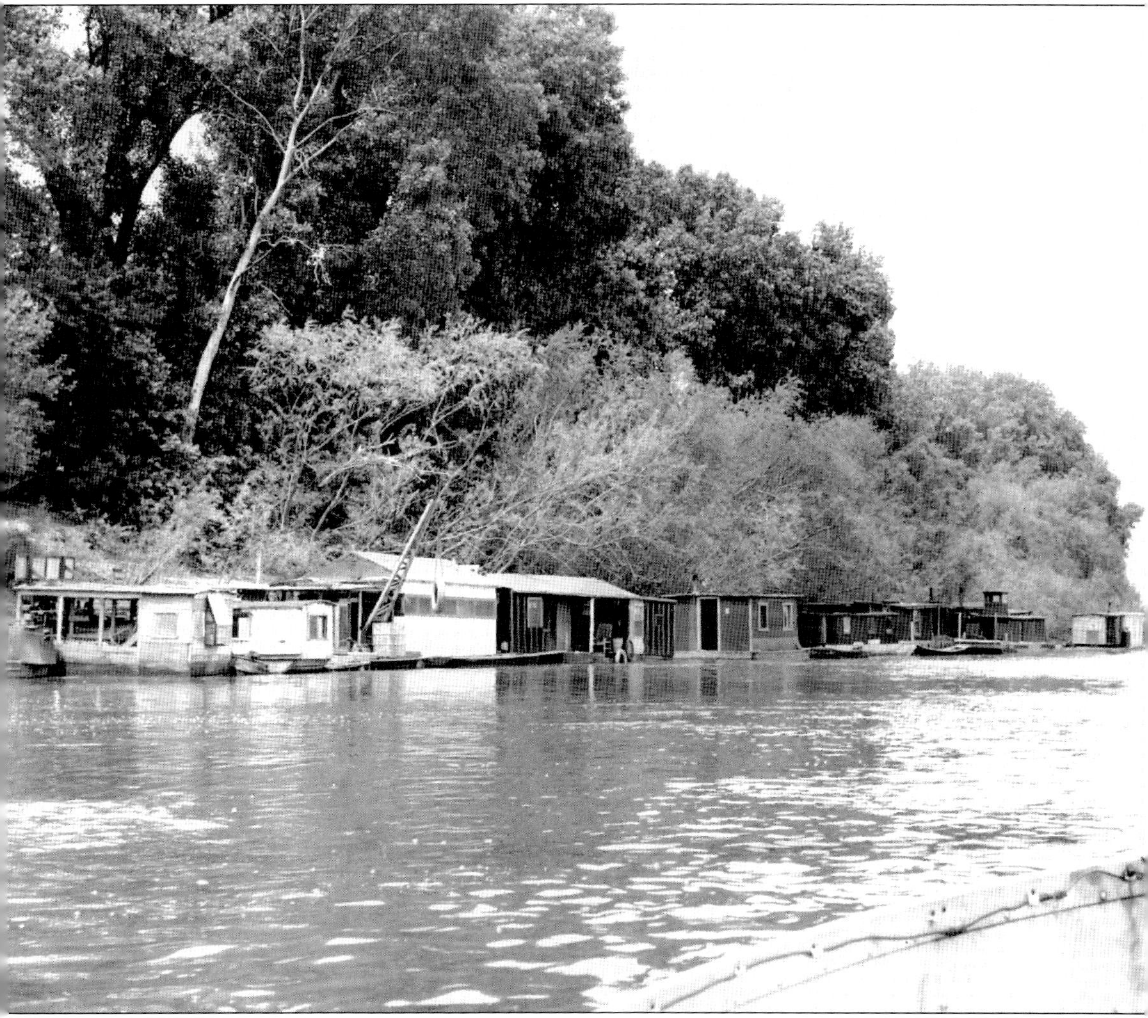

River camps, like this one photographed in 1957, dot the banks of the Ohio River. These houseboats provided an affordable weekend getaway for many families. (Courtesy of Willard Library.)

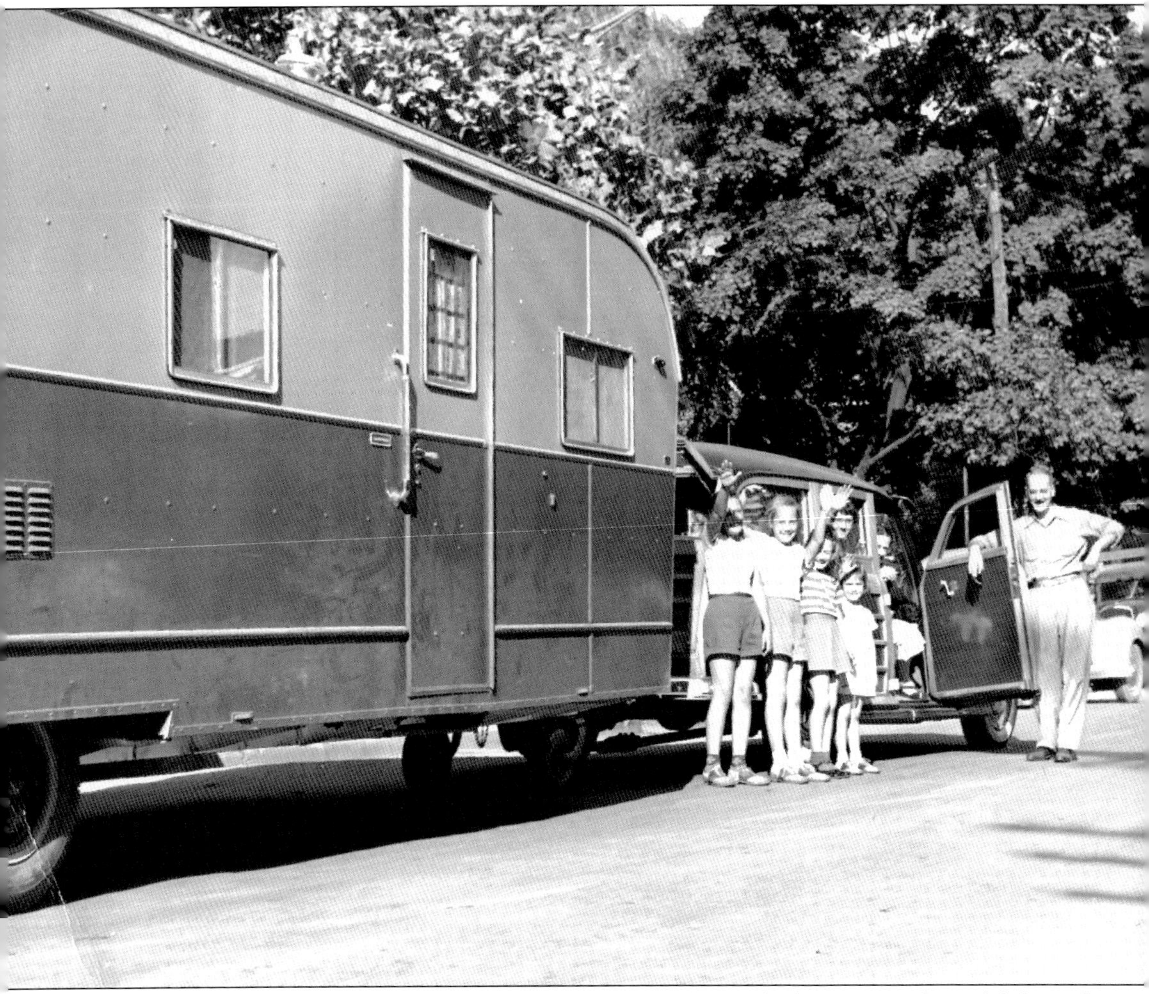

Camping was another pastime that became more popular with the increased availability of automobiles. Campers and travel trailers could be towed behind cars for added ease. Dr. Fred Applegate's family from Corydon prepares to leave for vacation with their camper trailer. Today camping is a popular activity along the Ohio River Scenic Byway. There are many state parks, and the Hoosier National Forest also offers campsites at many of its facilities. (Courtesy of the Harrison County Public Library.)

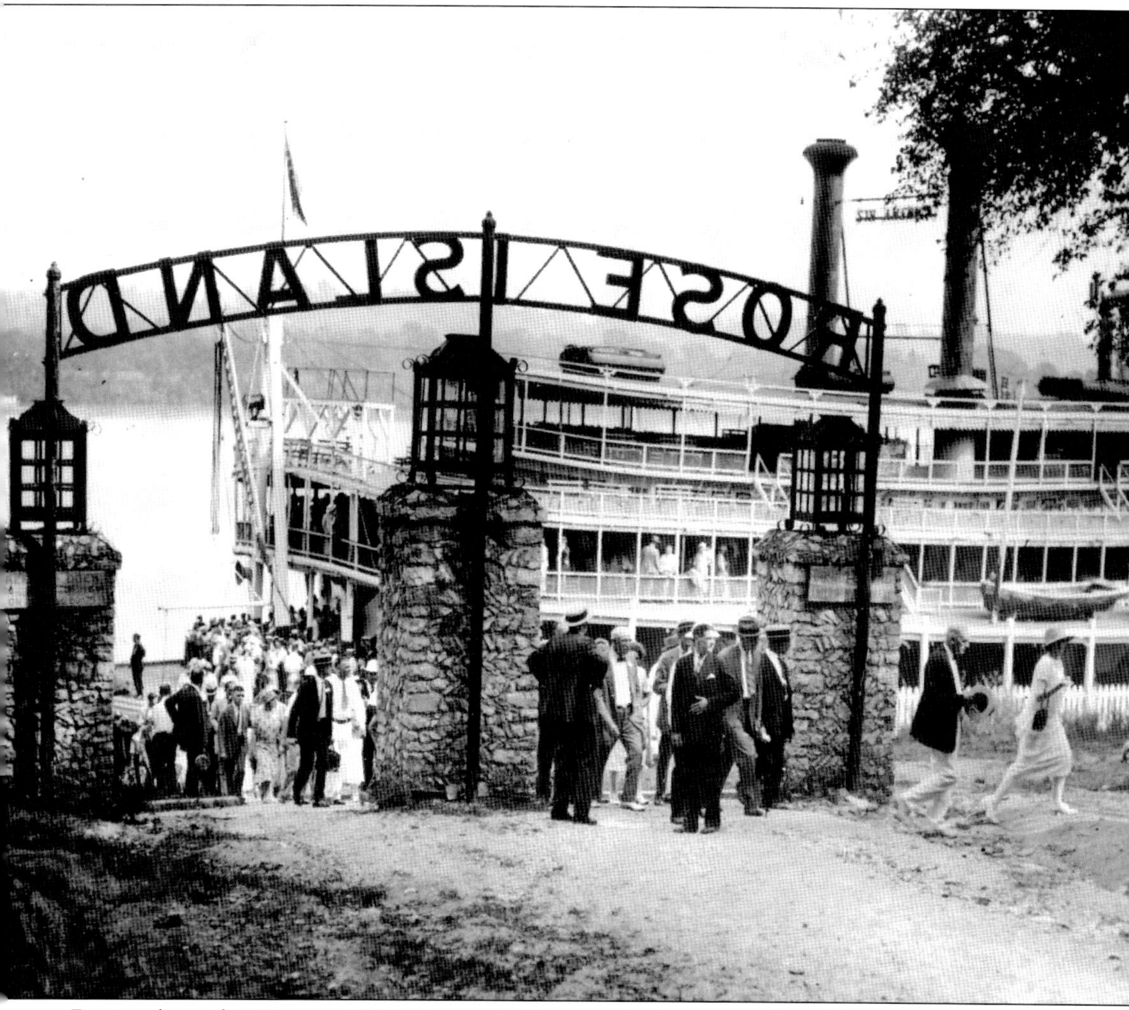

During the mid-1920s, over 135,000 annual visitors made their way to Rose Island, an amusement park just upstream from Louisville. Most people traveled to Rose Island by steamboat. Arriving passengers were met with a boat landing and impressive, electric lighted entrance sign. Rose Island visitors enjoyed many recreational activities. A hotel and furnished cottages provided lodging for overnight and week long visits. A restaurant, cafeteria, and delicatessen offered ample dining options. Recreational facilities included a swimming pool, dance pavilion, orchestra, merry-go-round, baseball fields, zoo, miniature golf course, shooting gallery, bird shows, row boat rentals, fountain, picnic tables for 1,600 people, hiking trails, and a pony track complete with 15 Shetland ponies. Rose Island fell on hard times during the Great Depression and was destroyed by the flood of 1937. It never reopened. (Courtesy of the Jeffersonville Township Public Library.)

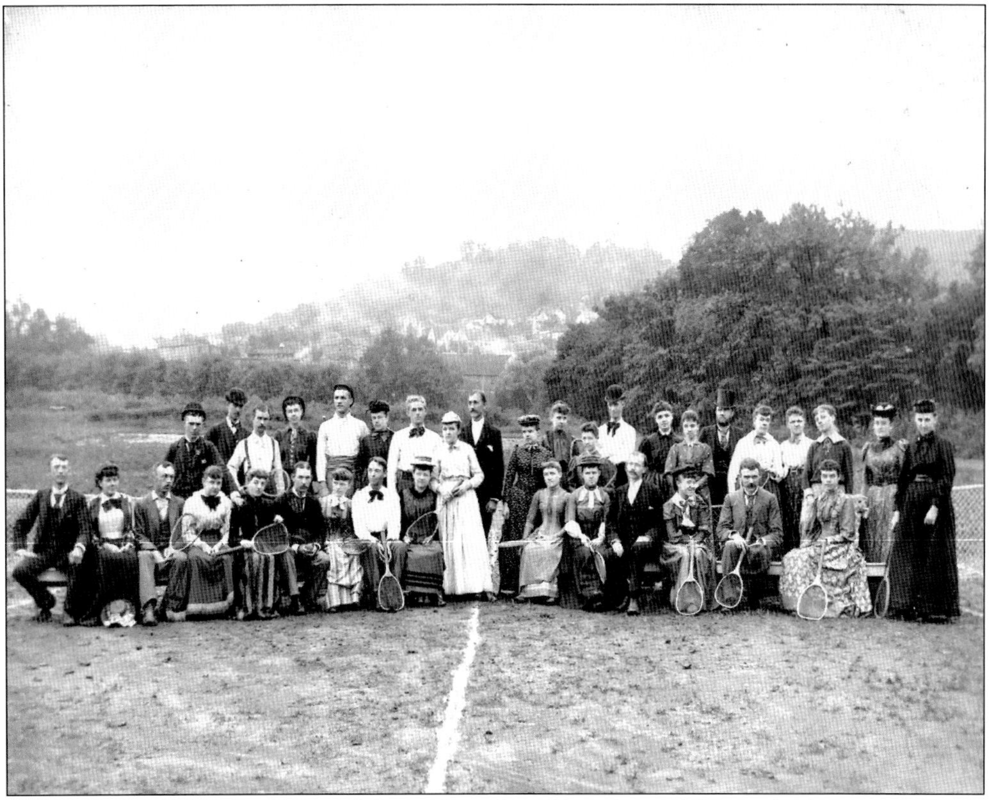

As work became more mechanized, more clerical, and less physical during the late 19th century, Americans became concerned with diet and exercise. With sedentary urban activities replacing rural life, Americans used sports and outdoor relaxation to balance lives that had become hurried and confined. Biking, and golf became popular for those who could afford them. Here a group of men and women gather for tennis in Dearborn County. (Courtesy of the Dearborn County Historical Society.)

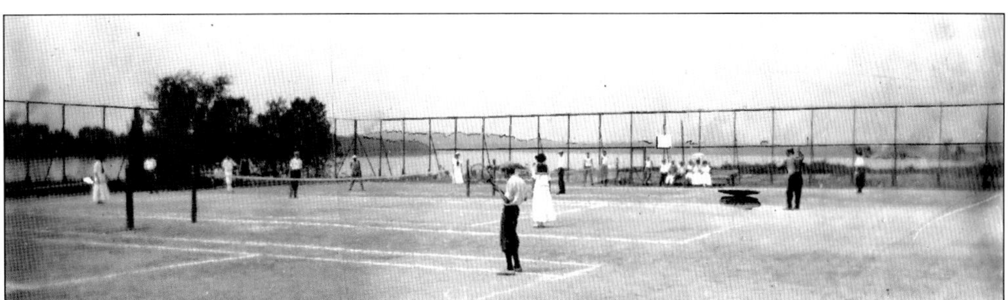

Tennis courts were a popular feature at Sunset Park along Evansville's riverside. (Courtesy of Willard Library.)

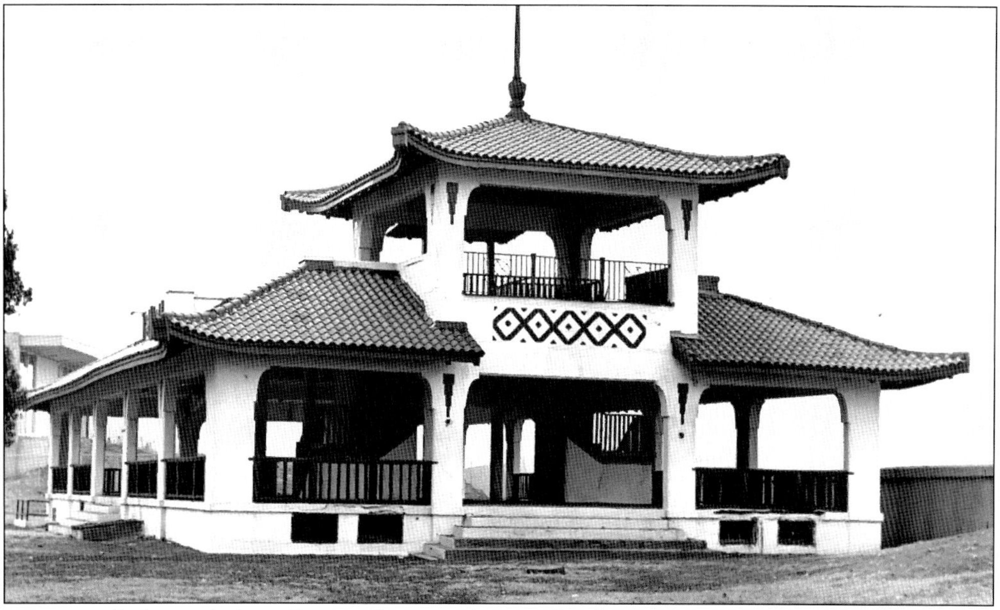

Sunset Park, located along Evansville's riverfront, offered an area for people to relax and enjoy the view of the river. The Evansville Pagoda was originally named the Sunset Park Shelter House. It served as an outdoor meeting place, where people could gather on its main floor for picnics and parties, enjoy the view of the Ohio River from either of its stories, and hear bands that frequently played on the second floor patio. The Sunset Park Shelter House continued in that capacity until the flood of 1937. During the period of recovery in the times that followed the flood, the restoration of a non-essential structure like this one, was not a top priority. The shelter had been boarded up, neglected, and vandalized for years. Renovation of the Sunset Park Shelter House began on August 1, 1995, and was completed the following year. Today it is called the Evansville Pagoda, where the main floor serves as the Evansville Visitor's Center, the upstairs patio still commands a breathtaking view of the bend in the Ohio River, and the basement serves as the offices of the Evansville Convention and Visitor's Bureau. (Courtesy of Willard Library.)

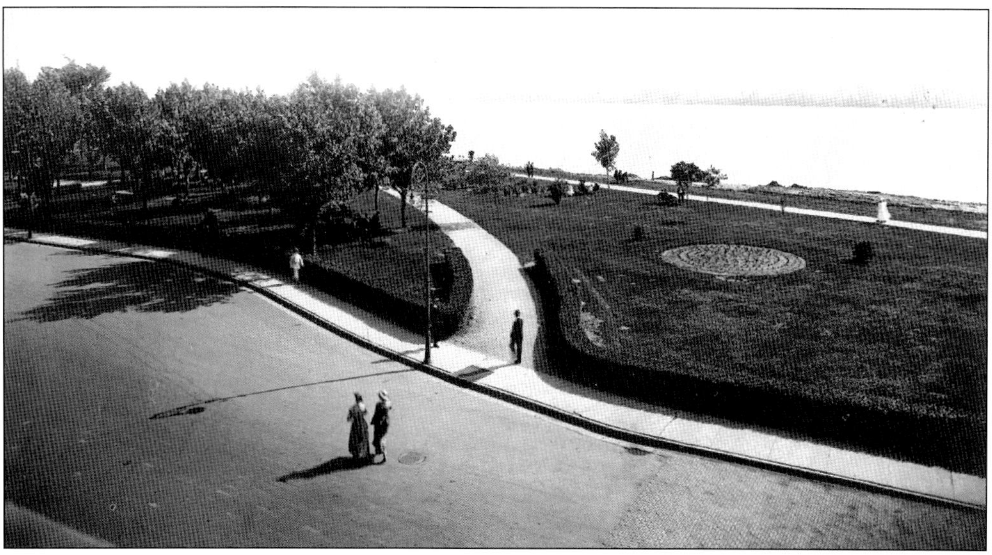

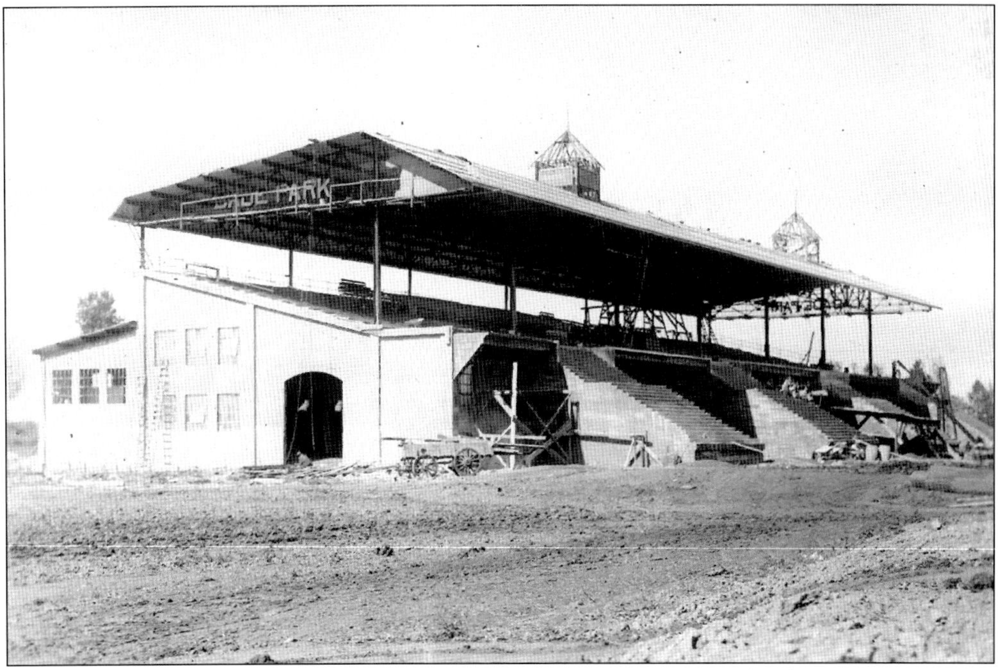

Dade Park was built by the Green River Jockey Club in 1922 but went bankrupt in 1925. That year, James C. Ellis purchased the track and changed the name to Ellis Park. Originally designed after Saratoga Race Course in Saratoga Springs, the circumference of Ellis Park's dirt track is 1.8 miles, the largest in Kentucky. An unusual fact about the track is that it actually lies north of the Ohio River by Evansville. However, the state border is based on the course of the river as it existed when Kentucky became a state in 1792. Due to the New Madrid earthquake of 1812, the Ohio River changed course to the south, leaving the land that would later house Ellis Park separated from the remainder of Kentucky by the river. (Courtesy of Willard Library.)

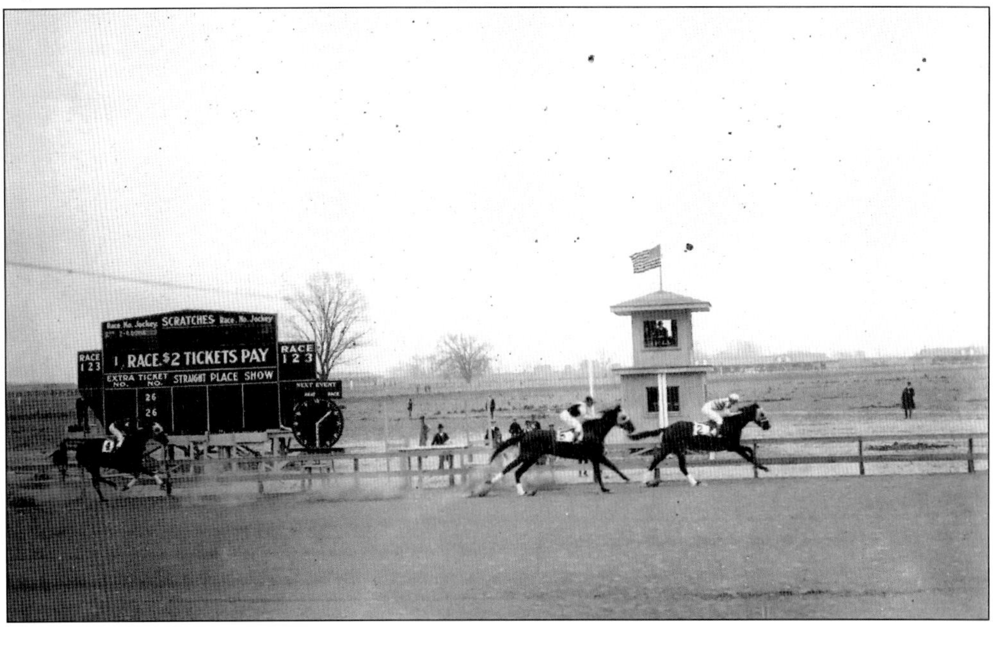

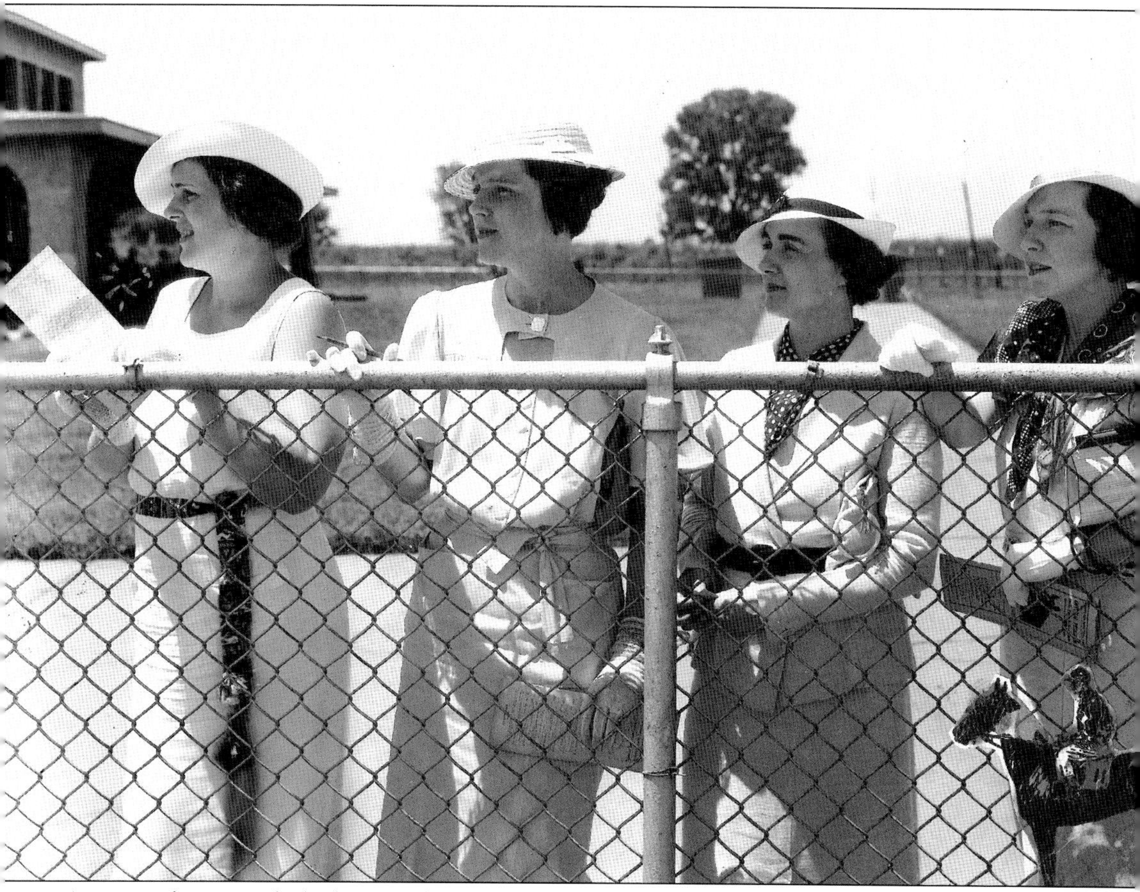

A group of women, decked out in their summer finery, enjoy a day at the races at Ellis Park. The racetrack draws regular crowds from Indiana, Kentucky, and Illinois. It still operates today and is open from mid-July through Labor Day. On November 6, 2005, a tornado caused extensive damage to Ellis Park and several racehorses were killed. The racetrack rebuilt and opened for the regular 2006 season. (Courtesy of Willard Library.)

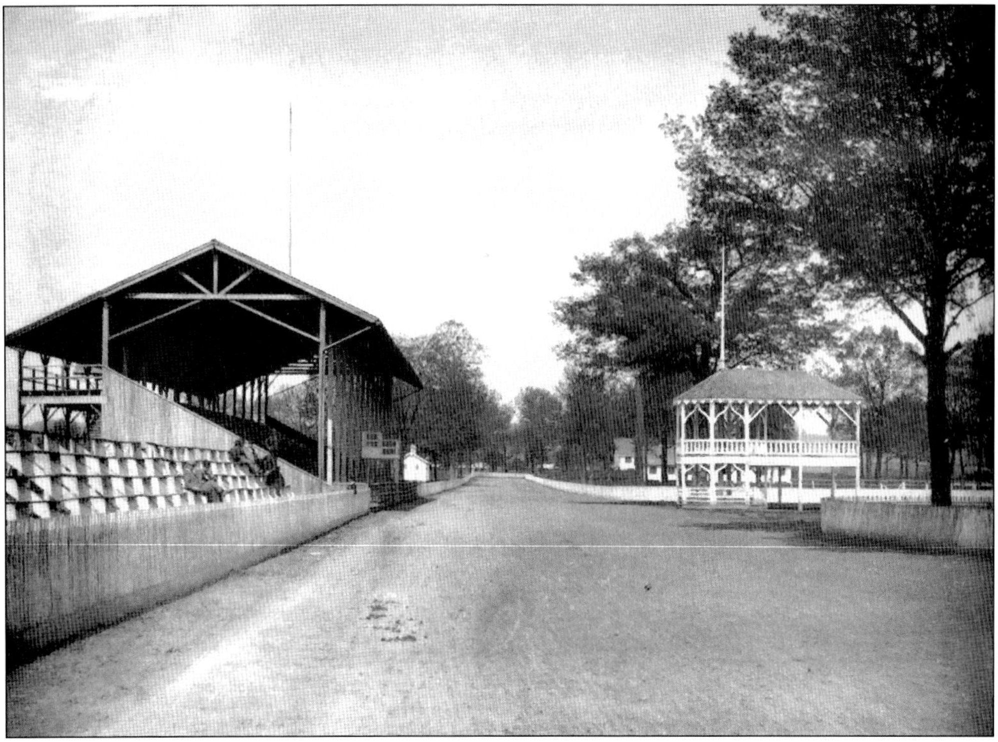

County fairs were, and remain, popular sources of entertainment for communities along the Ohio River Scenic Byway. This is a photograph of the race track at the Floyd County fair grounds in New Albany. (Courtesy of the New Albany-Floyd County Library.)

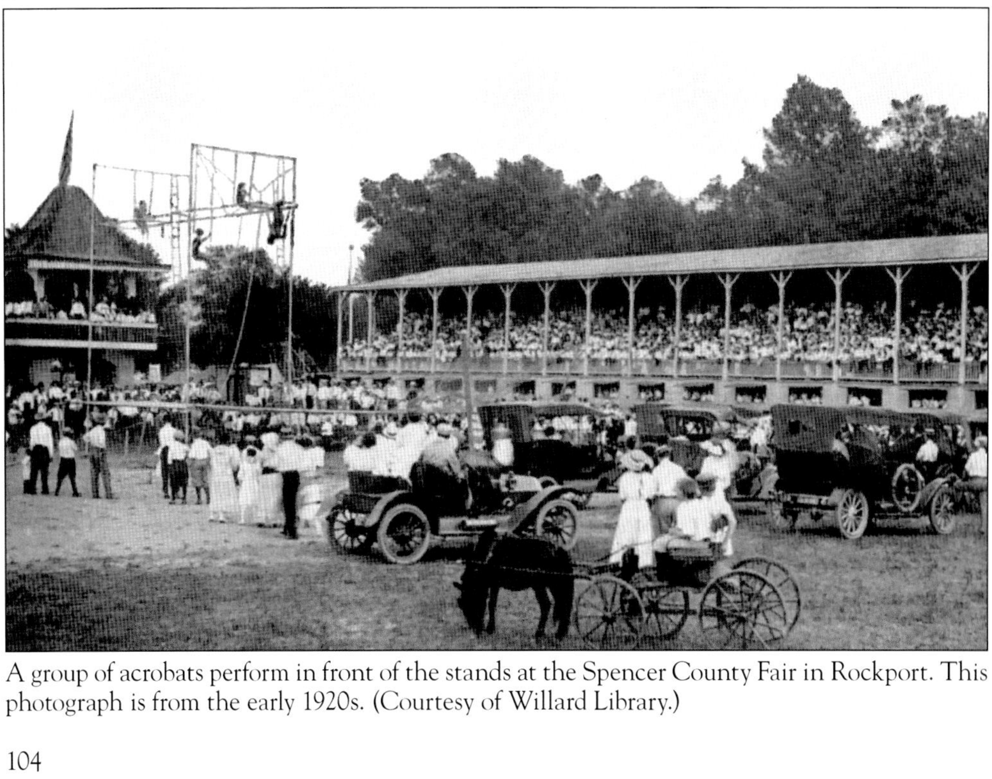

A group of acrobats perform in front of the stands at the Spencer County Fair in Rockport. This photograph is from the early 1920s. (Courtesy of Willard Library.)

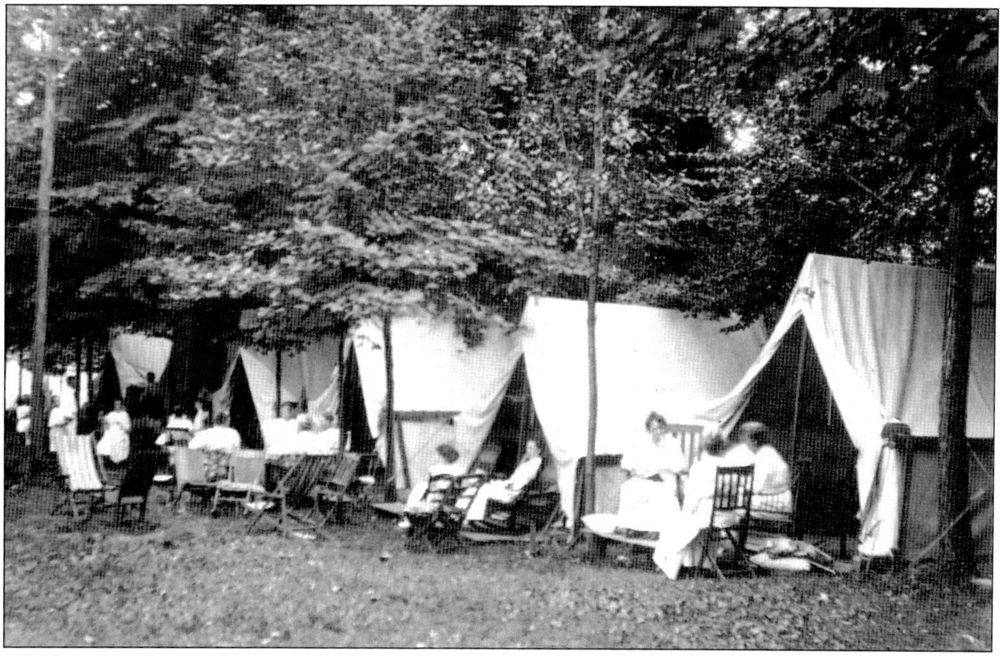

This photograph is from the Madison Chautauqua. Chautauqua gatherings were commonplace in southern Indiana in the teens. It was a chance for the community to gather for three to seven days to enjoy a course of lectures on a variety of subjects. Audiences also saw plays and heard a variety of music. The Chautauqua experience stimulated thought and discussion on important political, social, and cultural issues of the day. (Courtesy of the Jefferson County Historical Society.)

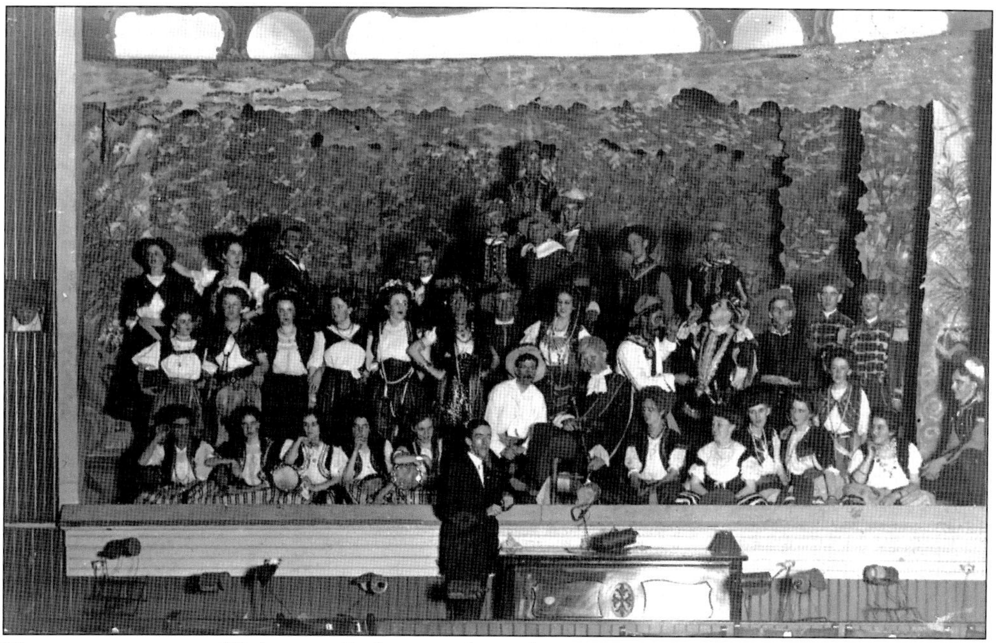

This summer opera of *Bohemian Girl* was performed in 1908 in New Albany's Glenwood Park as part of its Chautauqua. (Courtesy of the New Albany-Floyd County Library.)

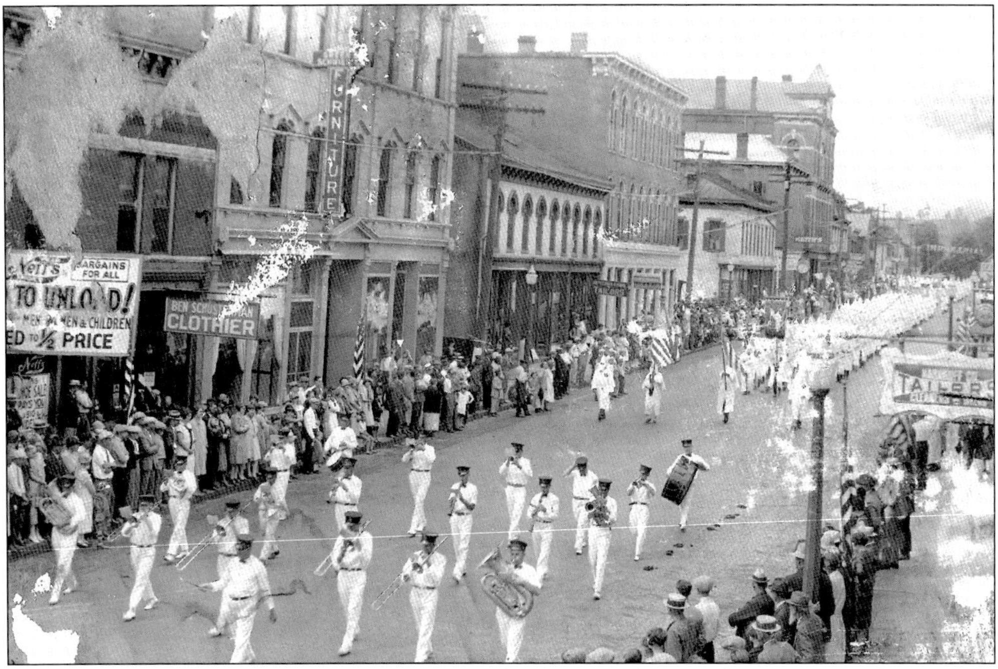

Parades were common forms of community celebration. At this parade in Lawrenceburg in the 1920s, Ku Klux Klansmen can be seen marching behind the band. In a dark piece of Indiana history, the Ku Klux Klan rose to prominence in politics and society after World War I. Nationally Indiana was said to have the most powerful Ku Klux Klan. (Courtesy of the Dearborn County Historical Society.)

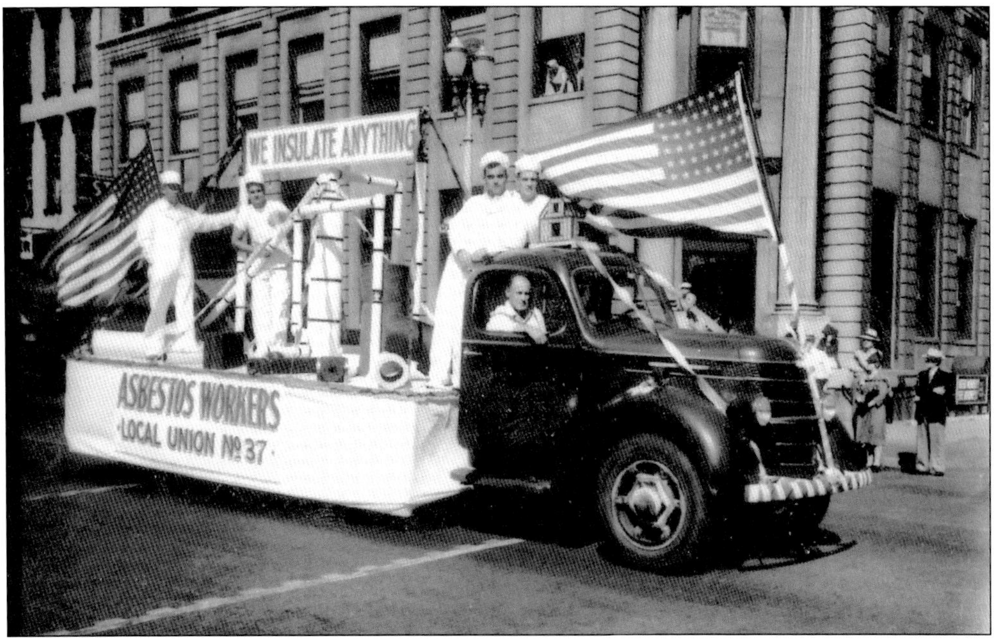

A group of asbestos workers from a local union tout their work in a parade in Evansville. This photograph evokes an eerie feeling, given today's knowledge of asbestos. (Courtesy of USI Special Collections.)

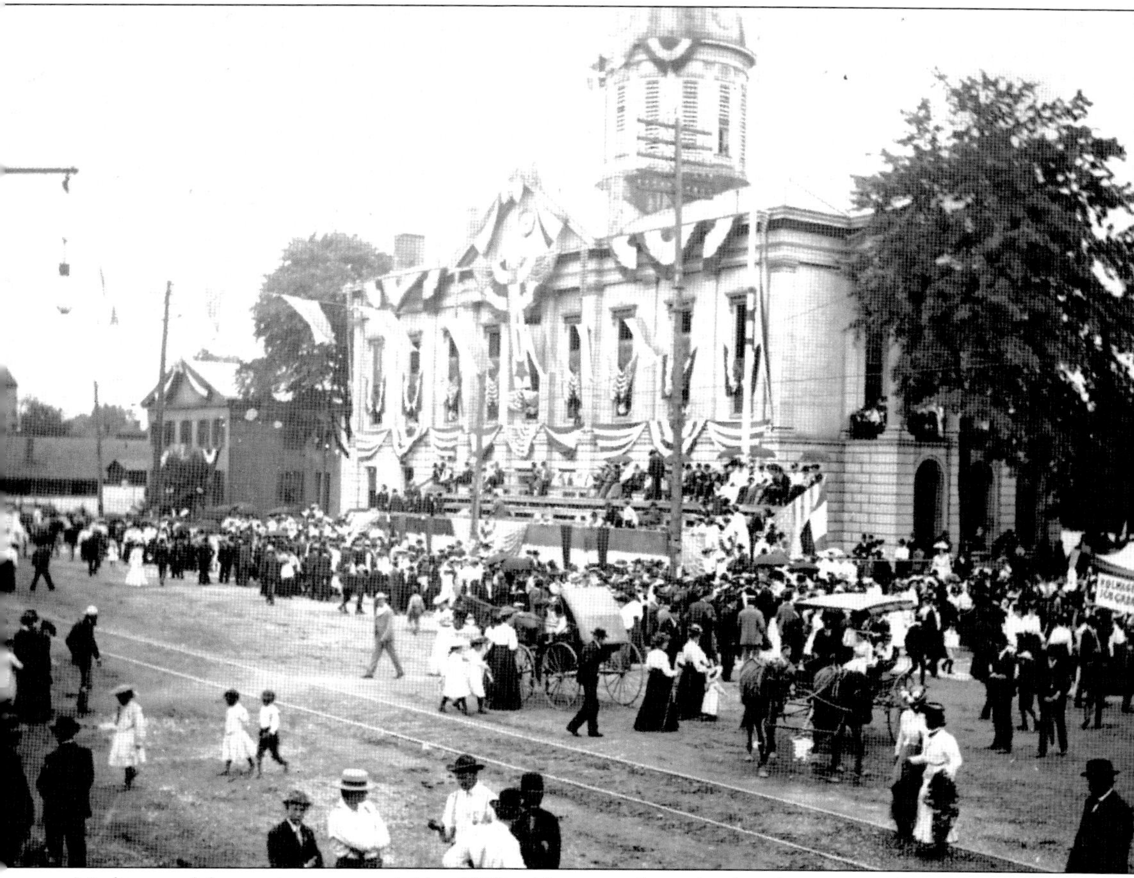

Madison celebrates its centennial in 1909 with a parade and other festivities. The courthouse and other buildings are decked out in bunting. Fair, parades, festivals, and other special events were big sources of entertainment in small communities during the early 20th century. (Courtesy of the Jefferson County Historical Society.)

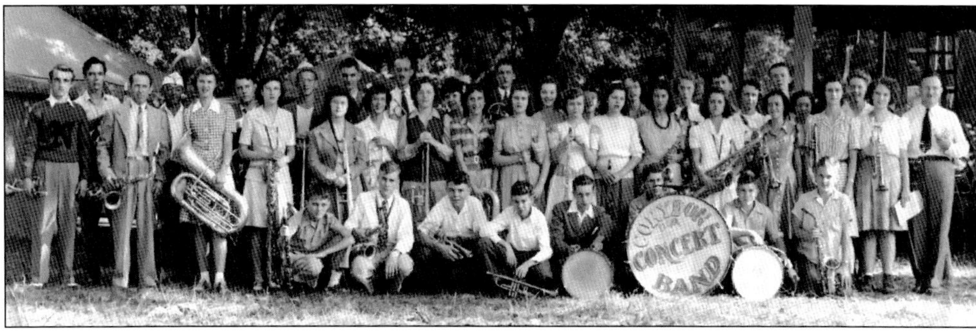

The Corydon Concert Band poses for a photograph before a performance. This band was comprised of high school students. (Courtesy of the Harrison County Public Library.)

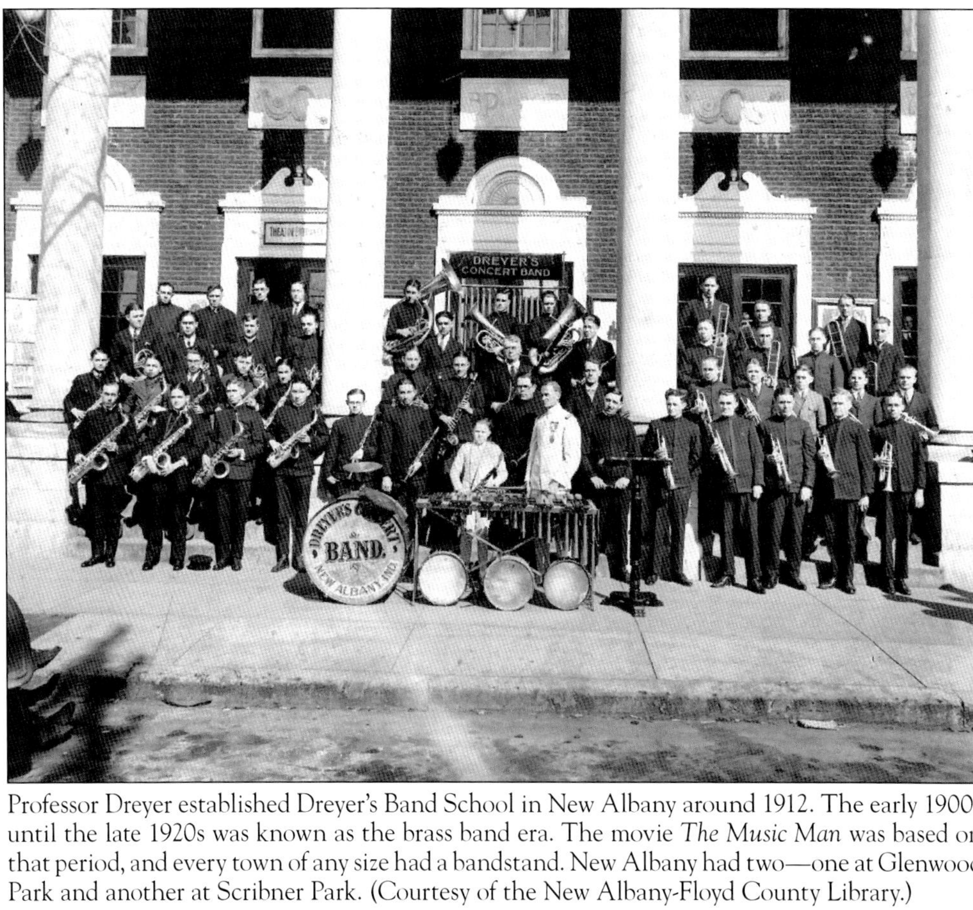

Professor Dreyer established Dreyer's Band School in New Albany around 1912. The early 1900s until the late 1920s was known as the brass band era. The movie *The Music Man* was based on that period, and every town of any size had a bandstand. New Albany had two—one at Glenwood Park and another at Scribner Park. (Courtesy of the New Albany-Floyd County Library.)

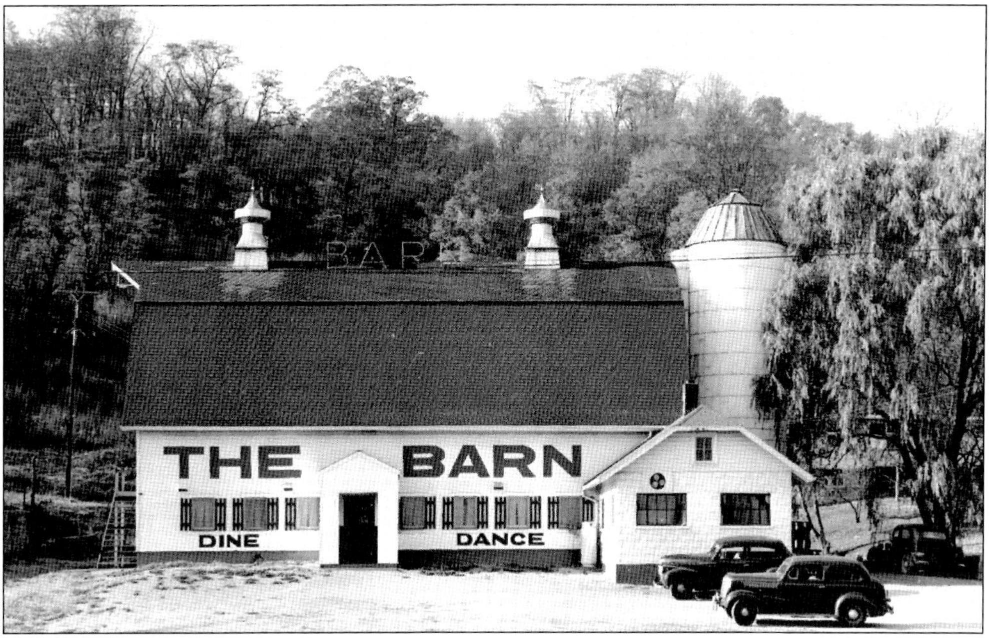

As long-distance road travel became practical and popular in the late 1930s, more restaurants began to dot America's highways. The Barn in Lawrenceburg offered visitors and residents alike a place to eat and enjoy some entertainment. (Courtesy of the Dearborn County Historical Society.)

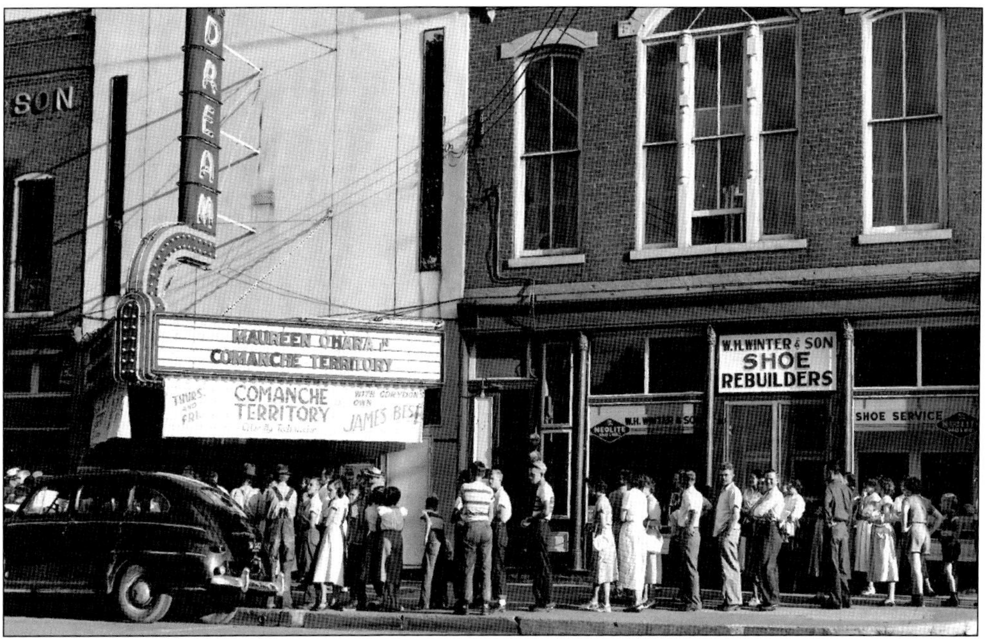

Most towns and cities in southern Indiana had their own movie theater for entertainment. The Dream Theater in Corydon hosts the movie debut of Comanche Territory, starring its own local, James Best. Best starred in several movies and television series in the 1950s and 1960s but is probably better known to more current audiences as Sheriff Roscoe Coltrane on *The Dukes of Hazard* television series. (Courtesy of the Harrison County Public Library.)

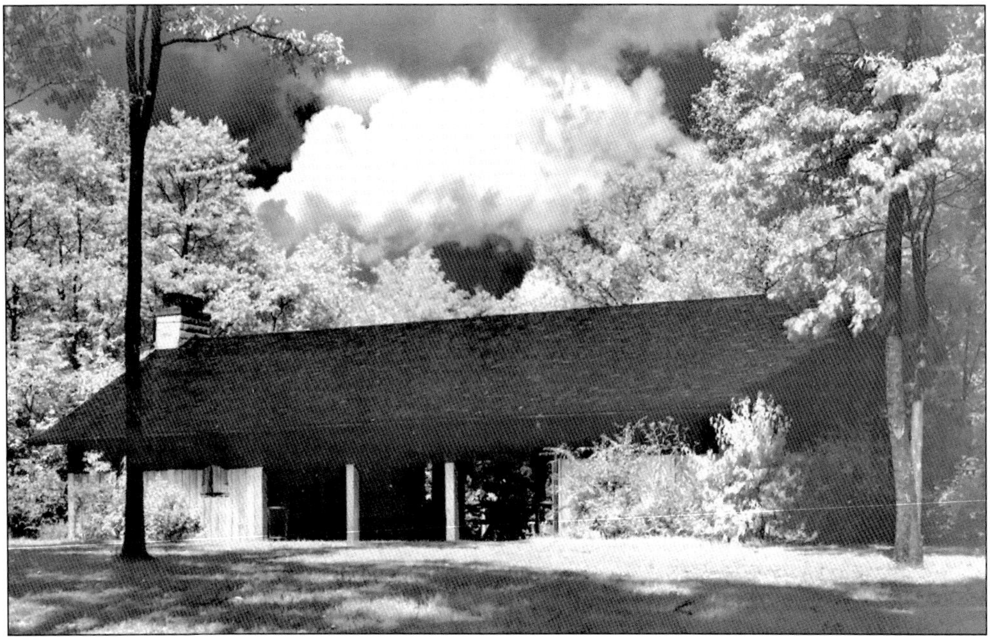

The Harrison-Crawford State Forest is located on the Ohio River Scenic Byway between the towns of Corydon and Leavenworth. It offers many recreational activities and has been a popular spot for hiking, camping, picnicking, and fishing over the years. Photographed here is one of the shelter houses on the state forest property. (Courtesy of the Harrison County Public Library.)

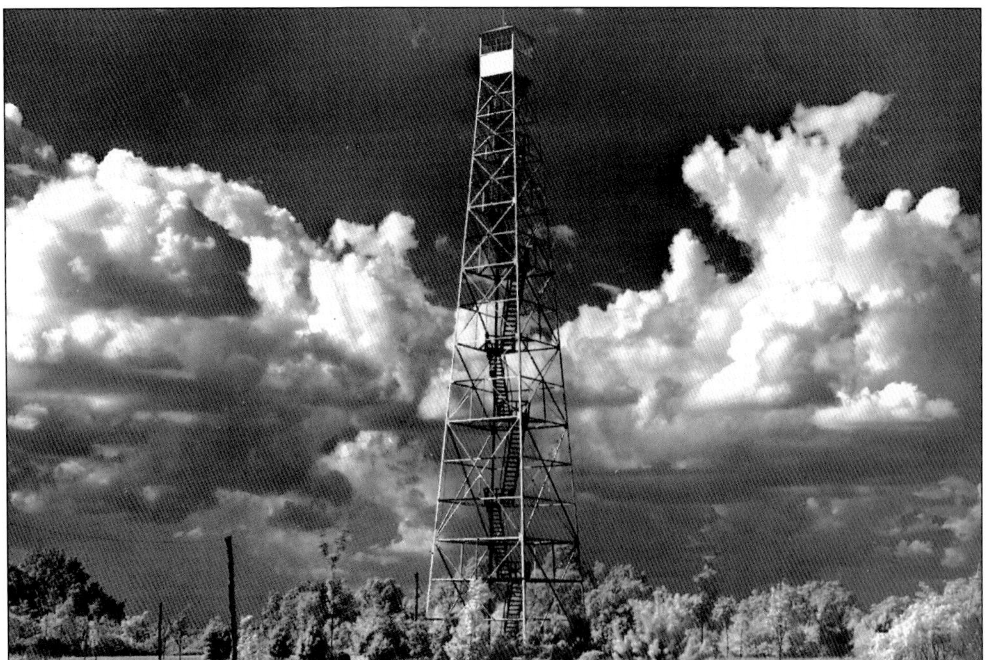

The Harrison-Crawford State Forest encompasses 25,600 acres of heavily wooded terrain. This fire tower helps park staff keep a lookout over the forest property. (Courtesy of the Harrison County Public Library.)

Four

SCENIC
VISTAS AND RIVER VALLEYS

The topography resulting from uneven glaciation, as well as the subsequent use of the landscape, has combined to leave the Ohio River valley in Indiana rich in scenic resources. The Ohio River Scenic Byway winds its way through rolling forested hills. Rocky bluffs and outcroppings offer breathtaking views of the river valley. This is especially true along the eastern end from Lawrenceburg to Madison and again along the central portion of the byway between Corydon and Troy. The river bottoms and cypress sloughs along the far western end of the byway are scenic as well.

The agricultural countryside, so prevalent in southern Indiana, possesses its own form of beauty. Well-kept barns, vineyards, and orchards dot the countryside. Fields of corn, soybeans, wheat, and in some places tobacco, are abundant along the byway. In many places, the river contributes to the rich, fertile soil.

Scenic qualities are not solely those found in nature. The quaint small towns and larger urban centers possess their own scenic qualities too, including the beautiful architecture in the churches, county courthouses, and other public buildings. They provide an aesthetically pleasing visual experience that offers an escape from the sameness of today's suburban landscape. Lavish 19th-century mansions like Hillforest in Aurora, the Lanier Mansion in Madison, the Howard Steamboat Museum in Jeffersonville, the Culbertson Mansion in New Albany, or the Reitz Home in Evansville give a glimpse to the charm and grace of a bygone era.

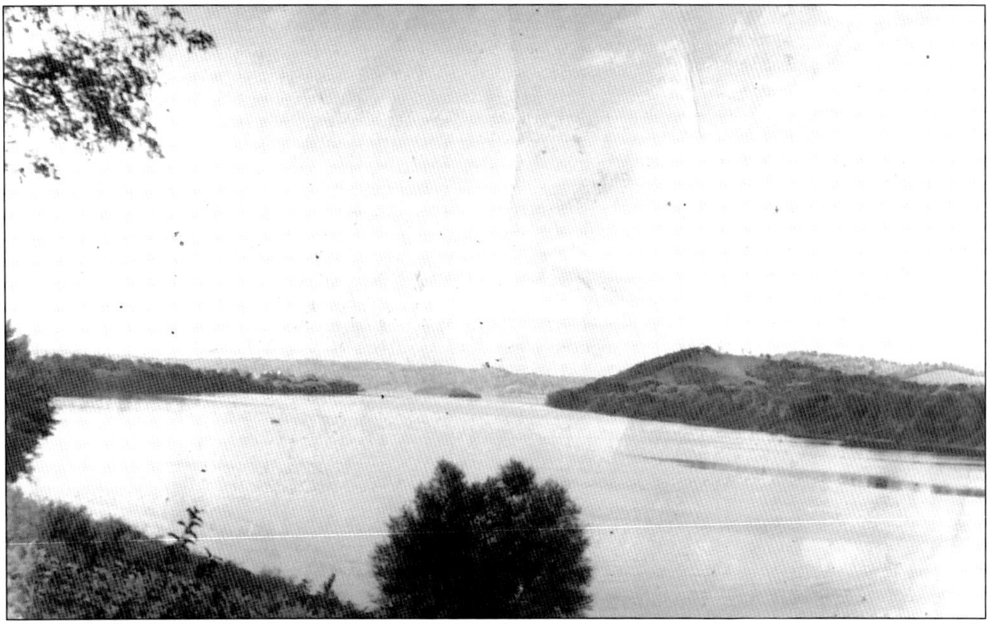

This panoramic view of the river shows Big Bone Island in the distance. The island disappeared sometime in the 1970s, most likely due to the rising water level from the Markland Dam near Vevay. Big Bone Island takes its name from nearby Big Bone Lick in Kentucky. This area is known for the fossil remains of large Ice Age mammals, such as the mammoth and the mastodon. Meriwether Lewis visited this area on his way to meet with William Clark on their expedition in 1803. (Courtesy of the Dearborn County Historical Society.)

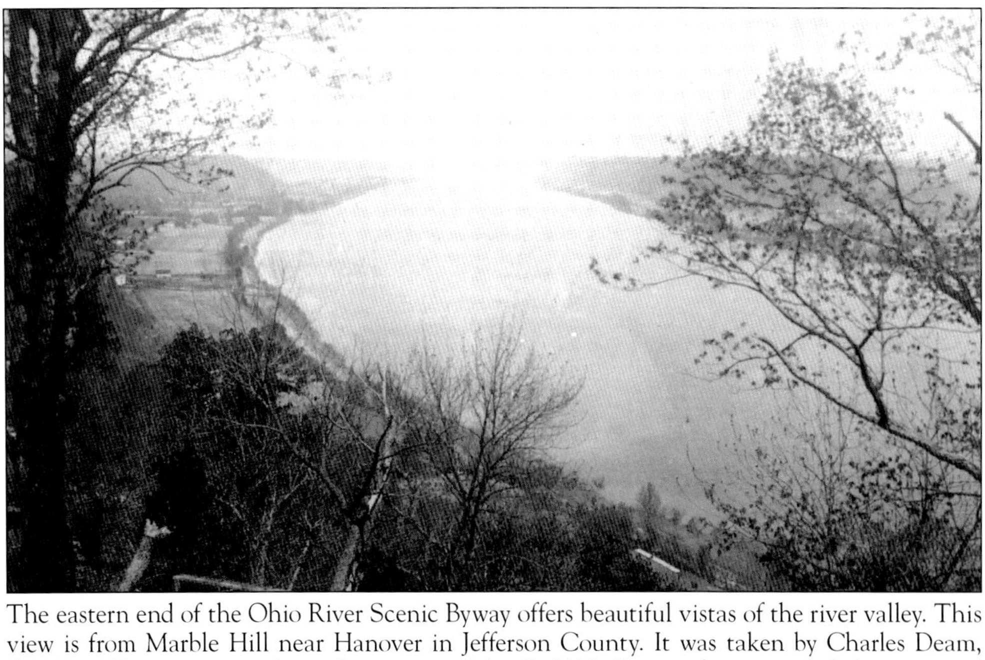

The eastern end of the Ohio River Scenic Byway offers beautiful vistas of the river valley. This view is from Marble Hill near Hanover in Jefferson County. It was taken by Charles Deam, the State Forester, on a clear afternoon on May 2, 1918. Deam often recorded the time and conditions when photographing. (Courtesy the Indiana Department of Natural Resources, Division of Forestry Archives.)

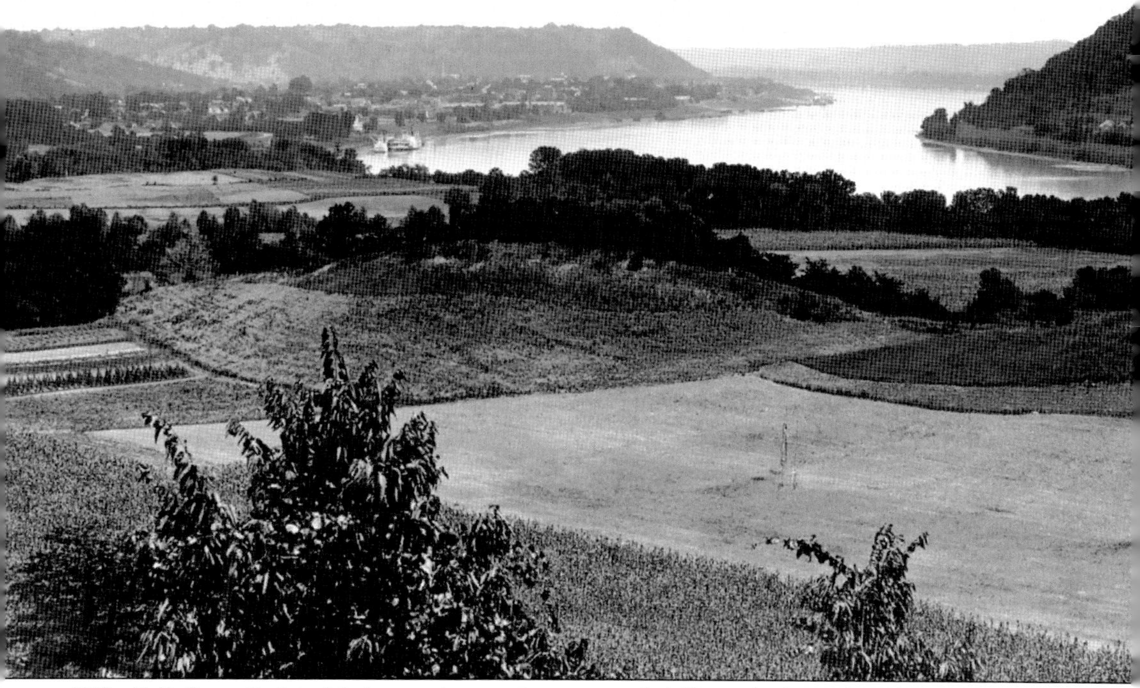

Clifty Falls State Park in Madison is known for its rugged cliffs overlooking the Ohio River. This photograph was taken from the overlook in the state park and offers a good view of Madison below. (Courtesy of the Jefferson County Historical Society.)

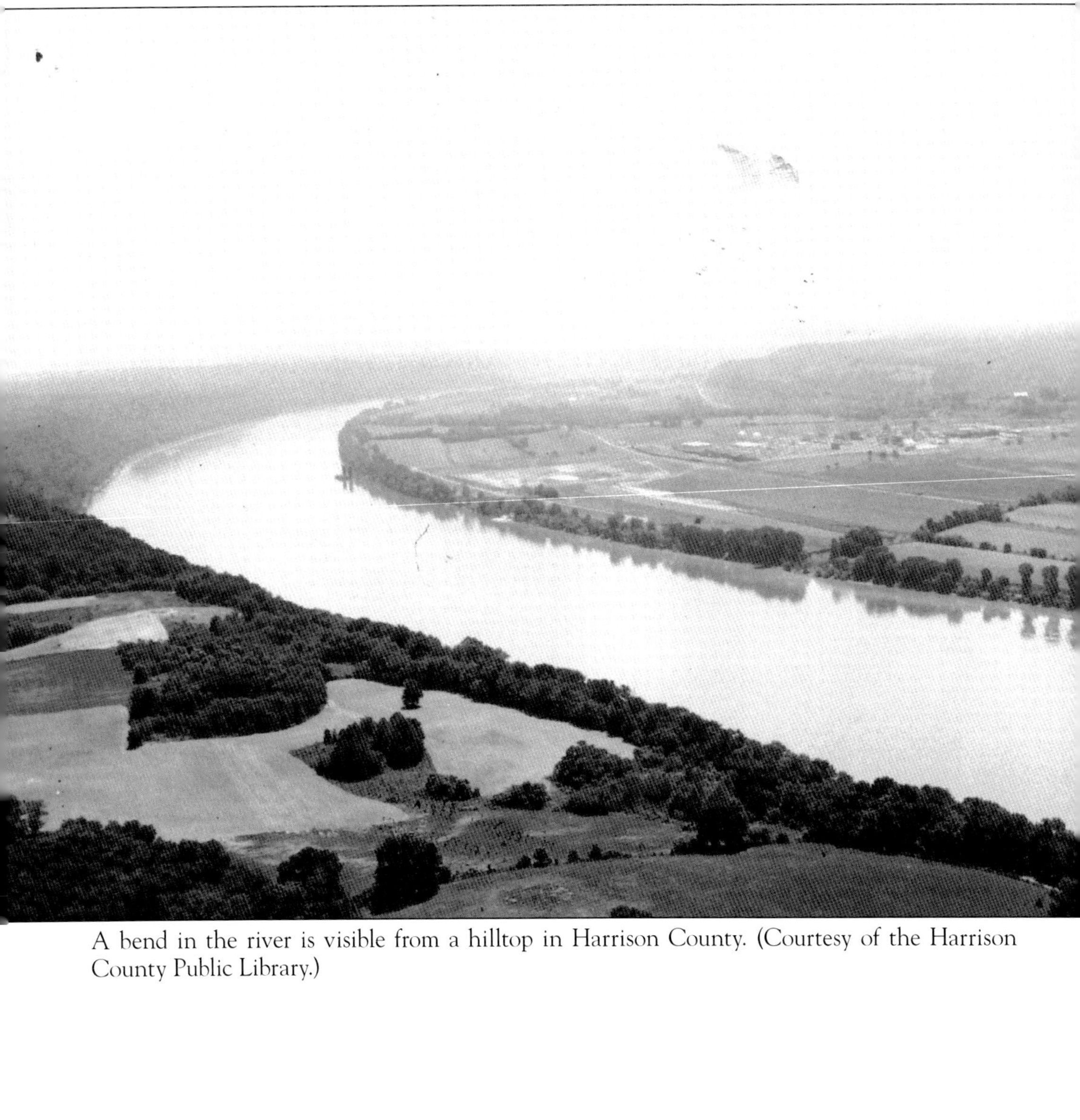

A bend in the river is visible from a hilltop in Harrison County. (Courtesy of the Harrison County Public Library.)

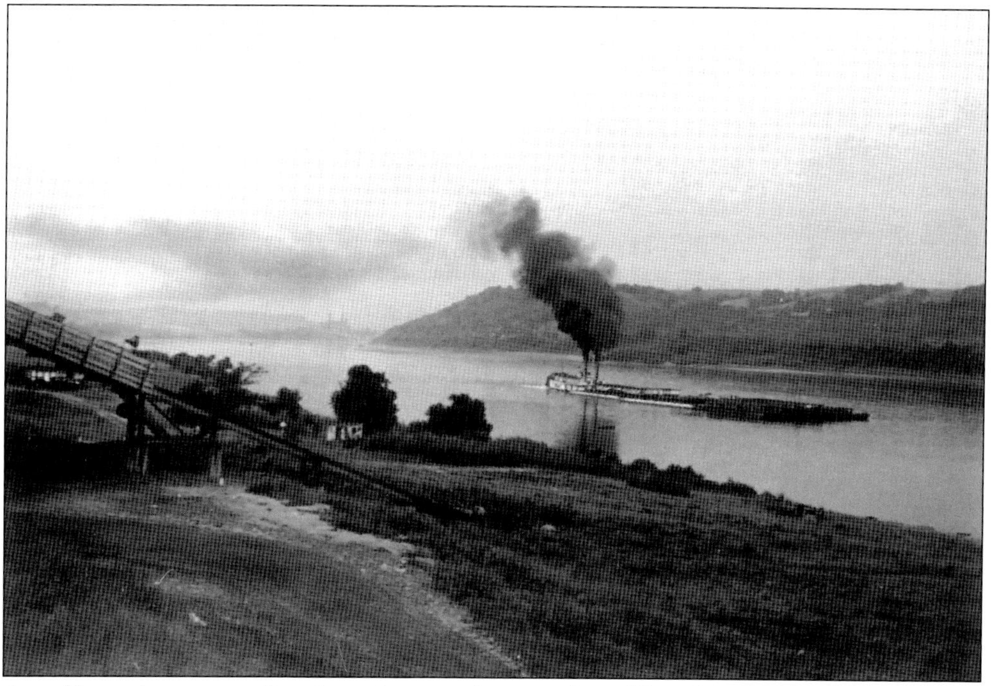

A coal barge is seen traveling downriver near Lawrenceburg. This photograph was taken in the early 20th century and this is still a common site along the Ohio River today. (Courtesy of the Dearborn County Historical Society.)

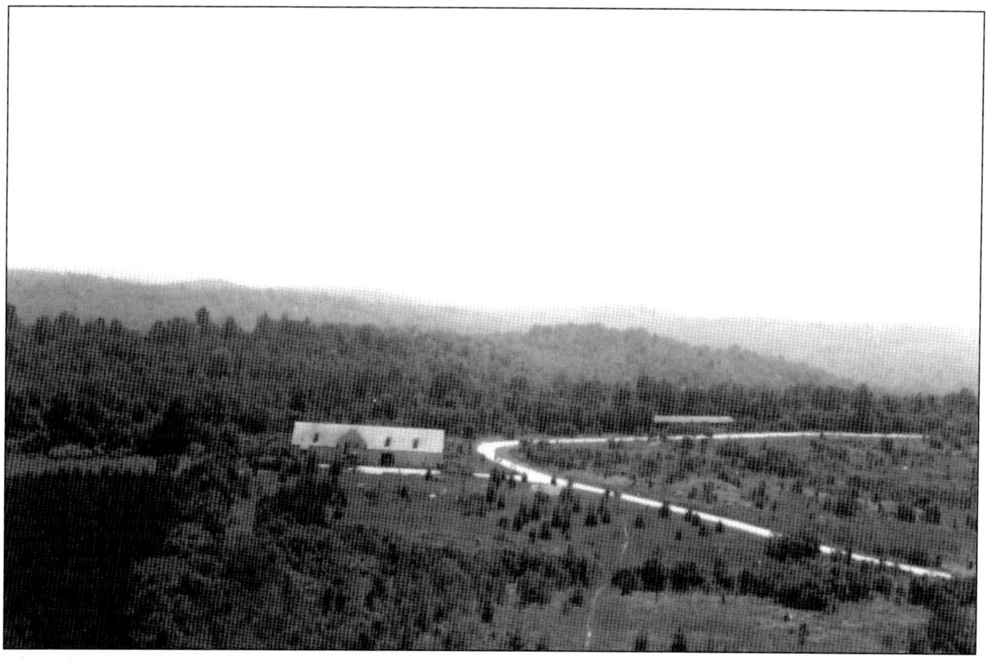

This photograph was taken from the fire tower at the Harrison-Crawford State Forest and shows the forested hills that are prevalent in this part of the state. A service building and wood shed are visible in the distance. (Courtesy the Indiana Department of Natural Resources, Division of Forestry Archives.)

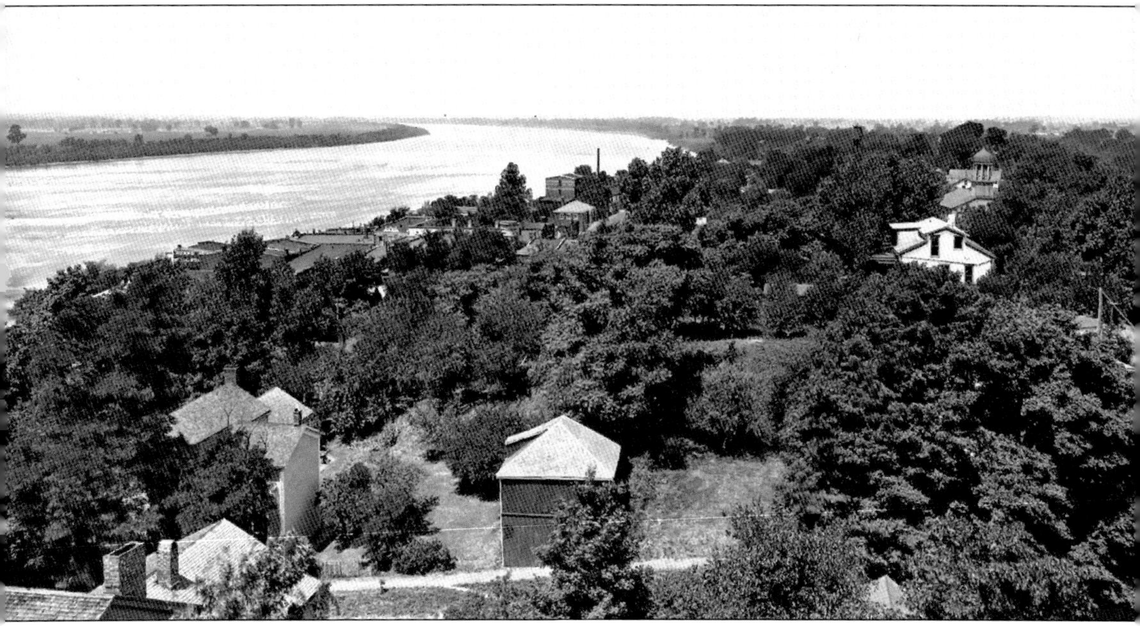

Rooftops peak through the trees in this view of the town Newburgh. Although trees are still plentiful, the landscape becomes considerably flatter than the eastern end of the byway. (Courtesy of Willard Library.)

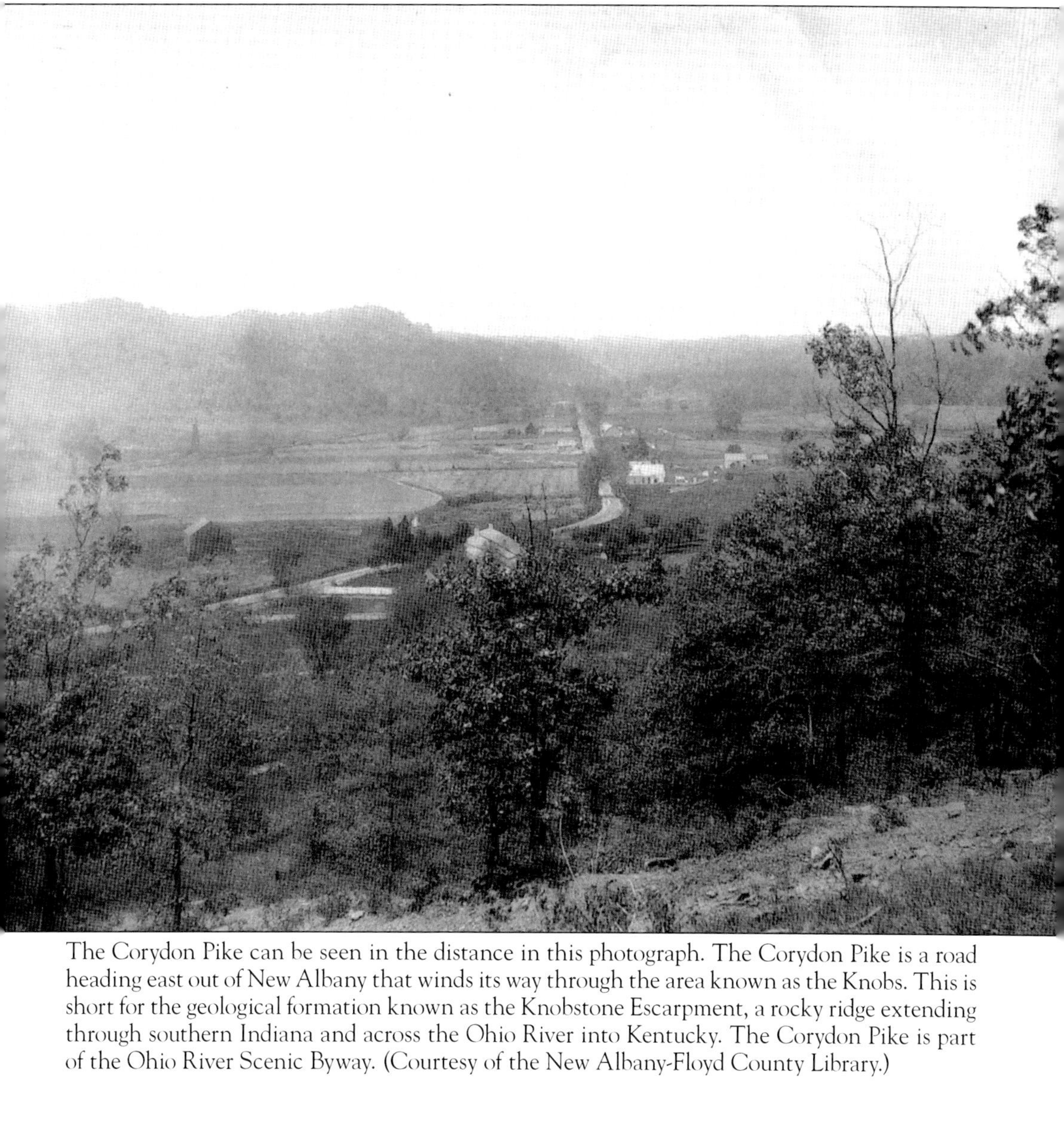

The Corydon Pike can be seen in the distance in this photograph. The Corydon Pike is a road heading east out of New Albany that winds its way through the area known as the Knobs. This is short for the geological formation known as the Knobstone Escarpment, a rocky ridge extending through southern Indiana and across the Ohio River into Kentucky. The Corydon Pike is part of the Ohio River Scenic Byway. (Courtesy of the New Albany-Floyd County Library.)

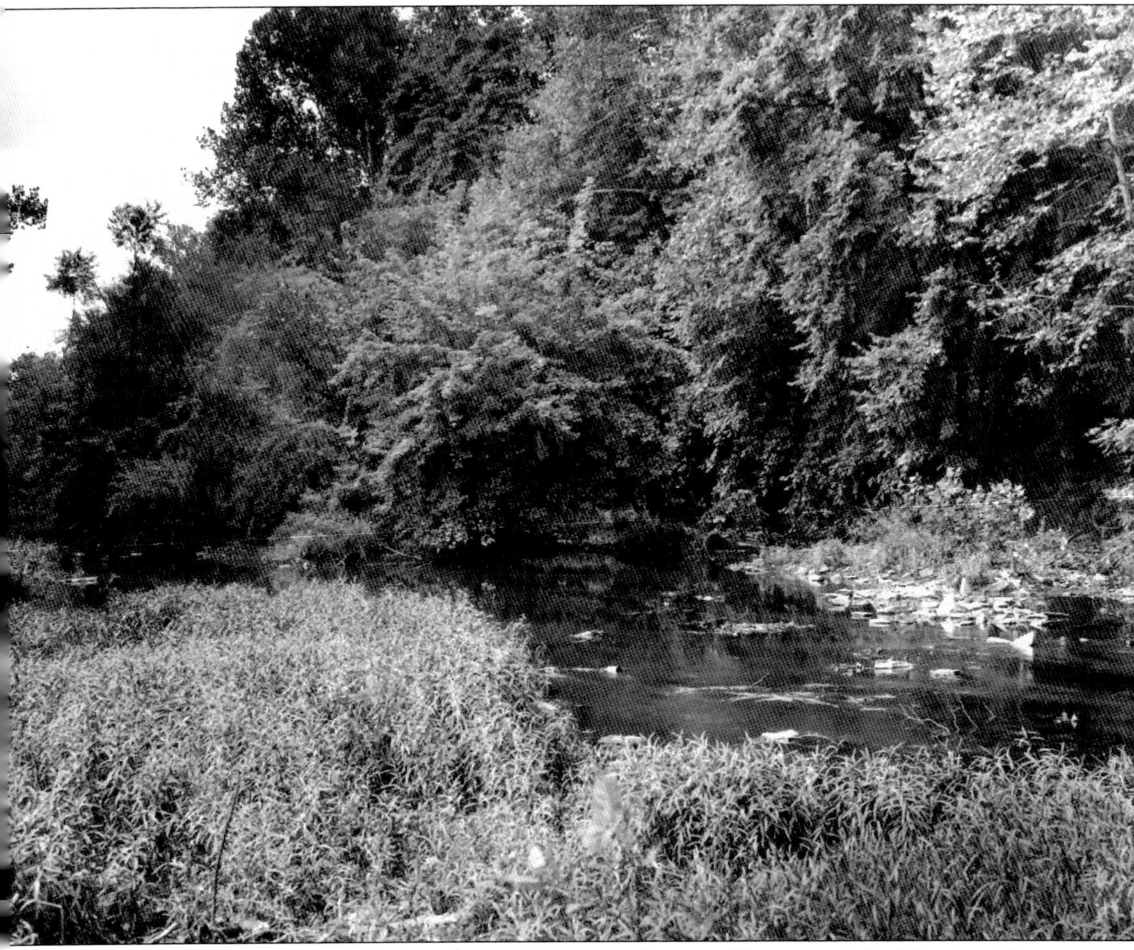

Indian Creek winds through Corydon and Harrison County. (Courtesy of the Harrison County Public Library.)

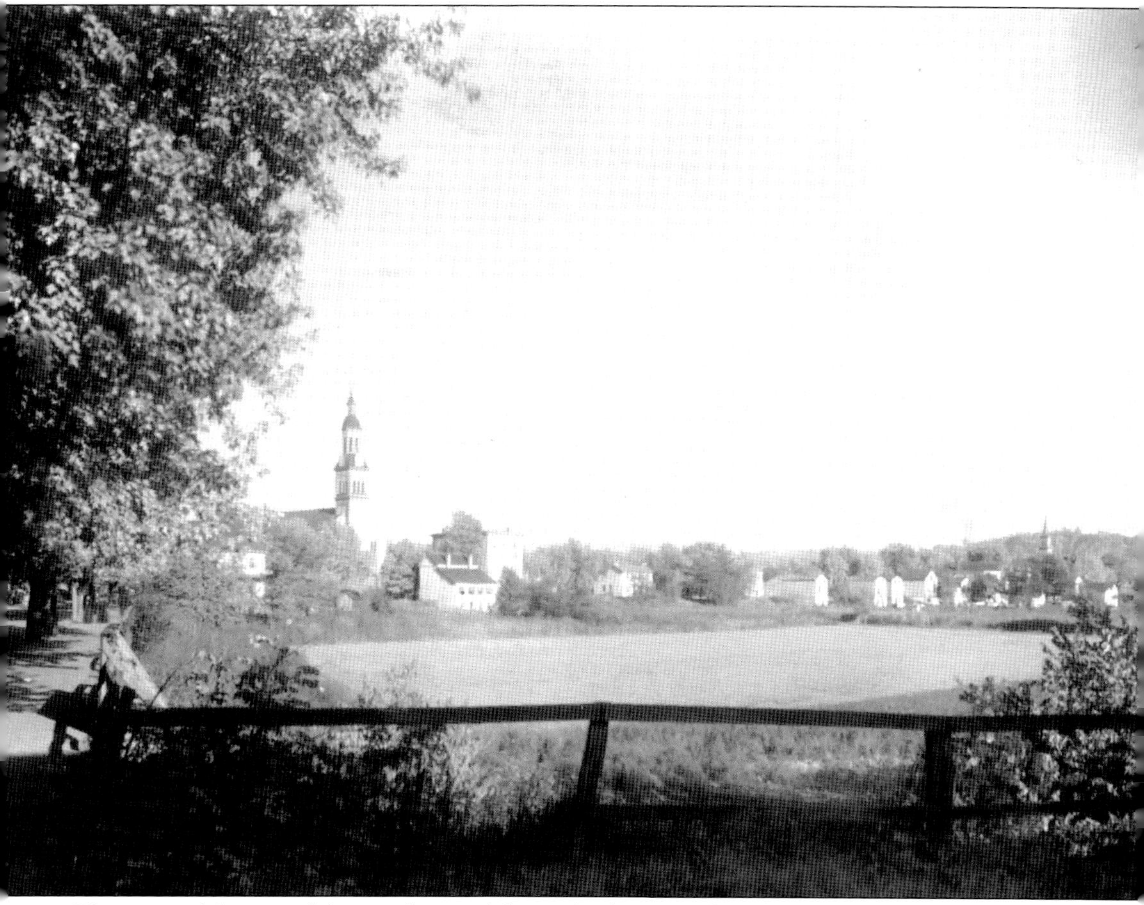

This view of the city of Aurora shows a lake in the foreground. Today the lake is filled in and a playground occupies the spot. (Courtesy of the Dearborn County Historical Society.)

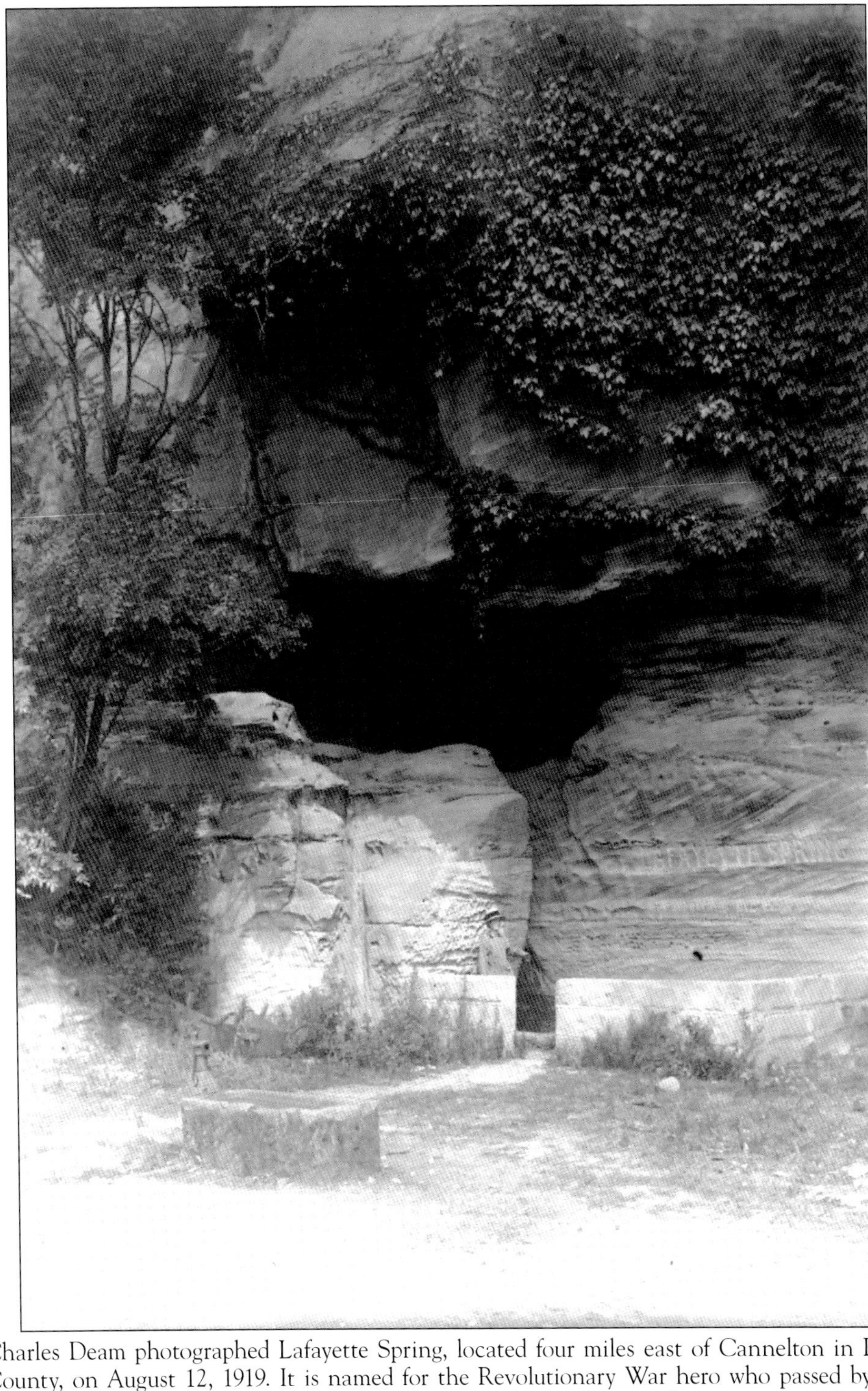

Charles Deam photographed Lafayette Spring, located four miles east of Cannelton in Perry County, on August 12, 1919. It is named for the Revolutionary War hero who passed by the area on the Ohio on a visit of the country in 1825. Lafayette Springs illustrates one of the most common geological features of the landscape in that region, the Crawford Upland. (Courtesy the Indiana Department of Natural Resources, Division of Forestry Archives.)

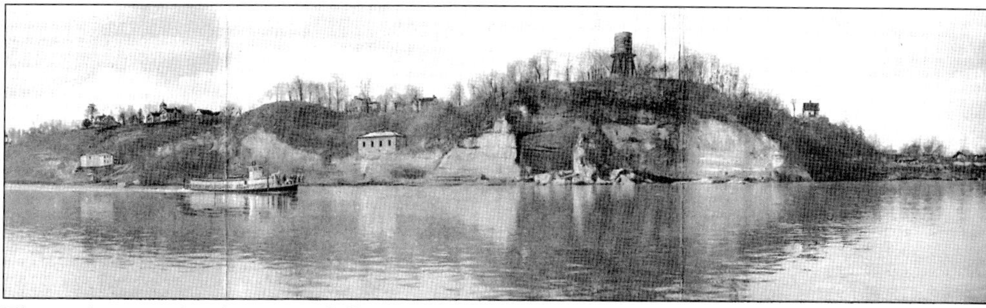

These photographs show two different viewpoints of the bluff overlooking the Ohio River at Rockport, early in the 20th century. Rockport's first settlers erected homes and businesses at the base of the bluff. (Courtesy of Willard Library.)

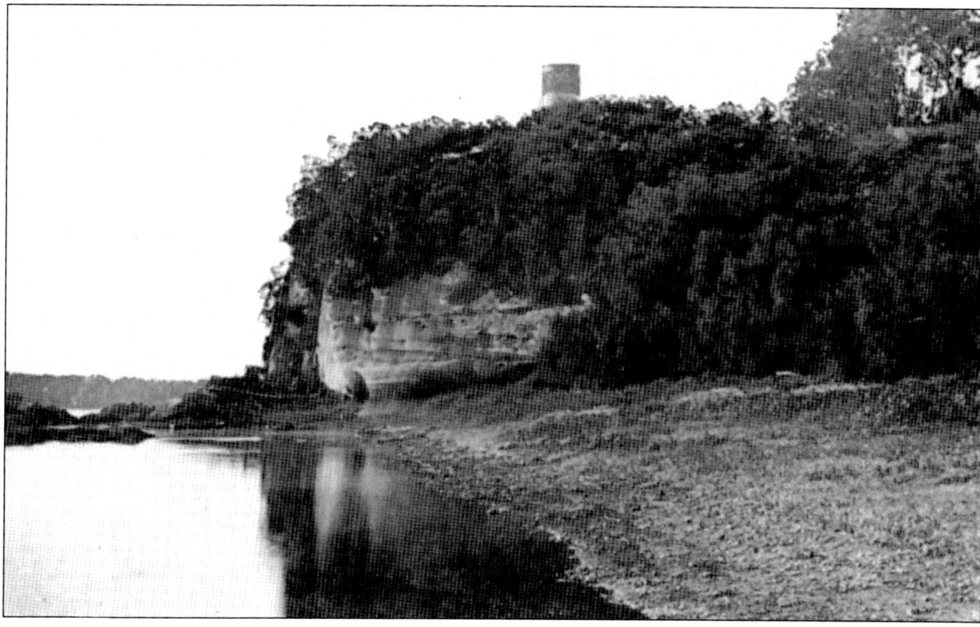

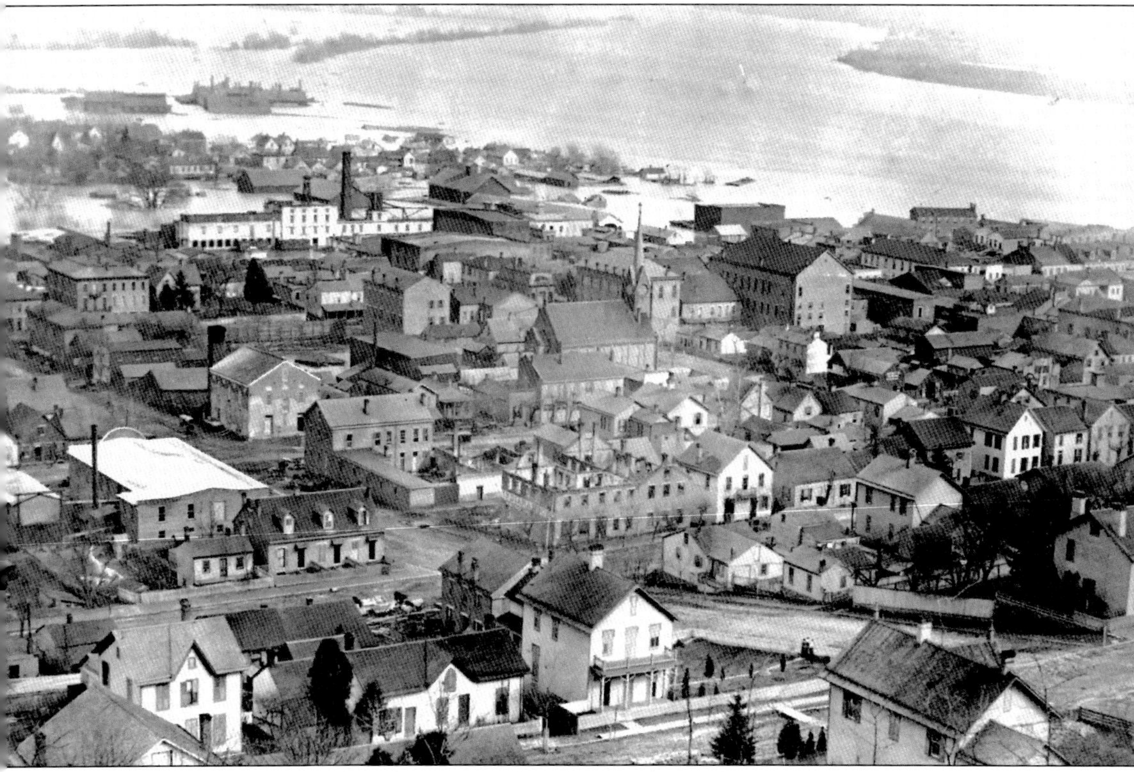

While scenic views of the Ohio River often show rolling hills or rocky bluffs overlooking the river valley, they also can illustrate the cities and towns that line the river. Here is a view overlooking Lawrenceburg, taken in the early 20th century. (Courtesy of the Dearborn County Historical Society.)

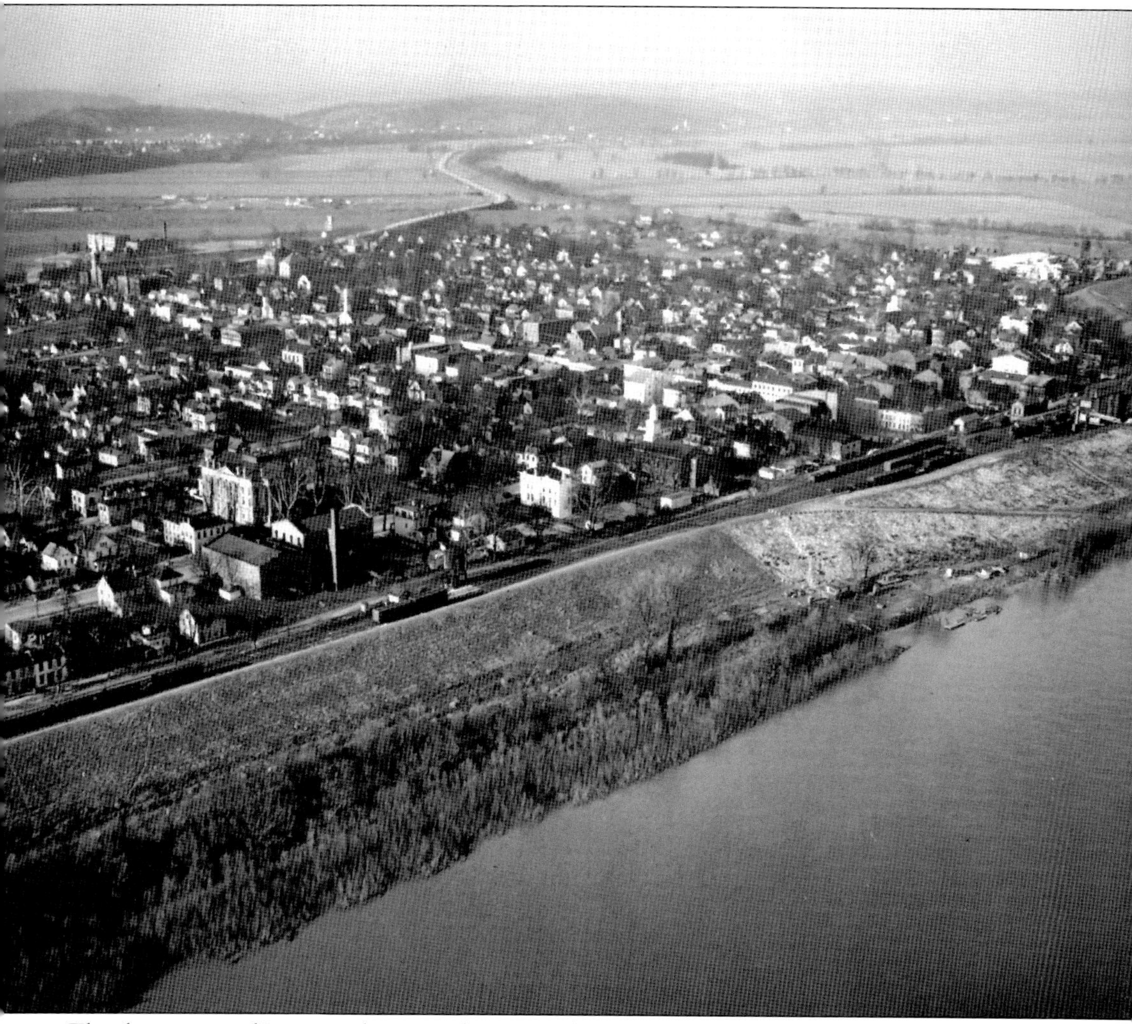

This later view of Lawrenceburg is taken over the river from the vantage point of Kentucky. (Courtesy of the Dearborn County Historical Society.)

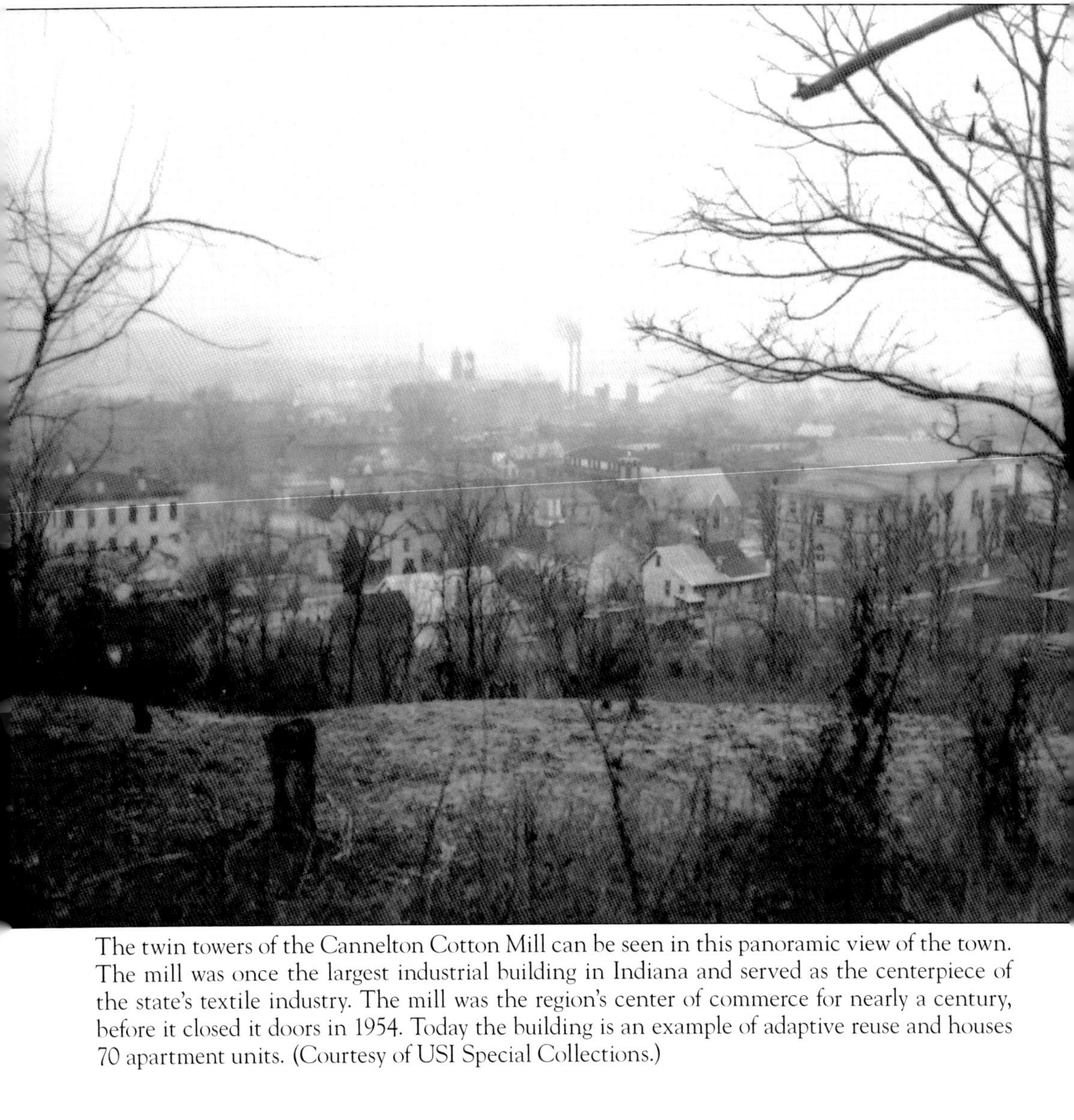

The twin towers of the Cannelton Cotton Mill can be seen in this panoramic view of the town. The mill was once the largest industrial building in Indiana and served as the centerpiece of the state's textile industry. The mill was the region's center of commerce for nearly a century, before it closed it doors in 1954. Today the building is an example of adaptive reuse and houses 70 apartment units. (Courtesy of USI Special Collections.)

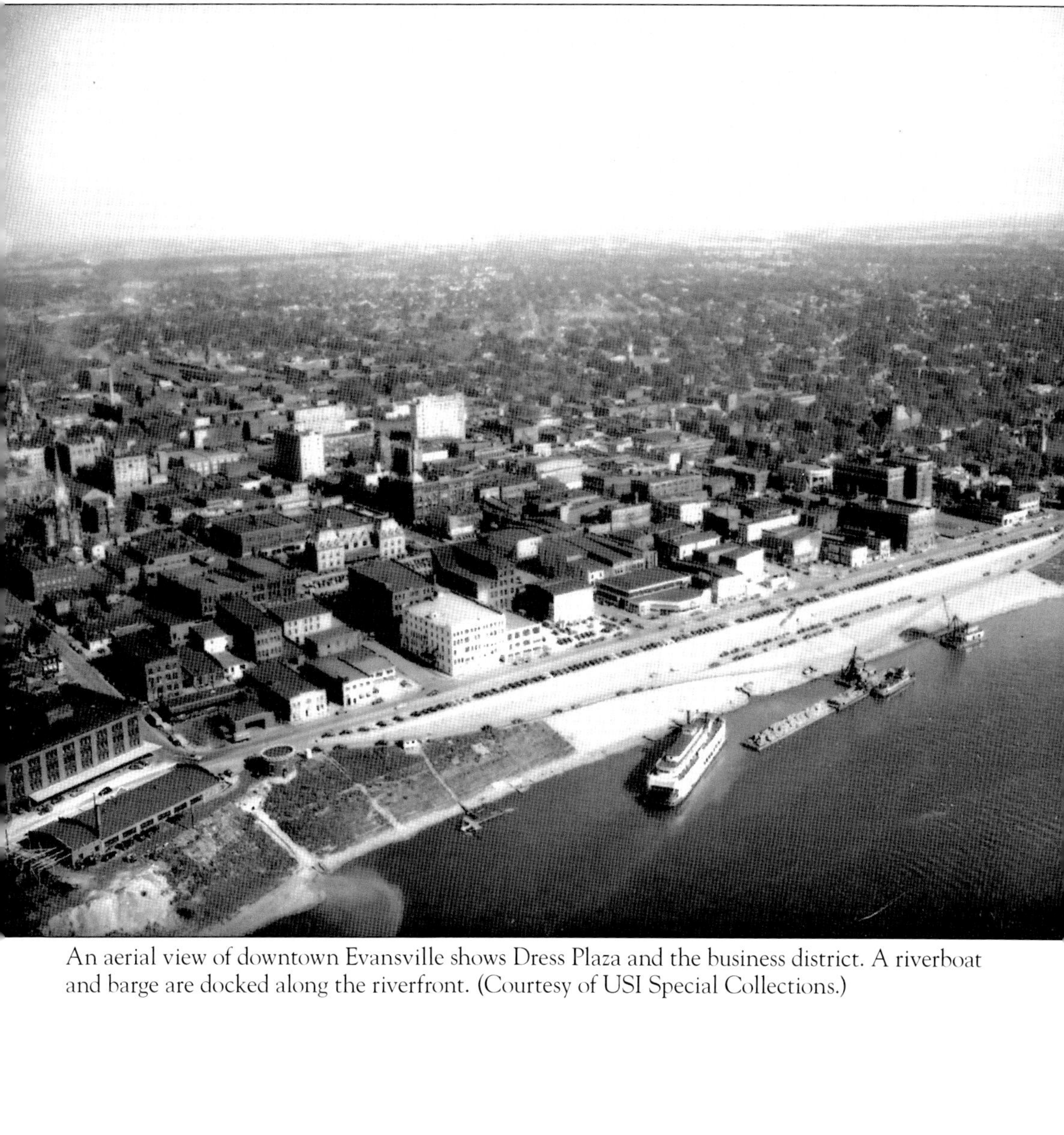

An aerial view of downtown Evansville shows Dress Plaza and the business district. A riverboat and barge are docked along the riverfront. (Courtesy of USI Special Collections.)

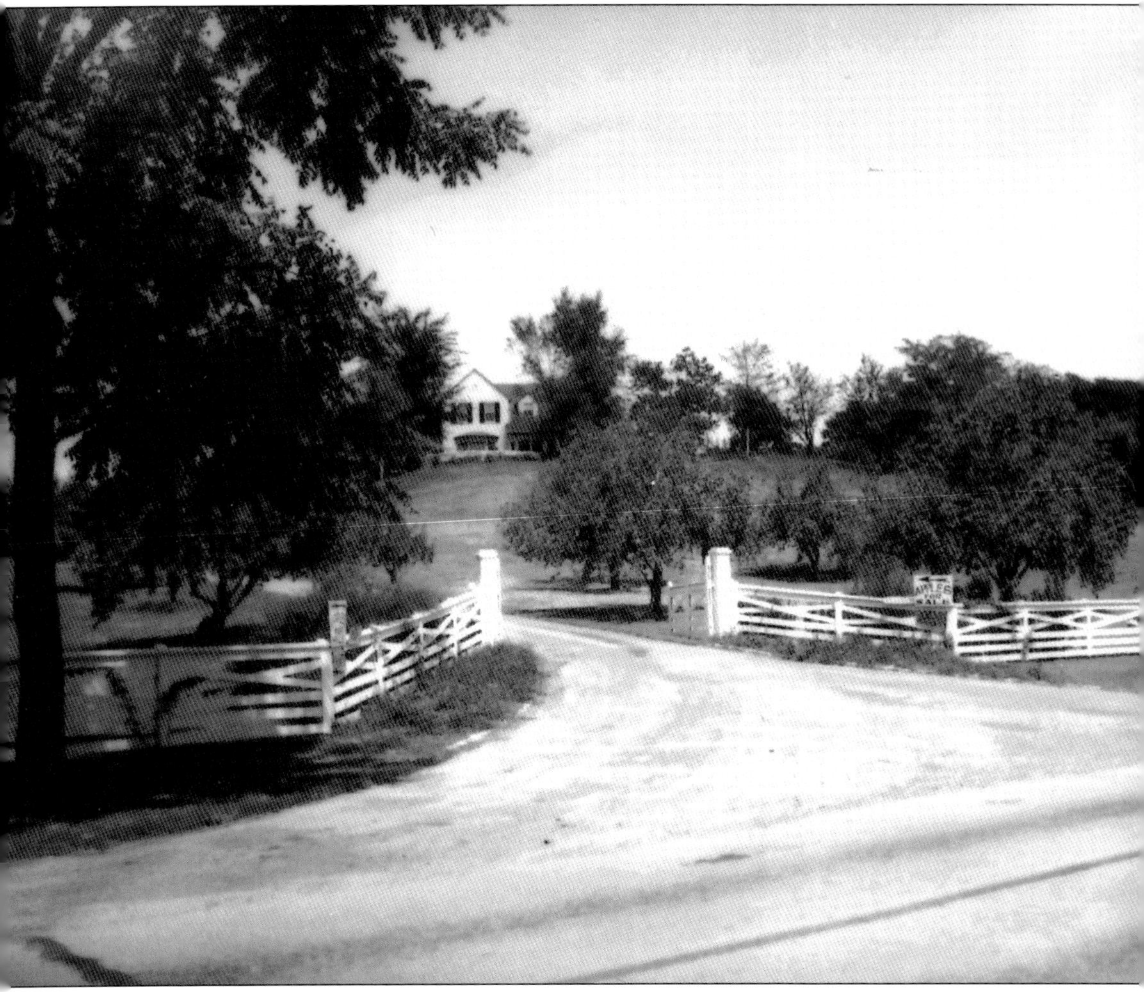

A large house overlooks the Ohio River in Newburgh. Many stately homes were located along this stretch, which is now part of the Ohio River Scenic Byway. (Courtesy of USI Special Collections.)

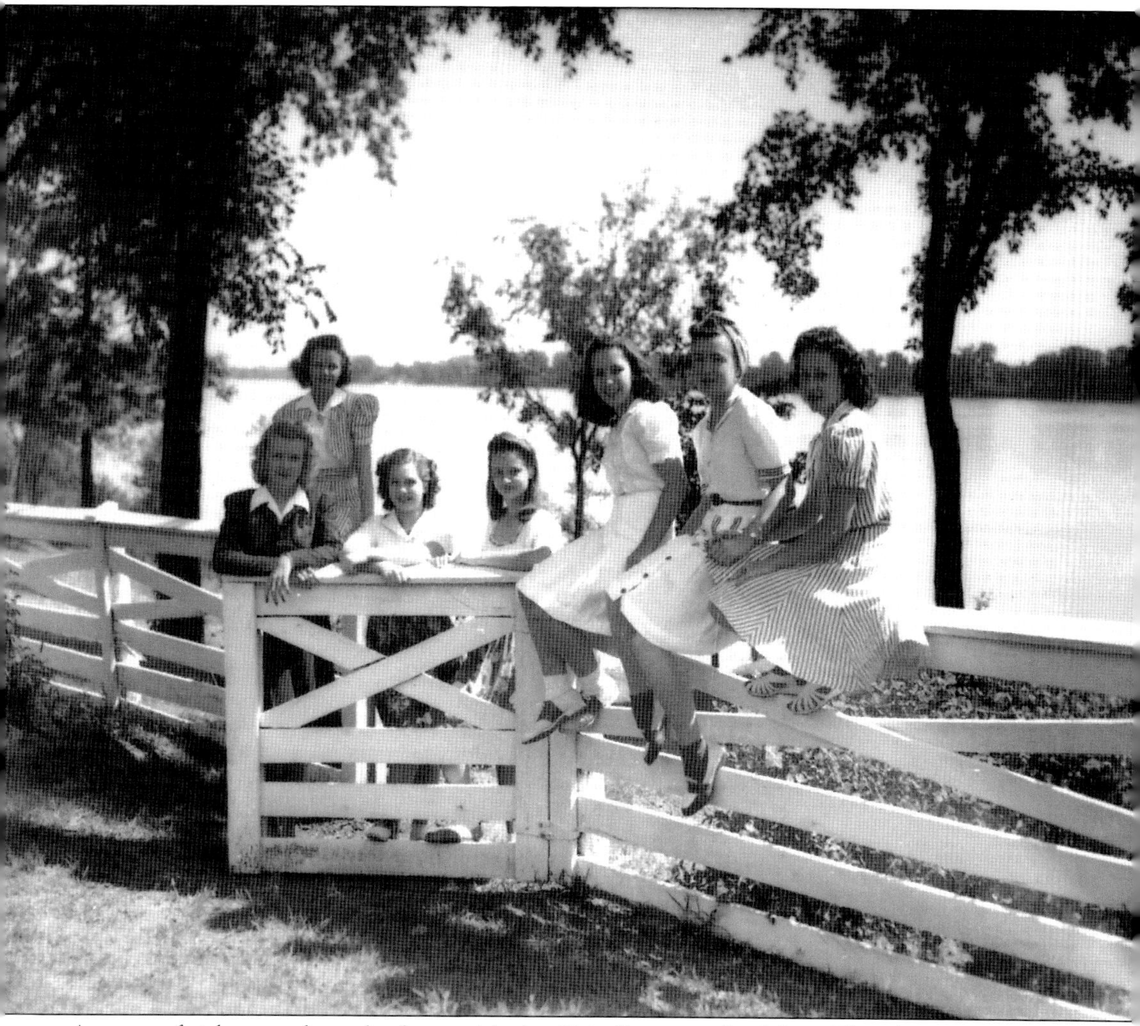

A group of girls pose along the fence with the Ohio River as a backdrop. The photograph was taken during the 1940s. (Courtesy of USI Special Collections.)